KIT BUILDING
For Railway Modellers

VOLUME 1 — ROLLING STOCK

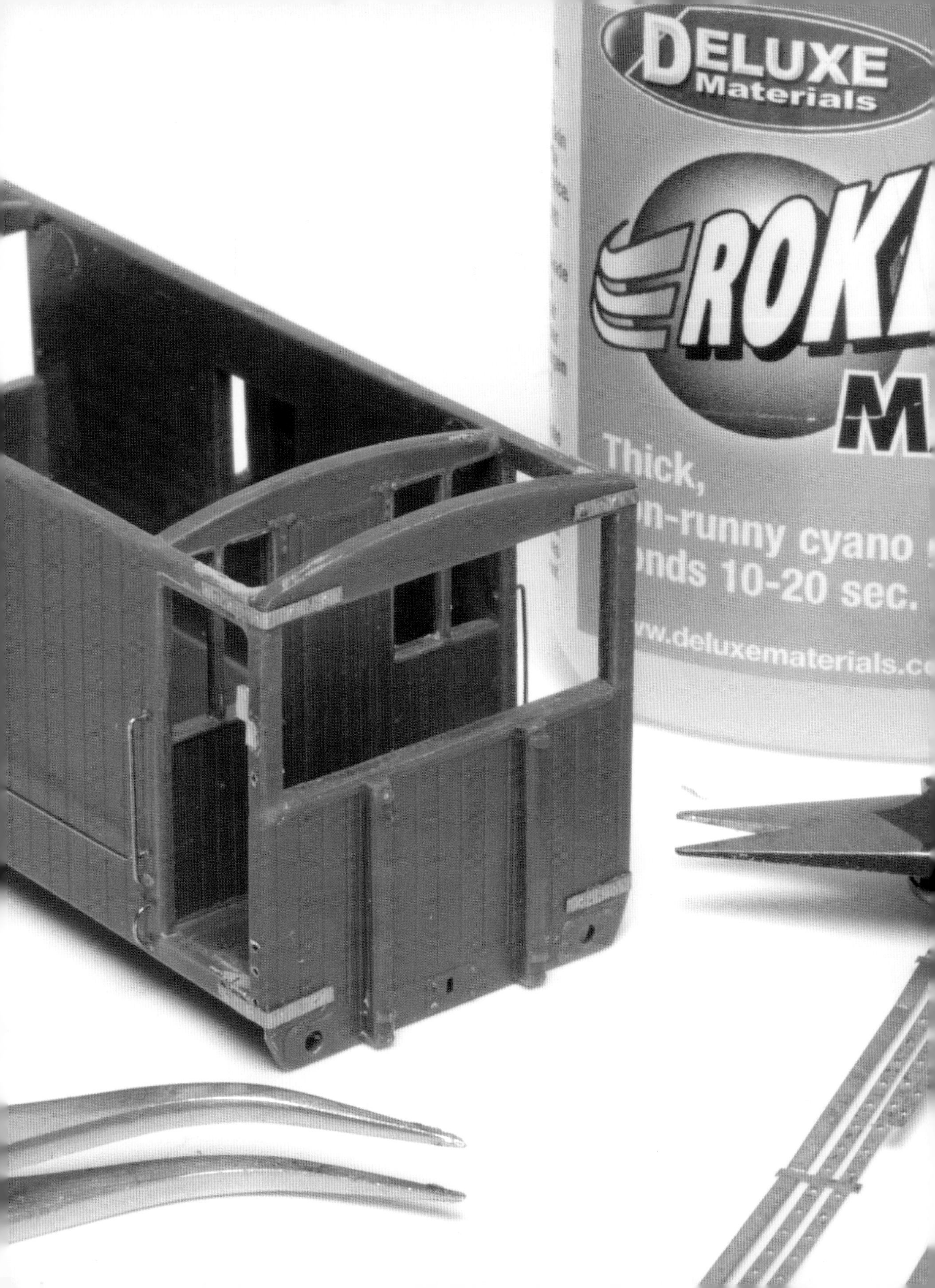
DELUXE
Materials
Thick,
10-20 sec.

KIT BUILDING
For Railway Modellers

VOLUME 1 – ROLLING STOCK

GEORGE DENT

THE CROWOOD PRESS

First published in 2013 by
The Crowood Press Ltd
Ramsbury, Marlborough
Wiltshire SN8 2HR

www.crowood.com

British Library Cataloguing-in-Publication Data
A catalogue record for this book is available from the British Library.

ISBN 978 1 84797 484 6

Typeset by Servis Filmsetting Ltd., Stockport, Cheshire
Printed and bound in India by Replika Press Pvt Ltd

CONTENTS

ACKNOWLEDGEMENTS

My special thanks go to Alex Medwell, Lisa Munro and the rest of the team at The Airbrush Company. Charlie Petty (DC Kits), Arran Aird (C-Rail), John Bristow (Deluxe Materials), Dave Young (Ten Commandments), Ken Bridger (Genesis Kits), Peter Harvey (PH Designs) and Mike Mazurkiewicz (Geoscenics) have all been generous in their supply of kits and materials over the past few years.

I must also thank my *Model Rail* colleagues for their support – Ben Jones, Richard Foster and Chris Leigh. Peter Marriott and Spencer Pollard have provided much in the way of inspiration and Dave Lowery remains a great source of knowledge and experience. I am also much indebted to Chris Nevard for the use of a number of his wonderful images and also to James Lavery, for the use of his 'Waytown' layout as a photographic backdrop.

As much of this manuscript was written on location in Settle, thanks are due, again, to Jeanne Carr, whose delightful cottage provided a stimulating ambience. Extra special thanks are due to Julie-Marie, Pepper and the rest of the Dent Collective.

This book is dedicated to the memory of Maude. There's still an empty corner of my workshop that will be forever yours …

Can a RTR model ever look as good as this? An O gauge Parkside mineral wagon, built by the author and weathered by Spencer Pollard, illustrates the great potential offered by plastic kits.

PREFACE

Like many young boys in the pre-computer era, building plastic kits formed a fundamental part of my childhood and early adolescence. Those first forays into Spitfires, stringy glue and enamel paints gave me a taste for model-making that is still with me today. The move towards railway-flavoured subjects came with the arrival of my first train set and a number of OO gauge Airfix building and rolling-stock kits. Thinking back, my father had probably bought those kits for himself. However, I soon got my hands on them and a cattle wagon and meat van duly appeared on my layout, sowing the seeds of a lasting passion for kit building and scale modelling.

I was lucky to be supported throughout my young life by my parents and sympathetic art and craft teachers, who allowed me to incorporate my hobby into my coursework. Although it's only twenty years since I left school, today's childhood seems a million miles away from my own experiences and I do wonder if youngsters are able to gain the same grounding in practical techniques. This seems to be an ongoing topic of conversation for those within the model railway industry. Yet, with the growth of digital control and ready-made products of the highest quality, the market continues to expand, confounding the argument that it is a declining pastime.

Are people still motivated to build kits in this day and age? I would wager that the answer is in the affirmative, with a large number of enthusiasts tempted to have a go, but with a lack of time, confidence and experience holding them back. Hopefully, this is where this book – and the forthcoming follow-up aimed at locomotive kits – comes in. With a wealth of clearly demonstrated hints, tips and techniques, there should be something for everyone.

ABOUT THE AUTHOR

Since 2004, when I became the in-house model-maker and all-round technical expert at *Model Rail* magazine, I have notched up hundreds of articles on every conceivable facet of model railways. I also teach courses on various modelling subjects and produce instructional DVDs. My work has also appeared in *Railway Modeller* and three previous Crowood titles – *Detailing & Modifying Ready-to-Run Locomotives in OO Gauge, Volumes 1&2* and *Airbrushing for Railway Modellers*.

INTRODUCTION

Is there still a place in the twenty-first century for the humble model railway kit, despite the ever-expanding ready-to-run (RTR) market now offering a huge range of subjects? The RTR scene will forever be constrained by mass-market appeal and manufacturers still scratch only the surface of the subjects open to them, especially in terms of rolling stock.

It is my view that kits will always have their place, although the breadth of choice in brand and subject is bound to fluctuate in accordance with market forces. Where RTR versions have appeared, kit versions have tended to bow out. That is, of course, assuming that the ready-made version is superior, which is not always the case. Scale is a pertinent factor too, as only OO gauge has enjoyed a massive influx of RTR products, with N gauge following some way behind.

Those with an interest in less mainstream scales, such as O gauge, 3mm scale or some of the finescale equivalents, find themselves facing kit building as the only viable option for creating key locomotives and rolling stock to suit their period and geographical location. Moreover, anyone with a leaning towards narrow gauge railways faces a similar prospect. Even the spoilt OO modeller must still make use of kits to produce copies of important subjects, especially if a specific location is being modelled.

Much of my own interests lie in the Settle–Carlisle, Peak District and South Wales Valley lines from 1950 to the present day and, while a great number of passenger and general-purpose freight stock is available off the shelf, there are some massive gaps in all scales. Those iconic ICI hopper wagons that plied their trade in and out of Derbyshire for sixty years have yet to tempt RTR makers (at the time of writing). Nor have the sulphate hoppers that worked between Long Meg and Widnes in the 1960s.

Granted, these two examples are limited geographically, perhaps explaining why the likes of Hornby, Bachmann and Dapol have steered clear of them so far, yet there are other items in their catalogues that are even more regionally specific (SR third-rail Electric Multiple Units for instance).

With advances in design and manufacturing, along with cheaper labour in the Far East, it is now viable for smaller brands, including a growing number of model railway retailers, to commission limited production runs of RTR models, with some very unusual prototypes being chosen. Firms such as REALTRACK Models, Hatton's of Liverpool, Kernow, Model Zone and TMC have each taken advantage of this situation to offer some superb products to the market. Indeed, *Model Rail* magazine has enjoyed great success with its range of commissioned RTR locomotives and rolling stock.

This is not the place for such discussions, however. What remains the case today is that there are many examples of locomotives, rolling stock and multiple units that can only be recreated in most scales by employing a kit as a starting point. Doom-laden tales abound of how the hobby is changing irrevocably, with everyone seemingly now interested only in off-the-shelf products; there's a massive 'skills gap' and nobody has the time to fiddle with a kit in today's time-poor society. How, then, can Airfix be enjoying an unprecedented renaissance, along with other military and aviation kit makers? Someone must have the time to build them and it cannot solely be youngsters or the retired. Can it be explained by the fact that these mainstream kits are produced to very high standards, while most railway-themed kits retain an image of homemade, cottage-industry fayre?

There's an element of truth in this, with many kits still available that are simply not up to today's

Modern advances in kit production allow an amazing level of detail to be offered as standard. This HO scale Steam Era Models kit hails from Australia and the beautifully rendered plastic components are a sight to behold. Sets of etched brass detailing parts and decals are also supplied.

expectations or the average modeller's skill level. Those days of the genteel enthusiast with a small engineering workshop in his shed are sadly all but gone. Now we prefer something we can glue together at the dining-room table, with clearer instructions and parts that actually fit together straight from the box.

Happily, at the same time that RTR products have advanced, so too has the quality of new kits, helped in part by computer-aided design and the reduction in production costs. Small-scale producers are now able to offer state-of-the-art injection-moulded, etched, cast or laser-cut components in a wide range

of materials. Moreover, computer-aided manufacture not only speeds up the process, but also promotes a higher level of accuracy and modeller-friendly assembly. Nowhere is this approach better typified than in Pete Waterman's 'Just Like the Real Thing' range of O gauge locomotives and rolling stock.

Others are catching up, with firms like York Modelmaking producing superb laser-cut plastic components, Chivers Finelines' hugely impressive injection-moulded plastic parts and Peter Harvey's amazingly accurate CAD-originated etched metal kits and accessories.

Computer-aided design and production have opened up plenty of new avenues, such as laser-cut plastic kits. With some extra detailing, these York Modelmaking kits can produce realistic models.

Kit building requires a number of skills and techniques which, once mastered, become second nature. The modeller can then expand his or her repertoire, moving on to more advanced projects. Furthermore, modifying the supplied parts or adding extra detail can produce something different. All of these facets are covered within this book, taking in the range of the most common materials and techniques.

Presented over separate volumes, this first instalment outlines all of the necessary foundations, with the accent on rolling stock, while Volume Two will look at techniques specific to locomotive and multiple-unit construction. The chapters are ordered roughly in increasing levels of difficulty, starting with a firm grounding in material properties, basic techniques and processes, before moving on gradually to more demanding tasks such as soldering, shaping metal and adding extra details. Accordingly, the first

few chapters concentrate on plastic-based kits, as these require far less in the way of experience, tools and equipment.

Writing this book has, in many ways, drawn me back to my roots. Indeed, I have approached the project as a tribute to the humble railway kit; a clarion call to all those modellers now worshipping the mass-produced, RTR product. How can you match the satisfaction and reward of putting the finishing touches to a newly built carriage or wagon that you have assembled yourself?

I hope that, by reading this book, you will be inspired to have a go and push yourself further than you may have previously ventured, to master a new technique that has hitherto vexed you and, above all, to enjoy yourself. Most importantly, I aim to convince you that there is definitely still a place for the kit in the model railway hobby.

Working in metal offers some unique possibilities and the bulkier material holds certain advantages over plastics. This whitemetal kit from Genesis portrays a 1970s-era nuclear flask wagon, something that is unlikely to appear in RTR form in the near future.

Dating back to the 1960s, the humble Airfix OO rolling-stock kits still make impressive models, especially if a few detail enhancements are added. This Meat Van kit is older than the author, but a new chassis and other fittings make it suitable for a twentieth-century layout.

It was the late 1970s-era Airfix kits that really got the author started in model railways, having cut his teeth on the same company's aircraft kits. Dapol still produces these kits, offering an excellent – and cheap – skill-building resource.

Etched-metal kits are perhaps the most difficult to assemble, especially subjects such as this Cravens carriage. The sides had to be formed into their distinctive bowed outline, matching perfectly with the ends. It took time to get them right, but rolling brass is easier than it seems.

CHAPTER ONE

RESEARCH AND PREPARATION

Research and preparation can be seen from two diametrically opposed viewpoints. Either it is a tedious necessity to be got out of the way as soon as possible, so that the practical work can begin, or it is an enjoyable undertaking in its own right, allowing for hours of interesting work amongst printed or digital resources. The degree of authenticity is a personal call, with 'rivet counters' assigning the highest priority to the research stage. But not everyone wants to be a slave to realism and many modellers will happily live with a few small detail omissions or indiscretions in the name of compromise.

I cannot boast to be the most meticulous researcher, with constraints of time and impatience often getting the better of me. Doing this job for a living is also a factor, as there is a limit to the time that people will pay a model-maker to sit in an archive. However, if an accurate model of a specific prototype is the goal, then you have to be prepared to put in the legwork and obtain all the relevant information before assembly begins.

Perhaps the most exciting aspect of researching is the injection of inspiration that can arise from unearthing a particularly arresting image or piece of information. Indeed, much of my rolling stock collection is made up of prototypes that have grabbed my attention, in terms of unusual modifications or *ad hoc* paint schemes. Often, it has been necessary to convert existing kits or even scratch-build components to create something a little different.

WHAT TO LOOK FOR

Some of the first considerations involve whether a particular vehicle is relevant to your chosen era or location. Most kits offer this sort of information in catalogues or on the packaging, allowing customers to answer this vital question before purchase. But, then again, maybe you really like the look of a kit, despite it not being strictly appropriate for your layout. In which case, one can usually come up with an acceptable excuse!

Research allows some variety to be built into a fleet of similar vehicles, introducing small modifications to axle boxes, suspension, brake gear and the odd livery variation to help create highly realistic rakes of carriages and wagons. Moreover, in the steam, early diesel and even the modern era, freight trains have rarely presented a completely uniform appearance.

Vehicle building and scrapping dates can be helpful in ensuring historical accuracy, although the former are easier to obtain than the latter. Goods vehicles, in particular, were once so numerous and varied that finding exact withdrawal dates for specific vehicles (or even types of vehicles) can be difficult. Again, the degree of your obsession for authenticity will rule your decision-making.

Build dates can also offer clues as to the detail variations to be found on rolling stock. For example, various freight wagons were built with roller axle bearings in later batches, in contrast to earlier versions with oil boxes. Similarly, build locations can also derive certain characteristics, with some outside contractors being able to supply only riveted wagon bodies, whereas the same 'type' of wagon could be built by another workshop with a welded shell.

Modifications to so-called 'standard' liveries are another important consideration, with the shade of 'freight grey' or 'freight brown' both being altered by British Rail during the 1960s and 1970s. The transition through corporate colour schemes also saw vehicles repainted at various times. Refurbishment dates and details of physical differences between original and modified condition are similarly important. Virtually all of this information is available to modellers. It is simply a matter of knowing where to look.

A good deal of relevant prototype information is often contained in a kit's instructions, so it pays to read them thoroughly before assembly.

period in which it is to be portrayed. These images will compliment a kit's instructions, assisting in identifying parts and locations, as well as ensuring that livery, markings and even weathering patterns are authentic.

Additionally, the images can be used to draw up a list of interesting details where the prototype may differ from the kit, or where the kit may have got some aspect wrong, for instance visible repairs to bodywork, non-standard location of lamp brackets and other fittings, brake gear, buffer and axle box types. Livery, lettering and numbering styles may also veer from the 'standard' specification. From this list, it can then be decided what work needs to be done to the kit before, during and after construction, with any additional parts sourced or improvised.

This latter point is important as projects can all too often stall while extra components are sought and, in many cases, making alterations to kit parts or substituting replacements can be tricky once construction has begun. So, planning the project through from the beginning pays big dividends; but more on this later.

INSPIRATION STRIKES

My personal preference is, whenever possible, to obtain as many images as possible of the vehicle in question, preferably captured while running in the

Introducing a little variety into a fleet of similar wagons adds visual interest and avoids the monotony of building several kits in exactly the same way. These two wagons are built from the same kit, but feature different brake apparatus, different buffers and even a slightly different shade of paint.

WHERE TO LOOK

Depending on the quality of the kit, the instructions may supply all the relevant information, such as livery and numbering details, plus variations in equipment or rebuilding dates. Brassmasters are a good example, albeit in terms of locomotive kits, whereby a comprehensive booklet of historical information is provided, with references to books and articles should the modeller need more details.

In contrast, other kits simply provide a few written instructions concerning assembly, so some sourcing of extra information will be helpful to ensure that the right parts find themselves fixed in the right places. Indeed, being faced with an array of disparate parts, many of which are difficult to identify and may only be suitable for a particular version of the vehicle in question (a choice of brake equipment is a common feature of rolling-stock kits), can lead to plenty of head scratching if the instructions are substandard. In which case, a few prototype images or plans, or even a written description, will take away any guesswork and make for a speedier and more enjoyable build.

These days, I am fortunate to be able to draw on the combined knowledge and resources of my colleagues at *Model Rail*, *Rail* and *Steam Railway* magazines, as well as having a decent library of books and journals of my own. These printed references have been amassed over twenty years, with newly released titles being supplemented by older tomes obtained largely by trawling through second-hand bookshops, charity shops and even car boot sales. Specialist booksellers can be a tad expensive, especially for highly specialized and rare titles, but chancing a look elsewhere – or on the Internet – can often bring results. It still comes as a happy surprise to me that there are many books in circulation on the most obscure facets of railway history or operation.

Old issues of railway magazines (such as *Rail Enthusiast*, *Modern Railways* and *Trains Illustrated*) can be a goldmine of information on locomotives and rolling stock, featuring lists of newly added or withdrawn stock, as well as illustrated articles on specific vehicle types and operations. Equally, back issues of modelling magazines are also invaluable, with articles to be found on the subject of building or enhancing kits in all scales. Furthermore, indexes of a number of modelling titles can now be searched online. Rolling stock lists from the likes of the RCTS (Railway Correspondence and Travel Society) or Platform 5, along with contemporary *ABCs* are also great resources, containing fleet numbers, liveries and other vital statistics.

Joining enthusiast societies, in line with your own interests, opens up a wide pool of free expertise. Groups exist for most of the various Big Four and Pre-Grouping railways; details are included in the Appendix. Regular journals and newsletters include articles on all manner of subjects, including rolling-stock design and operation, and most societies boast impressive archive collections that can be readily accessed by members. A good example is the Midland Railway Study Centre, based at the Silk Mill Museum in Derby, which contains a vast collection of photographs, plans and documents available for study.

Not surprisingly, modellers wishing to delve further back into history will face sterner challenges, purely due to less data surviving from the pre-1923 Grouping era, especially where rolling stock is concerned. However, archives held at the National Railway Museum, British Library and Public Record Office can prove fruitful, as can local authority archives in locations that once boasted large railway installations or workshops.

The Internet has certainly made railway research easier, with a wealth of information now at our fingertips. Those so inclined can spend hours trawling websites from the comfort of their armchairs, viewing images by the thousands. Posting a question on one of the many online forums can result in plenty of information being sent your way. While much of these resources, especially image-wise, are useful, there are no restrictions or checks on what is published online. Therefore, inaccuracies are widespread and can prove something of a pothole to the unwary. Books and magazines can just as often be guilty of making mistakes through misinformation or simply a typing error, so it always pays to double – or

There have been many books published containing a wealth of photographs, plans, build and withdrawal dates and many other details that a kit builder will need. Some of the best titles are now out of print, but they can be sourced cheaply over the Internet, or via specialist booksellers.

Plans, technical information and contemporary images are important, as are details of the interiors, especially with passenger stock, for example shades of wood panelling, upholstery, layout of seats and partitions, as well as the type of fixtures and fittings.

Stock lists are a little harder to come by, but they contain details of building and scrapping dates, regional allocations, modifications and liveries, greatly helping the modeller to choose a suitable prototype.

General Arrangement drawings, from museum archives, can be a terrific source of information. Dimensions, locations of fittings and equipment and lists of materials employed will all be invaluable. However, production vehicles often differed from the original plans, so they should not be used in isolation.

Magazine and society journals are another excellent resource, whether concentrating on a particular vehicle type or describing general operating procedures. Older copies can be obtained from specialist stores or via the Internet. Indeed, there is a number of searchable magazine indexes online, to help in tracking down that elusive article.

even triple – check certain facts or figures in as many sources as possible.

One of the best things on the Internet, especially for rolling-stock enthusiasts, is Paul Bartlett's amazing collection of photographs. This site contains thousands of images of British Railways freight vehicles from the 1960s up to privatization, mostly in colour and with many vital detail images that are perfect for the modeller. So good is his collection that many items of rolling stock in the catalogues of Bachmann and Hornby will look familiar to the dedicated viewers of his website. While the website is free to search, Paul also offers a print delivery service and there is some useful prototype information about each wagon type on there too. (See the Appendix for a range of useful website addresses that were live at the time of writing.)

It has to be said that Internet-based research and web forums are not everyone's cup of tea. Indeed, every hour spent on the computer is, to me, an hour less of modelling time and, personally speaking, I would rather spend the time in a library or museum archive or on a field trip, but that is purely a personal view.

Studying the prototype at first hand allows you to concentrate on the parts that most photographers tend to miss, such as underframe details. When the instructions are a bit vague, or you are looking for extra details to add, images like this help you to finish the job.

THE REAL THING

Getting out and about in pursuit of my hobby is one of the best parts of railway modelling as far as I am concerned, although it is not always the best

Vehicles in preservation are unlikely to be exactly how they were in regular service, but they can reveal a lot about the prototype, not least how they tended to weather and the building techniques employed. Note the canvas roof covering that has worked loose from the corners.

Identify what your kit is missing in terms of detail fitments and in-service modifications, such as these airbrake pipes. Obtaining some plastic rod or brass wire at the outset will allow such features to be added during the building process.

A vast array of buffers has been fitted to rolling stock, according to vehicle size, weight or type and braking arrangements. Your kit may not have the right type to suit your prototype, or they may simply be poorly rendered. There are many alternative sources from which to obtain them.

means of prototype research. Being amongst the real thing, especially in a working railway environment, is certainly inspiring, but recreating preserved vehicles is not a sure-fire way to achieving realism,

unless it is the restored version that you are aiming to reproduce.

Preserved vehicles are unlikely to be entirely original, with rebuilt bodies or reclaimed fixtures from different vehicles, but a field trip combined with other research can provide the raw materials for an overall picture to be developed and decisions

Wheel patterns varied according to period and the type of vehicle. Plain-spoke, split-spoke (seen here), three-hole disc and plain disc could be found, with some wagons even having a mixture as a result of ad hoc repairs. Axle boxes also varied, this type being the widely adopted Railway Clearing House (RCH) split oil box.

Roller-bearing axle boxes were a late development in Britain, being employed from the 1960s on vacuum-braked and later air-braked stock. Note the three-hole disc wheel and clasp brake arrangement.

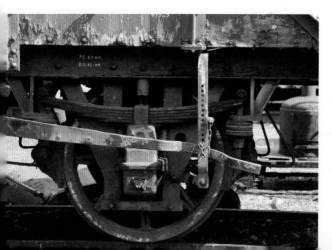

An enormous amount of detail information can be garnered from a single image: speedometer cable connected to the leading axle box; distinctive angled brackets along the chassis; locations of lamp brackets; water-tank filler pipes running either side of the windscreen; shape of the buffers (one of which is wonky); and orientation of the teak grain on each wooden panel. All are vital points for the modeller.

can then be made from an informed basis. A camera, tape measure, notepad and pencil, plus the authority to poke about with a particular preserved vehicle, are all you need.

For modern vehicles on the national network, modern safety regulations are virtually impossible to ignore and the privatized nature of the industry means that the humble enthusiast is seldom entertained. Gone are the days of 'bunking' loco sheds or gaining impromptu tours of goods yards by obliging ground staff. However, the modern railway does at least have public relations teams that may offer some degree of help, with freight companies such as Freightliner and DRS including useful information on their websites. Depot open days still occur from time to time and keeping an eye on the contemporary railway press will provide plenty in the way of inspiration and modelling material.

TECHNICAL KNOWLEDGE

A small degree of mechanical know-how can be a great help in kit building, though an engineering qualification is by no means a prerequisite. Simply having an idea of why certain parts fit in certain locations, as well as their purpose and means of operation, makes life much simpler. Wagon brakes are a good example, as it is easy to fit linkages in a manner that

would be impossible to operate in real life. Again, this is an area where a kit's instructions may make things either clear or cloudy, so some appreciation of how these parts interact with each other will remove any uncertainty.

Additionally, it is not only moving parts that can cause confusion. Chassis and bodyshells are often braced or supported in specific ways to absorb certain stresses or load characteristics. Accordingly, if your kit requires framing to be assembled, getting this aspect right is important for the overall effect. After all, our renditions of vehicles need to look as if they will actually do the job for which they were built.

Much of this knowledge will be gained through experience of building a variety of kits, especially those with clear, informative instructions. Alternatively, there are plenty of books and articles in circulation that contain all the relevant information. I have found some of the best instructors of railway engineering to be books from the 1930s to 1950s aimed at younger enthusiasts. Without the need to pander to a 'know it all' adult readership, these volumes offer a basic grounding in steam-age locomotive and rolling-stock design and operation, assisted by clear illustrations, diagrams and succinct language. As already mentioned, many such titles can be found for a few pounds in second-hand bookshops.

This model of B248701 depicts a BR 16t mineral wagon of the Diagram1/109 pattern, built as part of lot2795 by Hurst Nelson in 1959. The lot number is important as it reveals that this batch of steel-bodied wagons featured riveted bodyshells (Hurst Nelson could not weld bodyshells at that time). However, there were otherwise identical wagons, built by other makers to the same diagram, yet with welded bodies. As the photograph shows, this Parkside kit features a riveted body, so putting the right number on to the model is important.

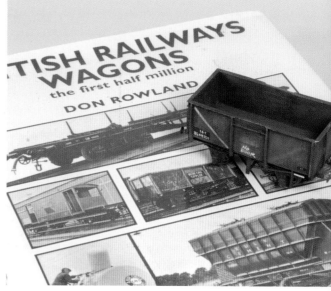

Being able to cross-reference the provenance of a specific vehicle helps to determine its own particular story and, for BR vehicles at least, it is not too difficult a task. Indeed, all of the information regarding B248701 was gleaned from one book, **British Railways Wagons by Don Rowland.**

A WORD ON DIAGRAMS AND LOTS

With the vast majority of subjects in this book deriving from British Railways and the preceding private companies, there has been much recourse to the study of diagrams and lots, especially in relation to freight vehicles. The common practice, up to the 1980s, was for railways to adopt a diagram number for each individual design and these were logged in the plan books of railway administrators and engineers for ready reference.

Consisting of a basic outline drawing of each vehicle, these diagram books contained essential measurements and specifications, but were by no means working drawings. Therefore, they are useful for gleaning basic information only, not least as the wagons or carriages tended to differ markedly in real life. Diagram books were published in great quantities and often turn up on stalls at railway shows, or the plans may be reproduced in books or magazine articles.

The lot number refers to the batch of vehicles built to a particular order and each lot may contain various detail differences, despite being from the same diagram. Confused? It is in fact a little more straightforward than it sounds and by also using the vehicle's running number (if known), it is possible to cross-reference the diagram and lot numbers, thus revealing a range of important data such as build variations and braking systems. The fitting of automatic or manual brakes determined the colour that the wagon would be painted, with bauxite red employed for 'brake fitted' and light grey for 'unfitted' stock. Discerning the equipment specification from the diagram and lot numbers is thus a great help when studying grainy or black and white photographs, where a vehicle may be obscured or its colour indeterminate.

SCALE CALCULATIONS

Working from original builders' plans or on-site measurements may be more pertinent for the budding scratch-builder or kit basher, yet an understanding of the calculations necessary to convert the full-size subject into a scale model will come in handy for many general modelling tasks. Adding extra details or modifying aspects of a model can only be done accurately by ensuring that everything is correct to scale.

The popular railway modelling scales tend to complicate matters by using a ratio between a metric and imperial measurement (millimetres:feet). The most prevalent scale is OO, whereby 4mm equals 1ft (the same as EM and P4); N gauge is expressed as 2mm:1ft; HO is 3.5mm:1ft; and O gauge is 7mm:1ft. This unsatisfactory situation is not a new one, coming as a result of trying to scale down measurements into fractions of inches, where millimetres gave a more precise and easy to communicate figure. For example, HO, originally envisaged to be expressed in ³⁄₁₆in:1ft (half of ³⁄₈in:1ft O gauge) was more of an approximation than an exact figure, whereas 3.5mm:1ft is more faithful.

The vast array of scales and gauges, each with their own finescale and narrow gauge offshoots, can be confusing. However, there are kits and products out there for virtually all of them and knowing how to convert real-life dimensions down to your chosen scale is an important skill.

Scale ratios employed by other modelling disciplines, such as 1:35 or 1:72, are often more logical as both aspects of the ratio are expressed in the same format. For instance, in 1:35th scale, a prototype vehicle measuring 10m in length would be 0.2857m when scaled down (ten divided by thirty-five equals 0.2857), or 0.29m (290mm) to two decimal places. The same process applies with imperial measurements – a 10ft long subject would be scaled down to 0.29ft (88mm).

Railway scales expressed as numeric ratios (as opposed to mm:ft) work out approximately as: 1:76 for OO/4mm scale; 1:87 for HO/3.5mm; 1:148 for British-outline N/2mm; 1:43.5 for O/7mm. Therefore, to convert figures into OO gauge, the measurements must be divided by seventy-six (in other words, the model will be seventy-six times smaller). So, if a real wagon has a 10ft wheelbase, dividing this by seventy-six gives a measurement of 0.1316ft (to four decimal places). To convert this figure into metric, multiply 0.1316 by 30.48. This gives a scale measurement of 4.01cm (or 40.1mm).

A further complication is that British railway vehicles used imperial weights and measures up to the 1970s, around the same time that the

Scale rules, available in various modelling scales, are a real boon when transferring measurements from plans or sketches.

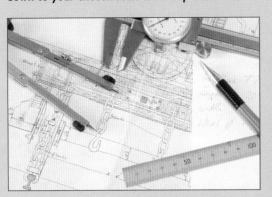

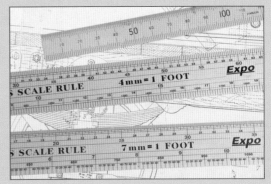

Collate all your research into sketch diagrams or working drawings to make it more accessible. These plans were drawn up from site measurements, photographs and reference to BR diagrams.

TOPS (Total Operations Processing System) numbering came into use. Instead of wheelbases and tare weights being expressed in feet and tons, they were now expressed in millimetres and kilograms. While mass is only relevant in terms of adding the correct weight markings at the livery stage, the following conversion factors will prove helpful when making any scale calculations.

Conversion Factors

* inches to millimetres: × 25.4; for example, 12in × 25.4 = 304.8mm
* feet to centimetres: × 30.48; for example, 12ft × 30.48 = 365.76cm
* millimetres to inches: × 0.03937; for example, 1,200mm × 0.03937 = 47.244in
* centimetres to inches: × 0.3937; for example, 12cm × 0.3937 = 4.7244in.

Therefore, if a plan drawing or vehicle data panel reads '14ft wheelbase', we can convert the imperial prototype dimension to a metric equivalent of 426.72cm (14 × 30.48). To then scale this figure down to OO gauge, we divide 426.72 by 76 (OO being 1:76 scale) to equal 5.6147cm to four decimal places, giving a more workable scale measurement of 56mm.

BEFORE YOU START

This book is not intended as a beginner's guide to model railways and, therefore, the question of scales and gauges will be touched on but briefly. Indeed, the assumption here is that a reader interested in building kits has already made up his or her mind as to what scale is the most suitable. However, there are still a number of important factors to consider before embarking on a rolling-stock kit, especially those that dictate how a kit may have to be altered during construction.

Issues such as wheel gauge are crucial, as making adjustments after assembly may be extremely difficult. Furthermore, if a higher grade of detail is required than offered by the kit, then identifying parts to replace or modify before assembly will also be advantageous. Even seemingly small considerations, such as whether or not an open wagon will be filled or left empty, can dictate how much – and where – extra weight can be added.

The choice of couplings is also of paramount importance, although this is too large a subject to shoehorn into these early chapters. Instead, the opening demonstrations will concentrate on getting the basics of plastic kits right before pausing for a full lowdown on coupling options in Chapter 8.

IS FINESCALE FOR YOU?

For an increasing number of modellers, established commercial gauges are an unsatisfactory compromise and finescale options now exist in 2mm, 4mm and 7mm scales. EM and P4 gauges have grown in popularity amongst the 4mm fraternity, due in part to the availability of ready-made track and points. OO gauge is really an anomaly, or, rather, it is a mixture of two scales: 4mm scale trains and scenery on 3.5mm scale track. The 16.5mm track gauge (distance between the inner faces of the rails) is a long-standing compromise first introduced into Britain by Bassett-Lowke and Stewart-Reidpath in the early 1920s. The rails are suited more to HO scale, yet the models themselves are a little larger, making them easier to assemble and handle.

Originally envisaged as a scale ideal for indoor model railways, HO was designed to be half the size of the contemporarily ubiquitous O gauge; hence the HO moniker, meaning Half of O gauge. While the smaller size of locomotives gave rise to difficulties in producing reliable electrical mechanisms (Bassett-Lowke's first HO set was clockwork-powered), the slightly larger size of OO gave manufacturers a little more room to manoeuvre. The choice to remain with the existing 3.5mm scale HO track gauge while enlarging the rolling stock to 4mm scale was presumably down to prudent economic reasons.

Writing in 1937, Ernest Twining, one of the early pioneers of serious railway modelling in the UK, saw little future in this 'stupid' arrangement, preferring to overlook the 16.5mm OO track gauge 'in the hope that it will in time be abandoned'. Twining may not have foreseen the proliferation of OO gauge as the 'standard' British scale in the second half of the twentieth century, but he did set out the case for more accurate 4mm scale modelling, albeit with a track gauge slightly oversize at 19mm. He certainly was not alone and finescale 4mm modellers have worked to implement closer-to-scale alternatives, resulting in the EM (or Eighteen Millimetre) and P4 (Proto-4mm) gauges. Being two variations on a similar theme, the latter could be said to be slightly more rigorous, given that EM has a gauge of 18.2mm and P4 a more exact 18.83mm. The variance of 0.63mm could be seen as negligible, especially as there is virtually no discernible visual difference to the casual observer, yet the two scales foster some passionate adherents. The very fine tolerances required in ultra-finescale modelling, especially in P4, demand close attention to mechanical detail, such as axles, wheels and rails. This can be very time-consuming, but it is often these technical factors that are of interest to many such modellers.

The inaccuracy of OO gauge may catch the headlines, but proprietary O gauge is not without its faults, with a track gauge 1mm too narrow (it should be 33mm for standard gauge track). Additionally, the proportions of locomotives and rolling stock from some quarters have tended to conform more to the generous Continental loading gauge, rather than the confined UK version.

Somewhat bewilderingly, the Gauge O Guild lists four distinct versions of O gauge – Standard; Coarse Standard; Fine Standard; and Scale Seven, the latter using a 33mm track gauge and more exacting scale dimensions. It is amusing to note that the late model railway designer and writer, Cyril Freezer, once described Scale Seven as 'only distinguishable from O gauge by the large notices attached to the layouts at exhibitions'.

British N gauge gets its name from the 9mm ('N' for nine) distance between the rails and this too has its compromises, leading finescale enthusiasts to build their models to a more precise version of 2mm scale, which calculates to a 1:152 scale ratio, giving a track gauge of 9.4mm.

All of these numbers can get a bit confusing and we have not even begun to deal with the various narrow gauge variations. Putting the head scratching to one side, pursuance of the finescale route is a decision best left to the individual and a number of useful contacts are provided in the Appendix. Despite the odd finescale dalliance, I have yet to change my OO ways, although the improved appearance of EM or P4 track over even the best quality OO equivalent cannot be ignored. Indeed, constructing the majority of rolling-stock kits to EM or P4 does not involve too much extra work, even if compensated axles are demanded (see Chapter 14). However, what continues to put me off is the chore and financial implications of having to rewheel RTR locomotives

Most proprietary gauges are not exact enough for some modellers, which is why a number of finescale equivalents have emerged. In 4mm scale, EM and P4 modellers use more realistic renditions of standard gauge track than that offered by commercial OO. The difference can be appreciated in this view of OO and EM track. Can you tell which is which?

Kit building in EM or P4 is not too difficult, as far as rolling stock is concerned. In most cases, it is only a matter of moving the brake gear to line up with the wheels. However, many finescale enthusiasts also prefer to add compensation units to their chassis.

and stock – especially steam traction – before they can enter service.

Whatever your views and aspirations are, the decision must be made before kit-building projects begin, not least as replacement wheel sets and compensation units must be obtained. Some kit makers who provide wheels with their kits also offer to exchange the standard units for finescale equivalents with only a modest charge (far cheaper than buying new stock), so make sure you read the kit's instructions or catalogue before sending off for new wheels from elsewhere.

FINISHING OPTIONS

Another factor to bear in mind at the beginning is the matter of how you will be finishing the kit once it has been assembled. Is the shade of paint available off the shelf, or will you have to mix your own? If so, how will it be colour-matched? Do you have a reference source to hand, such as a colour swatch?

More of the finishing process is discussed in Chapter 16, although some thought should be given to the painting stages before assembly begins, in case certain components or subassemblies will be easier to finish before the whole vehicle is put together. Indeed, various kits offer little in the way of help for detailing and painting interiors, as the carriage body may be designed to be sealed up before painting.

Many of these preliminary decisions are eased with the benefit of experience and hopefully the ensuing chapters will guide the reader in the right direction. Taking the time to plan the project from the beginning will lessen the risk of a half-completed kit sitting around forlornly after a snag is encountered. If extra wheels, bearings, detailing components, paints and decals are required, why not order them all at the outset so that they will all be in hand by the time the project is started? Similarly, do the research legwork now, so that you have enough images and information before making a start. The more prepared you are, the better job you are likely to make of the model.

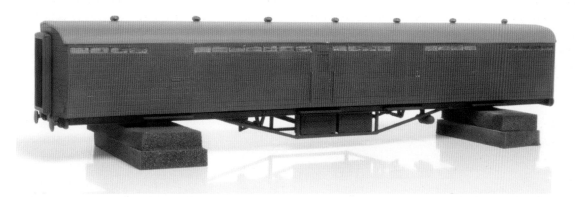

Forward planning helps a kit project to run smoothly and this extends to thinking about how a model will eventually be painted. The glazing had to be fitted to this van before the roof was attached, therefore careful masking was required before the model was finished.

CHAPTER TWO

TOOLS AND EQUIPMENT

Contrary to popular opinion, rolling-stock kit construction requires only a modest capital investment for the majority of what we might call 'intermediate level' tasks. If you are just starting out, only a handful of tools is actually needed and, if chosen carefully, these humble aids should last a modelling lifetime. Indeed, the core of my everyday tool kit dates back to my early teens. Even when progressing towards advanced undertakings, such as etched-metal kits, just a few extra tools are necessary, albeit of increased cost, such as soldering equipment. Aside from the fundamentals, there are a few 'luxuries' that can speed along or aid specific tasks.

There is certainly no reason to amass all the tools you will ever need in one go. Rather, adding to your arsenal gradually, as your experience and confidence grows, will prove more economical. Besides, the more familiar one becomes with the subject, making an informed purchase will save frustration and wasted pennies in the long run.

Throughout the following pages, we will look at what tools and workshop aids will be needed to get started, plus a few suggested products to help your skills develop. Adhesives play just as important a part in modelling as anything else in the toolbox, so a rundown of the relevant formulas is provided. Finally, we will also delve into the properties of each material that is likely to come your way.

As already mentioned, my trusty set of essential tools has stood me in good stead for over twenty years of intensive use. Few of them cost more than a few pounds each, even in today's money. Some types of tool have finite lifespans, especially edged tools that cannot be resharpened. However, choosing knives with replacement blades, for example, can offer great savings in the long run.

TWEEZERS AND CUTTING IMPLEMENTS

The most regularly used items in my toolbox are a set of small, angled-nose tweezers and a Swann-Morton No.3 scalpel handle, usually fitted with 10A pattern blades. They are vital pieces of equipment and were chosen carefully many years ago on the grounds of comfort and effectiveness. Tweezers, of straight and angled shape, must be positive in their sprung action, with the two jaws meeting correctly, and fashioned from quality steel – cheap ones simply distort at the slightest resistance.

Personally, I prefer angled-nose tweezers as they allow for greater accuracy and control, especially in confined areas. I use a No.7, 120mm long, stainless-steel set and these have proved more than able to cope with a vast variety of tasks over the years. Self-closing tweezers, working in the opposite manner whereby squeezing the arms open the jaws, are fine for clamping small objects lightly, thus reducing fatigue in the hand. Other tools are available with sliding clamps that lock the jaws closed, giving a greater grip, although I find a peg attached to my trusty tweezers does exactly the same job.

For ultra-fine work in smaller scales, there is a wealth of choice in size and profile of tweezers, with

The Dent Workshop could not function without this basic set of tools that fits happily inside a small metal tin.

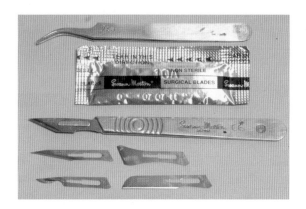

Invest in a good quality set of angled-nose tweezers and a Swann-Morton scalpel with a selection of interchangeable blades will suit many tasks and materials. Blades will need to be changed frequently, as anything other than a razor-sharp edge is asking for trouble in terms of sloppy work or potential injury. If the knife's not cutting, the temptation is to exert more pressure, with subsequent loss of control; it is far easier just to change the blade.

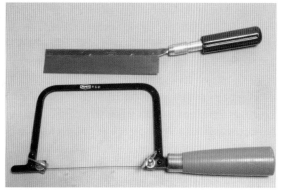

A razor saw, with a stiffened blade, is another tool-kit essential. Useful for accurate cutting of thicker plastics, resin, wood or metal, a mitre box is also helpful for more advanced tasks. Jeweller's piercing saws are great for cutting deeper or more intricate shapes, while junior and full-size hacksaws will also come in handy. Keep one or two spare blades in stock, especially for a piercing saw.

prices ranging from a few pounds up to about £50 for the more specialist devices. For workers in 7mm scale and above, larger jaws may be desired to cope with bulkier components, or longer arms to reach into deeper recesses. Either way, spend a little extra if you can, as a set of tweezers may well see far more action than any other tool in your kit, so needs to be up to the job.

Shears are a boon for cutting plastic and metal parts from the fret or trimming to size. Xuron offers tools optimized for use with certain materials, while some sturdier tin snips or shears will help with harder or thicker metals. Cutting accurately without damaging the material is a vital part of kit building, so investing in good-quality tools is recommended.

Legendary Japanese kit maker Tamiya produces a number of small but invaluable tools, including this handsaw for use with plastics, resin and wood-based materials. With a choice of two blade sizes, the tool is basically a miniature version of the Japanese carpenter's pull saw, or nokogiri. *The teeth are arranged to cut on the pull stroke rather than the push, as with Western saws, giving the user far more control and avoiding that hideous 'wobble' of the blade when tackling tough materials.*

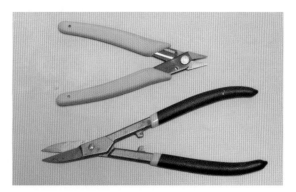

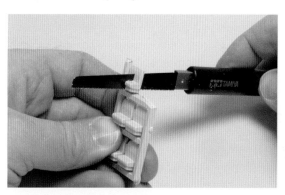

A knife has to be capable of work on various materials and able to be manipulated in awkward spots – so a bulky thing like a Stanley knife is good only for heavy-duty tasks. The ability to interchange blades, not only to keep a keen edge, but also to suit different tasks, is of immense help, with the Swann-Morton tool fitting the bill admirably. Only ever use a sharp blade and keep plenty of spares on hand. Persisting with blunt blades will just lead to poor results and a greater risk of injury.

For tougher jobs, where more pressure will be brought to bear on the blade, a light-duty scalpel may break and cause injury. Instead, a sturdier blade will be necessary, with a larger handle to provide more grip and control. For really thick lumps of material (more than 3mm thick), a set of shears or a razor saw will be far more effective than a knife. Shears provide leverage and safe operation and are excellent for cleanly cutting plastic or metal parts from their frets. Different tools are optimized for use with certain materials, although generally metal shears work just as well on plastics (but not *vice versa*). A razor saw, meanwhile, possesses a large number of fine cutting teeth and a straight reinforced blade, producing clean cuts through plastic, resin, wood or soft metal. Because the teeth are so small, they are liable to clogging, especially when cutting resin or plastic (though they can be cleared with a stiff brush and the blade's strengthening ribs limit the depth to which it will cut.

DRILLS

In general, hand-operated drills are preferable for the vast majority of modelling tasks, not least on cost and noise grounds. Pin vices, of varying sizes and capacities, offer far more control when drilling small holes in any material. Trying to maintain accuracy with a heavy power drill is not easy, even when the speed can be adjusted. When we are dealing with holes of only a fraction of a millimetre, the mismatch between the drill's bulk and the fragile bit usually ends with the latter breaking. There is also the risk of the bit wandering off from its intended destination, unless a centre punch is used beforehand. Even then,

Drilling is an inevitable task, whether it be opening out moulded apertures or adding extra details like handrails or brake rigging. A set of pin vices and bits can be obtained fairly cheaply, although you must expect breakages of smaller bits and keep a spare of the more commonly used sizes. The ideal set to have consists of bits from 0.3mm up to 3mm, in 0.1mm increments.

the power tool still offers more chance of the hole being misaligned than when cut patiently by hand. Friction is an important factor, with a drill generating considerable heat when rotating in a power drill, even on a low speed setting, which can be disastrous if drilling into plastic or resin.

This is not to say that powered drills do not have a place in our toolbox; quite the opposite, in fact. For larger holes, especially in harder materials, they can sometimes be preferable, particularly if you have the luxury of a bench-mounted pillar drill; but more on this subject in later chapters.

General-purpose twist drill bits, sometimes referred to as 'jobber' bits, are fine for the majority of tasks, the tips of these being ground to an angle of 140 degrees. However, for better results in sheet metals, a flatter angle of 110 degrees is preferable to lessen the risk of the bit snatching the material as it cuts through the surface and causing distortion. Again, with careful use in a pin vice or hand drill, this effect can be minimized, but we have much less control over such matters with a power tool.

A set of bits ranging from 0.3mm up to 3mm, in 0.1mm increments, will cover all bases and a number of spare smaller bits (1mm and below) will cover for

Powered mini-drills, as offered by the likes of Dremel, have many uses but are not recommended for use with sub-1mm bits. The heavy tool and delicate bit combination invariably ends in tears and accuracy is often sacrificed for the sake of speed. However, as will be seen in later chapters, power drills are great for tasks such as milling and abrading. A cordless tool usually proves easier to handle.

any breakages – much grief can be saved by having a few extra bits, rather than trying to make do with the wrong size if the one you are using breaks.

MEASURING UP

It is probably not surprising that accurate measuring and marking are of vital importance, so investing in a decent steel rule and a scriber tool will be rewarded with superior results. Calipers are also a worthwhile addition, offering the facility of accurate measuring, down to fractions of millimetres or inches. Some also offer a depth gauge and the method of reading off the dimensions varies according to the type of tool – dials, Vernier scales and digital read-outs are all available, at varying costs. Imperial or metric scales (or both) can be chosen according to preference, with digital tools offering the convenience of instant conversions.

Modeller's scale rules are a real blessing, saving precious minutes spent in head scratching, pencil chewing and brain churning mental arithmetic. Available in all of the popular modelling scales (2, 3.5, 4 and 7mm), they offer a ready-reckoning service for instant checking or setting-out of the correct scale measurements.

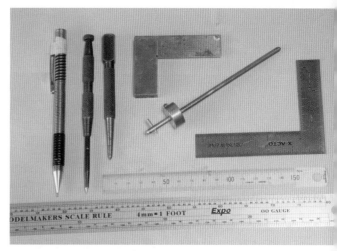

Another area where a little extra investment pays dividends is in measuring and marking tools. A quality steel rule with imperial and metric measurements, a mini-set square and a scribing tool are recommended. Ground to a slightly shallower, angled tip, a scriber can also double as a centre punch, marking holes accurately for drilling in soft materials. Modellers' scale rules are also a great help, available for N, HO, OO and O gauges.

Calipers, in digital, Vernier or dial format, are luxuries that ease the measurement of complex 3-D objects. Great for gauging thicknesses, depths and lengths, they make quick work of divining whether a sheet of brass is 0.005 or 0.0010in thick, something nigh on impossible with a ruler!

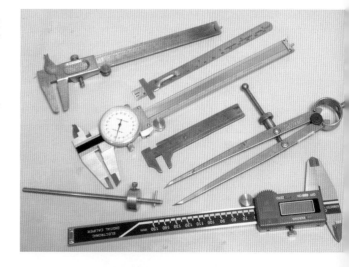

Another excellent use for a set of calipers is in gauging the right size of drill bit for the job at hand. Unless you keep your set in clearly marked wallets, choosing the right bit from a tin full of drills can be tricky.

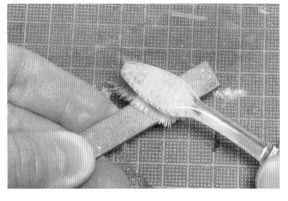

Older plastic or metal kits sometimes call for massive amounts of excess material to be removed before assembly and a 'bastard cut' file will make quick work with less clogging. Cleaning files after use will keep them keen, with a steel brush recommended following work on whitemetal. An old toothbrush will shift plastic or resin deposits.

ABRASIVES

Needle files, of varying shape, are cheaply obtained, although a good-quality set will last longer. The teeth will wear out when used with tough materials like metal, but softer plastics and wood will clog the faces, requiring the intervention of a stiff brush. Whitemetal, being a soft alloy, is also prone to clogging files and requires a steel- or brass-bristled brush to clear the teeth effectively.

A set of needle files, of different profiles, can be obtained cheaply and a couple of larger, flat files will prove useful for dressing larger surfaces, especially wagon or carriage body sides or underframe components. Engineers' files are offered in the delightfully termed 'bastard cut', with coarse teeth, or 'second cut' for a gentler abrasive surface. Sanding sticks and pads are a great alternative to sheet abrasives and can be used wet or dry.

Files, no matter how fine the teeth may be set, are bound to leave a fairly rough surface, so should be followed with sanding sticks or wet-or-dry abrasive paper. For particularly fine results, especially on plastics or pre-painted surfaces, micromesh abrasives are hard to beat. With a rubber-coated backing, the sheets should be used wet whenever possible to avoid clogging and grades are available from 3,600 down to 12,000grit. Used properly, they can produce a mirror-like shine.

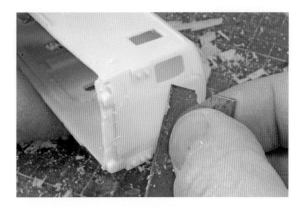

Scraper blades are handy for flattening surfaces or removing unwanted detail without 'digging in' like a knife can. They must be used and stored with care, however.

Abrasive sheets, preferably of the wet-or-dry variety, will be needed to smooth surfaces after working with files. It is common practice to work through the grades, beginning with a 120grit for shaping or removing heavy surface scratching. A 240grit will then smooth the marks left by the 120grit and so on, working down through 360, 600 and 1,000grit grades.

Super-fine abrasives, including the excellent Alclad2 Micromesh brand, offer grades from 3,600 to 12,000grit that combine to leave a perfectly burnished, glass-like surface. Micromesh is backed with a rubberized coating, in contrast to the paper or cloth-backed wet-or-dry varieties, giving it a much more flexible and long-lasting character.

For best results, all of the above abrasive sheets should be used wet, being rinsed at regular intervals to clear away debris that will eventually clog the surface. The water also acts as an effective lubricant, making the job a lot easier and quicker.

THE WORKSHOP ENVIRONMENT

The use of sharp implements and toxic adhesives, while at the same time aiming for accurate and detailed kit building, requires a decent work surface. A workbench, after all, provides the foundations for modelling, although it need not be big – just a square foot will do. A desk is the optimum, or a dining table if the rest of the household does not object. Covering with a protective layer is recommended and a cutting mat will preserve the life of sharp tools, as well as offering a non-slip working surface.

Adequate lighting is another vital factor, if eyestrain and fatigue are to be avoided. Working in plenty of natural light is the ideal, but this is not always possible, especially for the evening hobbyist. Instead, daylight-simulating bulbs and lamps are the next best thing, offering a clean, gentle light as opposed to the harsh glare of regular household light bulbs or fluorescent tubes. Most importantly, avoid working in the shadows. Remember that comfort and safety are of paramount importance.

Ensuring adequate ventilation is also vital and cannot be overstated. The majority of adhesives that we will be using, as well as soldering and painting, can create some nasty fumes that may be injurious to health. It is all too easy to get carried away with assembly, not realizing the extent to which solvent vapours have built up in the room. Only upon leaving and re-entering the room do you realize just what a toxic environment you have been sitting in for the

You may as well be comfortable while practising your hobby. A decent table (not wobbly), plenty of light and ventilation, plus a cutting mat to protect the surface and your tools are all that are required.

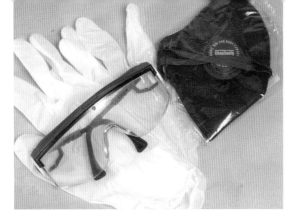

Eye protection is essential whenever drilling or cutting with powered tools, as well as protecting against flying debris when trimming metal (especially wire). A dust mask is always recommended when sanding or filing plastics or resin, as the ultra-fine dust irritates the nasal passages and may cause respiratory problems. A mask is also vital whenever spraying paint, with a correct grade of filter employed. Vinyl gloves are perfect for protecting the skin from solvent-based glues, paints or liquids without affecting the ability to handle delicate objects and tools.

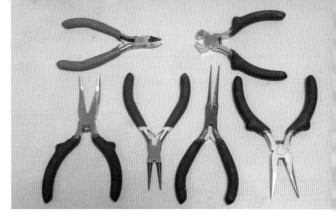

I have become quite a connoisseur of miniature pliers over the years, with an array of different tools to suit different tasks. Round- and flat-nosed, straight or angled, serrated and smooth jaws; they each have their role in holding, locating, shaping and pulling. End cutters are equally useful, allowing near-flush cuts against a flat surface.

past few hours. Unless you want to do irreparable damage to your body, always work with a nearby window open.

Continuing the health and safety lecture, a good set of goggles will protect against flying debris from power tools and a facemask is a necessity when spraying paints or creating dust from cutting, filing and sanding plastics and, especially, resin. Protecting your skin is also something to consider if using solvent-based paints or adhesives and a box of disposable latex gloves will be a worthwhile addition to the workshop. The following chapter highlights in greater detail the risks involved with particular materials and adhesives.

AIDS AND DEVICES

Miniature pliers are another very important set of tools. Bending, shaping, holding and twisting are all functions made easier with a decent set of long-nosed pliers. Jaws with serrated inner faces are great for providing extra purchase on their quarry, but they can also damage softer materials; pairs of smooth-jawed pliers help in this regard. Furthermore, round-nose tools allow for easier shaping of wire, strip metal or plastics.

Pliers with a sharp cutting area at the base of the jaws help with trimming wire, although these tend to leave a fairly rough edge to the cut. If you have a set of shears or snips (mentioned earlier), use these for accurate, clean cuts instead. End-cutters, on the other hand, allow for almost flush cuts against a surface; great for trimming handrails or brake linkages *in situ*.

Other invaluable items can be classed more as aids than tools, in that they may not actually perform a direct cutting or shaping function. However, they will allow operations to be performed with greater accuracy and convenience and, therefore, will soon earn themselves a place in the workshop's front line. A vice takes the place of the modeller's best friend – the third arm. How we all wish we had an extra limb when fumbling with awkward parts that simply will not sit still while we work on them. A vice, with cushioned jaws and the ability to cope with uneven shapes, can prove invaluable.

Some vices can even be tilted or rotated without disturbing the workpiece and these come highly recommended. Similarly, hand vices can hold parts steady during drilling or shaping, or even perform useful tricks such as pressing wheels on to axles. Again, this can be viewed as something of a luxury, but a selection of vices – large and small – can help greatly with specific tasks, as will be demonstrated throughout this volume.

Clamps, of varying pattern, help in keeping parts correctly aligned while measuring or bonding and

Table vices, such as this wonderful tool from Dremel, act as an extra hand and make life much easier for the modeller. Being able to rotate and tilt the workpiece without disturbing it makes this vice irreplaceable. The plastic jaws offer a tight grip with a reduced risk of damage and the base can also double as a mount for a Dremel mini-drill. Hand vices, of varying sizes, are also welcome additions, as is a small mitre box for use with a razor saw.

can assist when making 'dry runs' prior to gluing or soldering to ensure everything fits as it should. Spring clamps offer great convenience and are offered in different sizes at bargain prices, although cheaper still is the humble sprung clothes peg. Elastic bands,

A range of clamps to hold parts still during assembly can be most useful. Spring clamps can often be found in your local pound shop, while sprung wooden clothes pegs are equally useful. Mini-sash and G clamps are also cheap and highly versatile.

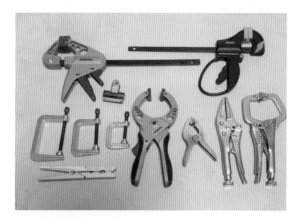

sticky tape and Blu-Tack also have their light-duty applications.

We will look at more specialist tools and devices in later chapters, as they become relevant to the tasks at hand. In brief, though, a Hold & Fold is one of those tools that, once having used it, you wonder how you ever managed without one. Designed for accurately shaping sheet metal, they are not the cheapest devices around, especially the larger sizes. However, it will pay for itself soon enough, with faster and better quality results every time.

Smaller and cheaper aids abound in the form of back-to-back wheel gauges, handrail folding jigs, nut and rivet formers, plus wheelbase measuring and alignment jigs. Aside from the back-to-gauge, none of these is essential and similar tools can be fabricated from scrap materials or improvised. However, they do allow for easier, faster and more uniform results. So, if you are planning on building a lot of kits over the coming years, their presence on the workbench will be more than justified.

A sheet of glass acts as a perfect reference surface to ensure that a vehicle is sitting on all wheels correctly and a short length of track is also handy, especially if working away from your layout. A number of other fancy tools and devices will become necessary as we tackle more advanced techniques, but these will be discussed in later chapters.

CHAPTER THREE

MATERIALS AND ADHESIVES

'To be forewarned is to be forearmed.'

This excellent piece of advice is highly relevant to the budding kit builder. Indeed, the attainment of knowledge will open the door to successful modelling. An understanding of materials and their properties allows one to anticipate how they will behave in certain situations. Choosing the most appropriate adhesive or bonding method, selecting the right tools for the job and knowing which materials are compatible or suited to a specific task will avoid costly mistakes.

Some apparently innocuous materials may demand precautions in handling, bonding or painting, while others may need special treatment before assembly can even begin. Some adhesives will destroy certain plastics yet will adhere perfectly to others. Oil or heat resistance may be of paramount importance, while damp conditions may render other materials useless.

With all of these variables in mind, this chapter looks into the materials and manufacturing processes employed in kit production, explaining how and why certain substances are suited to specific tasks. It is also wise to develop a working knowledge of adhesives.

COMMON PLASTICS

Plastic, or more specifically polystyrene, will have provided the vast majority of modellers with their first experiences in kit building. How many of us cut our teeth on Airfix 'Spitfires' and 'Hurricanes', spending our early years wrestling boxes full of plastic parts and tubes of stringy glue?

Polystyrene is employed for the majority of components within most model railway rolling-stock and scenery kits. In its original form, polystyrene is a hard, brittle compound perfectly suited to forming clear parts, such as glazing. With the addition of a rubberized additive and opaque colouring agents, the material takes on a more flexible composition. Also known as high-impact polystyrene, or just simply styrene, this flexible variety can also be moulded, extruded into rod, tube or section (as found in the Evergreen or Slater's ranges), or pressed into flat sheets of smooth or embossed plastic card. Polystyrene can also be expanded with air to form lightweight packaging foam or scenery products.

Styrene forms the perfect raw material for the injection-moulding process, with the ability to take extremely fine detail. It is also very easy to work with – cutting, trimming and filing require very little effort and parts can be 'welded' together with liquid solvents to form incredibly strong bonds. On the downside, styrene does not have a high resistance to oils, nor can it withstand high temperatures without melting or distorting. This does have some benefit, as deformed parts can be straightened by immersing in warm water.

Tougher, oil-resistant plastics like Acrylonitrile Butadiene Styrene (ABS) are commonly employed

For generations, the humble injection-moulded plastic construction kit has given countless youths a taste of model-making. Pungent, stringy glue, enamel paints and wonky wings on a Spitfire ... what sweet memories are made of these!

The same injection-moulding principle is employed on the vast majority of plastic rolling-stock kits. Polystyrene forms the superstructure and fine details, while the underframe is often rendered in self-coloured, oil-resistant ABS.

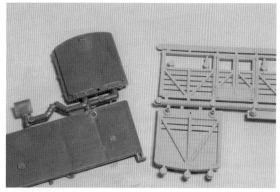

Raised disc shapes reveal where the molten plastic entered the moulds and such features may be harmless enough if they will be hidden inside a closed bodyshell. However, they can often impede the fitting of other components. The kit on the right (from Slater's) boasts less intrusive, 'off-stage' injection points that can be simply trimmed away.

where some form of lubrication will be required. Due to its extreme flexibility, ABS is also perfect for parts that need to be resistant to handling or stretched for assembly/disassembly, such as detachable bogie frames and certain detailing parts supplied with ready-to-run locomotives, such as brake pipes and linkages. It can also be found in a number of plastic rolling-stock kits, especially in the form of wagon and carriage underframe components. ABS also boasts a superior surface finish to most other plastics.

An ever-present factor of the injection-moulding technique, 'flash' needs to be removed from components before assembly. In many cases, older tooling is more prone to the phenomenon, brought about by wear on the faces of the moulds.

Because of ABS's resilience against oils and solvents, paints and adhesives may struggle to form a bond with the surface. However, it can be dyed in all manner of colours during production, so, from a manufacturer's point of view, there is no need to

Radial marks such as these are fairly rare and can be tricky to remove after assembly. Caused by the faces of the moulding tools not being cleaned up properly after milling, a file and abrasive paper will remove them, although care must be taken not to damage any delicate moulded detail. Happily, this hopper base is barely visible once the wagon is finished, so the marks can be ignored.

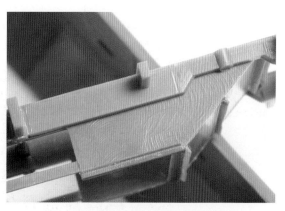

While styrene is the material du jour of the majority of injection-moulded components, underframes and bogies tend to favour the use of tougher plastics such as ABS or butyrate. These bogies are formed from the latter and require a strong solvent to bond them securely.

paint it afterwards. For us, though, who may want to change the colour, add weathering or extra components, we need to choose the correct adhesives and paints, as well as ensuring that the surfaces are properly prepared.

ABS cannot be produced in transparent form and lacks sufficient weather resistance to be suitable for prolonged use outdoors, due to its slightly porous nature. Indeed, fluctuating temperatures and

Styrene is also favoured for creating plastic sheet, strip, section and rod in the ranges of Slater's, Evergreen and Plastruct. Keeping a selection of sheet and strip on hand helps with detailing work or joint reinforcement.

humidity can cause ABS components to expand or become distorted.

Acetate is another common form of clear plastic that is sometimes employed for model glazing. Cellulose Acetate Butyrate, commonly referred to as butyrate, is formulated to be free-flowing, with high-impact strength, and is less prone to cracking than regular acetate. Plastruct makes use of a coloured version of this material in certain lines of tubing and moulded fittings. The high viscosity also lends butyrate well to the injection-moulding process, being found in high-grade, low-production kits such as offered by DC Kits.

FORMING PLASTICS

By far the most prevalent means of forming plastic kit components is the injection-moulding process. The roots of this technique can be traced back to an 1872 patent lodged by the Smith & Lock Company. However, the idea failed to take off until the advent of Leo Baekeland's invention of Bakelite in the 1920s, which went on to revolutionize the manufacture of all manner of everyday objects.

The injection-moulding process consists of metal moulds, or 'tools', produced usually in two parts. When these are brought together, small lead-in holes allow the liquid plastic to be injected into the mould under pressure, running throughout the tooling via a series of channels that form what we call the 'sprue', from which the various components are suspended.

With small-scale models, the mould tools invariably feature tiny, intricate shapes. Accordingly, the plastic must find its way easily into these tight spots and this is where the flexible properties of polystyrene, ABS and butyrate come in handy. These plastics are usually obtained by the manufacturer in pelletized form, liquefied in heated hoppers above the moulding machine and then forced into the moulds by compressed air.

The moulds also feature ejector points, where small pins push out the solidified plastic when the mould is opened. On many kits, the injection lead-in points and ejector-pin location can be traced by the

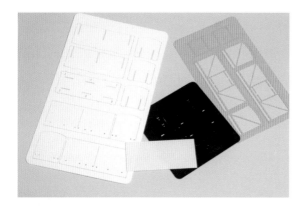

Laser-cut plastic kits and components are becoming increasingly popular. The process is not great for rendering intricate 3-D shapes and the amount of surface detail is limited by the flatness of the material. However, with careful design, kits can be created in several layers to produce a pleasing amount of relief.

circular marks that are left behind. A sign of a quality kit is the ejector-pin marks (if any) being located in inconspicuous areas, whereas the majority of kits leave the modeller with a certain amount of cleaning up to do before the parts can be assembled.

On the subject of tidying up mouldings, the issue of 'flash' is important. This excess plastic seeps between the two sides of the mould and usually signifies aging or poorly machined tools. A little is

It is hard to believe that these wagons were once simply sheets of flat plastic. Providing the 'bare bones', these York Modelmaking kits have received a variety of cast and etched-metal parts.

almost inevitable due to the nature of the process, but excessive tracts of unwanted material can prove a real bore for the customer, who has to trim it all away before any parts can be glued together.

Vacuum forming is a process seldom seen in railway modelling, especially rolling-stock subjects, although I have come across a few carriage roofs, clear glazing packs and the odd scenic kit so-rendered. The technique consists of thin plastic being warmed and then sucked down over a mould, the plastic retaining its new shape as it cools and the mould is removed.

Laser cutting of plastic is an area that is currently enjoying something of a boom, with a number of new manufacturers offering a variety of off-the-shelf kits as well as a bespoke cutting service. Suited especially to flat sheets of plastic, kits are generally built up from several individual layers to form attractive models with plenty of relief.

Incidentally, plastics can be crudely divided into two main categories – thermosetting and thermoplastics. All of the materials mentioned above are thermoplastics and offer much in the way of workability and recyclability. They can be melted at relatively low temperatures and cured repeatedly without losing any of their inherent properties.

Conversely, thermosetting plastics are usually liquid in their original form and are cured by means of heating or chemical reactions. Once solidified, the effect is irreversible, so limiting their usefulness and recycling potential. Thermosetting plastics are not frequently encountered by modellers, except in the case of certain adhesives or casting mediums that make use of a thermoplastic ingredient and setting compound, such as polyurethane or epoxy resins.

RESIN

Resin models have grown in popularity over the past decade or so, seeing use in anything from detailing components to complete kits. Ideally suited to small-batch production, they are mainly offered by the smaller 'cottage industry' suppliers and have been a staple for DIY and limited-run military and aviation kits for many years.

Anyone who has ever had any contact with this material will testify both to its excellent potential and its limitations. The resin itself is based on a polyurethane polymer and is a cheap material, both in its procurement and in the production and operation of the moulding process. Supplied in two parts, namely the resin and a hardening compound, these must be mixed carefully in specified proportions and poured into a prepared mould. Depending on the material, no heating or pressurized feed is required.

A mould master must be produced in plastic, wood or metal, which is then placed inside a container and surrounded by cold-cure silicone rubber. In the case of hollow forms, such as bodyshells, an inner and outer mould will be formed. Silicone has the potential to form itself around even the most intricate details and shapes, allowing high-quality reproductions if the work is carried out properly. Naturally, the quality of the original master and the mould directly influences the quality of the finished product.

The completed silicone rubber mould is then filled with a mix of polyurethane resin and a hardening compound. The resulting chemical reaction produces a warming effect within the mould, thus helping the material to harden. However, this heat also works to degrade the silicone mould, reducing its lifespan to anything between fifty and one-hundred castings. For the cured resin to be ejected without damaging any delicate details, the mould must be coated in a chemical release agent.

While the production process negates the need for expensive machinery, the resin casting process has its drawbacks. Air bubbles, trapped inside the mould, are a common problem, especially on complex forms. That said, a producer who knows his job will find a way of avoiding these pitfalls in the first place, resulting in castings with only the most minor of flaws.

Sadly, such expertise is not universal in rolling-stock kits and the modeller can sometimes be faced with hours of remedial work before assembly can even begin. Moreover, the design of the kit must allow for the material's limitations. Brittle, soft and liable to warp, resin is not ideal for long, thin

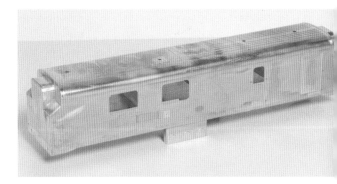

With one-piece resin kits, a master has to be created by scratch-building, or by other means such as this assembled set of brass etches. Put together by the author for DC Kits, the brass parts were created using computer software and based on the plans and measurements of the real thing. The inside of the shell had to be 'beefed up' with plastic card to give the resin copies sufficient strength.

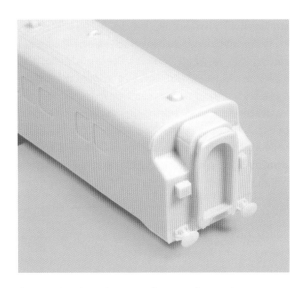

All that hard work to get the complex ends correct has paid off with a lovely, crisp resin moulding. This is how it looked straight from the box, illustrating the great potential of resin kits.

components, or those where straightness is vital, such as vehicle chassis. It will be found that the best kits offer a brass or plastic chassis rather than one rendered in resin. With this in mind, I heartily recommend buying only the best-quality resin cast models and being sure to inspect a kit's components carefully before purchase.

Polyurethane resin castings are fairly durable and resistant to oils and most solvents. It cannot be coloured at the production stage, hence the reason why all castings are supplied in a yellowish shade. Polyester resin is a cheaper and softer material that is also used in kit making, but is even more prone to the formation of air bubbles within the moulds. Also, it cannot reproduce delicate detail as well as polyurethane.

METALS

There are instances where plastics are not suitable, for example when the material must be entirely rigid and resistant to mechanical wear, while also being rendered in ultra-thin section. In these cases, metal is the prime candidate, with a number of alloys (an amalgam of different metals) being commonly found in rolling-stock kits, either in the form of castings, turned components (produced by turning on a lathe), or etched sheets. They may form the bulk of the kit's contents, or may be included as extra-fine details, where the metal offers specific advantages over the predominant kit material.

Metal kits offer an advantage in terms of the material's weight, negating the need to add extra ballast, as is the case with virtually all plastic or resin kits. However, in larger scales, this can result in a supremely heavy vehicle and baseboards must be constructed with this in mind.

BRASS

This popular alloy consists mainly of copper and zinc. Its strength and hardness varies according to its composition and the nature of the heat or chemical treatment during manufacture. Brass possesses a moderate weight, is bright yellow in colour when clean and oxidizes to a dirty brown or green in extreme circumstances. It can be joined either by soldering, brazing or with suitable adhesives.

Available in sheet, tube, rod, bars, angle strip and wire, the material lends itself well to model-making and particularly the production of etched or turned

Brass kits can be expensive and appear daunting, yet can be surprisingly simple to put together. Once again, though, it all depends on the quality of the kit's design and production. Some are designed for elite modellers, with impenetrable instructions and parts that refuse to go together without the intervention of expert hands and fancy tools. On the other hand, kits like this MARC Models product are thoughtfully produced, with tab-and-slot joints and immaculately rendered components.

detailing and kit components. Its low melting point also suits it to the creation of cast components.

When in thin sheet form, brass is highly flexible and can be folded and rolled to intricate shapes and can be rendered in a variety of thicknesses, in some cases down to just five-thousands of an inch.

COPPER

A pure metal, it is red-brown in colour and fairly soft, but can be hardened by hammering or bending. Copper possesses superb thermal and electrical conductivity, hence its common use in power cables. Available in sheet, tube, rod, bar, angle strip and wire, it can be soldered, brazed and glued.

STEEL

Steel comes in various forms, being an alloy of iron and carbon as well as a variety of other metals. Varying the proportion of the ingredients and the type of heat treatment used during production creates widely differing materials. Mild steel, for instance, contains little carbon and is relatively soft and lightweight.

Carbon steel, however, has a higher carbon content and is very hard yet brittle. It can be toughened by tempering (reheating to a specific temperature) and is often used to make tools. Silver steel is another high-carbon steel, with added chromium for a lustrous finish; stainless steel contains both nickel and chromium, allowing it to resist corrosion.

Steels are seldom involved in rolling-stock kits, other than in the form of weights and the odd detailing component in stainless steel. It cannot be readily soldered, although adhesives are effective.

NICKEL SILVER

Despite the name, there is no silver content in this alloy, being a mix of 60 per cent copper, 20 per cent nickel and 20 per cent zinc. However, its appearance is bright and silver-like and it was used in ancient China as a decorative material. Its popularity in the West grew in the nineteenth century, initially in Germany, and it was subsequently used for bodywork on early motorcars.

Popular for model railway track, it is resistant to corrosion and, although prone to oxidization, it remains highly conductive to electrical currents. Harder than brass, it can still be folded or rolled, albeit requiring more effort. Nickel silver is also regularly used to produce lathe-turned items such as buffers and handrail knobs.

Commonly offered in etched-sheet component form, it can be worked, machined and soldered easily. Even when supplied in thin sheets, its rigidity makes it ideal for chassis frames. Indeed, many kits offer certain vital structural parts in nickel silver, with less important components in the cheaper, softer brass alloy.

WHITEMETAL

Whitemetal is not a specific material, rather a generic term for a number of similar lead- or tin-based alloys. Common ingredients include tin, antimony, lead, cadmium, bismuth and zinc, while copper may also be added (especially to tin-based pewter). The format is dictated by the intended use of the product. Anything from jewellery to engine bearings can be formed from whitemetal alloys.

Its low melting point (typically 150°C) makes whitemetal particularly well suited to casting. For model-making purposes, the material must be able to flow freely into small and intricately shaped moulds, so the alloy's ingredients must reflect that. Soft and fairly flexible, whitemetal can also be brittle, depending on its formulation. The material is dense and is commonly found in rolling-stock kits in the form of cast buffers, air cylinders, underframe components and other similar parts. Entire bodyshells and chassis may also be rendered in whitemetal, assembled from various parts to produce a sturdy model. However, excessive weight can be problematic, especially on layouts with gradients and tight curves. By way of comparison, a typical OO gauge four-wheel wagon in whitemetal will tip the scales at about 100g (3.5oz), whereas a plastic equivalent weighs in at around 25g (0.9oz).

The low melting point also means that care is needed when soldering, with a temperature-

Whitemetal kits are bulkier and sometimes a little cruder than etched-brass or nickel-silver versions. However, there is still some good stuff out there and small producers like David Geen and Genesis offer some real pearls in this medium. The material certainly has its foibles, but the inherent weight comes in handy and, if assembled correctly, whitemetal kits make for sturdy models.

controlled iron and special solders required, although glue can be employed effectively. Whitemetal containing lead must be handled with great care, as this toxic material can cause serious health problems.

ETCHING AND CASTING

My first experience of etching metal was back in Art School, while creating lithographic illustrations, using a wax-covered sheet of aluminium. The reversed image had to be scribed into the wax and the plate submerged in a bath of ferric chloride. The exposed areas were chemically etched for a specified period of time, which dictated how deep the acid worked into the metal. Once cleaned of the etchant and wax, the plate could be used to transfer the image on to paper using inks; just like the prints found in old books.

Etching metal components uses a similar principle, whereby the plans are transferred to a sheet of brass or nickel silver. Until recently, the job was done photographically (the technique known more formally as photo-etching), but these days a computer-controlled system is employed to transfer the 'negative' on to the material. This leaves a resistant coating on the areas of the metal to be retained, while the exposed areas are attacked and destroyed by the chemical etchant.

By limiting the amount of time the metal is in contact with the acid, parts can be etched only halfway through, known as 'half-etches', allowing detail relief or folding lines to be rendered. A good example is in the production of etched nameplates, where the half-etch system renders the numerals and characters.

When sheets of metal require repeated baths in the etchant to produce varying layers, a ridge can often remain along the edges of the components, as if the parts have been laminated from several sheets. On high-quality kits, this ridge will be barely discernible, yet it will still need flattening to allow parts to be slotted together accurately. On poorer kits, inaccurate alignment of the resist on subsequent 'dips' leaves parts requiring plenty of remedial work before assembly can begin.

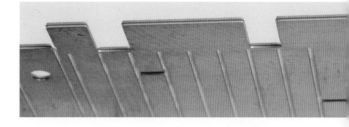

When sheets of metal require repeated baths in the etchant to produce varying layers, a ridge can often remain along the edges of the components. This will need flattening to allow parts to be slotted together accurately.

As my student experiences testify, etching thin sheet metal requires little in the way of expensive equipment and modern computer programmes mean that patterns can be produced on a home computer. Etching fluids are available from electronic hobby outlets (such as Maplin) and, as long as care is taken, decent results can be obtained. However, this is a subject for a book on scratch-building rather than kit building.

Casting in metal offers the chance to render parts in three dimensions, such as air tanks, buffers and valve assemblies. As long as the mould is prepared to a high standard, extremely intricate shapes can be produced en masse. The low melting point of whitemetal alloys allows silicone rubber to be used to create moulds, while casting brass requires a material with better heat resistance.

Lost-wax casting dates back centuries and refers to a process whereby a mould is created in several stages, resulting in a wax copy being bathed in silica and baked to form a tough ceramic-like shell. The wax then melts away, leaving the inside of the mould complete (hence the term 'lost wax') and ready for molten metal to be poured in.

Brass is the commonest material to be cast in this fashion and the resulting components are incredibly tough and capable of taking extremely fine detail. Often, a number of parts are cast in one mould, linked together with a sprue, similar to plastic kits. These require care when cutting apart and some casting marks may need removing prior to assembly.

Lost-wax casting allows supreme levels of detail to be achieved and kits may include a sprue of detail components. As the material is incredibly tough, hand cutters or shears will struggle to cut the parts away cleanly. A carborundum disc in a mini-drill will do the job, but be sure to wear eye protection.

naturally suited to the production of specific parts, such as a chassis in etched nickel silver, cast-brass detail parts and moulded plastic seats. The material may also be dictated by the proposed method of construction. Weight or labour saving may be relevant considerations, with a hefty metal chassis adorned with a resin body, for example. Indeed, it is becoming the norm rather than the exception to find modern kits presented with a variety of materials.

Moreover, kit makers have different preferences, according to their own expertise and production facilities. Dave Alexander, for instance, is a former model-maker for the north-east shipyards and has the ability to create some of the highest-quality whitemetal castings around. Not surprisingly, therefore, the majority of his kits are rendered in this material. In contrast, Just Like the Real Thing offers resin-cast bodyshells in its O gauge rolling stock, complemented by etched and cast-metal components, all produced using state-of-the-art computer-controlled design and production processes.

MIXED-MEDIA KITS

Not all kits are rendered in the same material, be they plastic, resin or metal. Different materials are

OTHER MATERIALS

Wood offers the pleasure of working with a natural material and close-grained timber, such as box or

These days, it is common to find a mix of media within a kit, each material being chosen to suit a specific need. This Model Irish Railways rendition of a cement wagon features a resin body and chassis, with brass and whitemetal detail components.

Timber still has a place in modern kit building, with thin veneers being perfect for wood flooring on open wagons, while sawn stock is the ideal source of ultra-realistic wagonloads.

lime, is perfect for small-scale models. The traditional timber-bodied goods wagon is a fine example, especially in O gauge and above, where using the real material may offer far superior results to plastic or metal.

Indeed, real wood retains a colour and texture that is very difficult to replicate with paint or other materials. Making use of wood dyes simplifies the finishing process and the ease with which it can be worked is another point in wood's favour. All manner of wood varieties are available in strip form – in varying sizes and shapes – from model shops, while veneer can be obtained from specialist craft suppliers. A wood veneer will certainly enhance the decks of wagons and carriage interiors.

Card was once popular for rolling-stock kits, with firms such as Peco offering embossed card overlays and bodyshells for its range of wagon underframes. Cardboard and paper still have their uses, as will be demonstrated in later chapters, such as wagonload formers and van roof coverings.

Card kits used to be all the rage and a few lingered on into the twenty-first century, including this embossed card wagon body from Peco, designed to be cut and folded to shape before mounting on to a matching plastic underframe.

JOINING MATERIALS

Choosing the right adhesive to suit the material and application is important, not only for the short-term goal of getting the bits to stick together, but also for the long-term reliability of the bond. To understand why certain glues are suited to certain materials and situations, it helps to study each of the main adhesive types that we are likely to come across in model kit assembly.

In basic terms, adhesives fall into two main categories – 'mechanical' and 'non-mechanical'. 'Mechanical' glues work to form the interlocking bond with the surfaces of both materials being joined, creating a permanent, intermediate layer. These are ideal for porous materials such as wood or card. Non-porous surfaces may need roughening-up a little to give 'mechanical' glues something on which to gain purchase. 'Non-mechanical' adhesives work best on closely fitting parts, the surfaces being softened by a chemical solvent, fusing them together. The adhesive then evaporates, leaving no trace of any film between the surfaces.

PLASTIC CEMENT

While many of us will have started building plastic kits using tubes of thick polystyrene cement, this adhesive really has no place in scale modelling. It may be fine for beginners, with the advantage that the viscous fluid is less liable to spillage than a thin liquid, but it is almost impossible to achieve neat joints with this stuff. Consisting of a strong methyl-based solvent, tube cement is thickened with dissolved particles of plastic (usually styrene). It is prone to stringing, blocked nozzles and is difficult to apply to small or awkwardly shaped parts, as well as being so powerful that it can actually melt the plastic if applied too thickly.

Liquid plastic cements, on the other hand, contain only the solvent and are thin enough to be applied by brush. Therefore, as much or as little glue can be applied exactly where it is needed and there are various precision applicators available for ultra-fine work. Brands such as Plastic Magic (Deluxe Materials), Plastic Weld (EMA), Mek Pak (Slater's)

and Liquid Poly (Humbrol) are all recommended. Each brand is excellent on styrene, but, with the exception of Humbrol's formula, they can also be used to great effect on tougher plastics such as ABS and butyrate.

Liquid cements work by fusing the two plastic components together, rather like the act of welding metals. With parts prepared and held together, applying a small amount with a brush will allow the liquid to be drawn into the joint by capillary action. The plastic will visibly soften and the bond will begin to form immediately, with just a few moments needed before the joint can be left. It may take several hours for full strength to be achieved, but, in practice, assembly can usually continue within minutes.

This type of adhesive is only truly effective when both mating surfaces are already in contact. When it is desirous to apply glue to one surface before the parts are brought together, a slightly thicker formula is useful. Humbrol's Precision Poly, Revell's Contacta and the non-toxic Roket Plastic are all perfect in this instance.

As may be appreciated, the softening of the plastic can have potentially harmful effects if too much

Liquid poly-cements, such as Mek Pak (Slater's), Plastic Weld (EMA), Liquid Poly (Humbrol) or Plastic Magic (Deluxe) contain a powerful solvent that practically welds the plastic parts together. Evaporating in seconds, the solvent leaves incredibly strong bonds. Suitable only for application on bare plastics, they will destroy painted finishes and certain brands are optimized for particular materials.

The beauty of using thin liquid adhesives is that they can be applied with precision, using a fine paintbrush or a Pin Flow applicator from Deluxe Materials.

Deluxe offers a non-toxic alternative to liquid poly, Roket Plastic Glue. The longer curing time allows for much more control over positioning and it is ideal for use on pre-painted surfaces, such as this Walthers container kit.

solvent is applied. While the plastic will harden again once the adhesive has evaporated, delicate moulded relief may have been damaged. Additionally, it should be mentioned that all types of plastic cement are only truly effective when applied to bare plastic surfaces and are likely to damage painted finishes.

CYANOACRYLATE

Colloquially known as superglue, cyanoacrylate adhesives are available in various formulas to suit different materials and applications. The bog-standard tubes found in supermarkets and hardware stores are fairly crude with a short working life and are best avoided. Brands tailored specifically to modelling use are far more reliable.

The viscosity of the liquid differs according to the glue's projected use. Slow-setting (10–20sec), gel-type 'cyano' is perfect for bonding larger parts, or those that may need a degree of repositioning before the glue sets hard. At the other extreme, ultra-thin versions can penetrate into awkward joints and set within one to four seconds, leaving little chance to adjust the parts.

In the middle lie the majority of general-purpose formulas, offering a few seconds of working time and

an easily managed consistency. Effective for use on virtually all plastics, resin, metals, wood and card, there are a few formulas that are specifically tailored to plastics, such as Roket Poly (Deluxe Materials), Tamiya and Plasti-Zap.

Cyanoacrylate contains some nasty ingredients (including cyanide) and must be used with great care and in an area with plenty of ventilation. It can also damage painted surfaces and clear plastics by leaving a white 'blooming' effect that is very difficult to remove. In enclosed spaces and near glazing, an odourless formula is recommended and, with all cyano-type adhesives, only the bare minimum of glue is required; excess glue can actually weaken the bond.

Activator sprays are helpful additions, speeding up the bond upon application from a spray bottle or eye dropper. These are great for use with slow-setting cyano glue as the parts can be held in place and, when perfectly positioned, the activator is added to cure the bond instantly. Filling powders also exist, designed for mixing with cyano to effect gap-filling.

For when things do not go to plan, debonder liquids are also available. These are good in

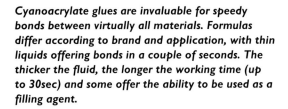

Cyanoacrylate glues are invaluable for speedy bonds between virtually all materials. Formulas differ according to brand and application, with thin liquids offering bonds in a couple of seconds. The thicker the fluid, the longer the working time (up to 30sec) and some offer the ability to be used as a filling agent.

Epoxy glues are available in different formulas, catering for long or short working times (five minutes to one hour). As it takes a few minutes to mix the two parts together, the five-minute stuff has to be used immediately, but a ten- or twenty-minute formula gives enough time to make adjustments before it starts to 'grab'. Clamping may be necessary, as full strength usually takes much longer to achieve. Excess glue can be wiped away with white spirit before it sets. Note also that fast-setting formulas tend to have a shorter shelf life. Glues are invaluable for speedy bonds between virtually all materials. Formulas differ according to brand and application, with thin liquids offering bonds in a couple of seconds. The thicker the fluid, the longer the working time (up to 30sec) and some offer the ability to be used as a filling agent.

emergencies, but can seriously damage plastic or painted surfaces if used in large quantities. For best results, always choose activators, fillers and debonding agents from the same range as the adhesives to ensure full compatibility. Furthermore, cyano-based products benefit from storage in cool, dark conditions. Many modellers recommend keeping them in the fridge, which is fine if the bottles are unopened. However, once in use, taking the glue in and out from a cold store promotes condensation inside the packaging that will ruin the glue. Instead, try to keep your glues in stable, cool conditions as much as possible and accept that, once opened, a jar may only last for about a year in full working order.

EPOXY

This versatile glue is suitable for a great many tasks and materials. Supplied as two separate components, a resin and a hardener, they must be mixed thoroughly in equal measure before the glue becomes 'activated' and begins to harden. Incredibly sticky, it will adhere to almost any surface, provided that it is clean and oil-free and working times are governed

by the formula in use. Commonly, five-, ten-, and twenty-minute formulas are available, as well as more specialist brands that may offer up to an hour before the hardener starts to take effect.

The adhesive is invariably thick and gloopy, so making it an awkward medium for use on very small detail parts, but the resulting bond is tough and waterproof without any discernible shrinkage. Epoxy joints also offer a degree of flexibility, which can be advantageous to mechanical parts under stress or items likely to be handled frequently, in contrast to the tough but brittle bond offered by cyano adhesive. Epoxy is also resistant to fairly high temperatures and is a useful electrical insulator.

CONTACT ADHESIVE

Household names such as Evo-Stik, UHU and Bostik are designed for bonding different materials, including metal, plastic, wood or card, and best results are achieved by spreading a little adhesive on to each surface and allowing them to become slightly tacky. When the parts are brought together, an instant bond is achieved.

Some formulas set clear, but others may cure to a yellowish appearance. Most brands emit fairly strong odours and are liable to stringing, thereby making them difficult to use with precision on smaller parts. However, they do have many uses, especially in scenic modelling. They must be used with care on soft plastics, such as styrene, as some formulas will soften the material and damage raised details.

PVA-TYPE GLUES

Polyvinyl Acetate is a popular form of 'white' glue that is happy bonding wood, card, paper, fabric and plastics. Providing a flexible joint, it can be thinned with water when greater penetration is necessary.

Aliphatic Resin and PVA-based glues have many uses in kit building, as they will bond many materials, including paper, card, wood and plastics.

It is available in many different forms, offering fast or slow curing times, water- or non-waterproof versions and different viscosities for woodworking or specialist craft use.

Commonly referred to as 'wood glue', most brands set to a white film, but others may offer a clear finish. Indeed, liquid glazing compounds are often PVA-based and are perfect for applying clear plastic glazing or used on its own to form crystal-clear films across small apertures.

Aliphatic Resin adhesives are similar in many ways to PVA, but with the added benefit of greater moisture resistance, faster curing and harder, less flexible bonds. Thick glues are ideal for joining wood (the Titebond brand includes some of the best wood glues around), while thinner, penetrating formulas, such as Super 'Phatic! or Roket Card Glue (both Deluxe Materials), are useful for binding loose materials, such as weighting ballast in rolling stock, or joining small timber or card components to like materials or plastics.

FINAL CONSIDERATIONS

There is more to consider when working with each of the materials and adhesives mentioned here, but this extra information will follow in later chapters, described with direct relevance to specific projects and techniques. Moreover, we have not mentioned solders and soldering yet, but this is explained in Chapters 12 and 13.

Cost is also a pertinent factor, especially as the past decade has seen massive hikes in the wholesale price of metals and petrochemicals (used in plastics manufacture), which has inevitably pushed up the cost of kit building. It certainly makes those kits where wheels and bearings are supplied look like great value. Add the cost of painting and finishing products and some kit projects take on the air of an expensive commitment, so it pays to know what you are doing before making a start.

CHAPTER FOUR

FIRST STEPS IN PLASTIC

As mentioned in the Introduction, plastic rolling-stock kits formed my first forays into 'real' railway modelling. Those early attempts to get vans and mineral wagons to sit squarely on the rails and running smoothly, without derailing, offered a steep learning curve. Hitherto, it had not really mattered if parts were misaligned slightly on static aircraft models. But for working railway vehicles, a more careful approach was required.

Attainment of square corners, with neatly executed glue joints, takes time to achieve, as does correct alignment of buffers and couplings to match other vehicles. The outward appearance is of equal importance as fitting the axles correctly, so that they are parallel to each other and turning smoothly in their bearings. Wheel sets must also be correctly gauged with the appropriate back-to-back measurement, while the weight of the vehicle is also an issue.

As with any practical undertaking, a thorough grounding in the basics is never wasted. Therefore, this chapter aims to take the reader through a foundation course in assembling working rolling stock, using the humble four-wheel freight wagon as a base. Cheap and freely available in virtually every gauge or scale, plastic wagon kits are great fun to put together, with much of the assembly possible in a couple of modelling sessions. Indeed, they offer the ideal evening project and each of the techniques described here is relevant to plastic wagon kits in any scale.

PRELIMINARY CONSIDERATIONS

It may sound like stating the obvious, but the best place to start with any kit is to study the instructions. Not only will they give you an idea of how the parts are meant to go together, but it is important to make sure that everything is present in the packaging. Run your eye over the parts list and check that all of the materials are there. If not, contact the retailer or manufacturer; there is nothing worse than making good progress only to have to abandon work until the missing components can be acquired.

As the quality of model railway kits varies, so does the quality of their instructions. Some can be down-right baffling, while others are a joy to work from, complete with step-by-step illustrations. In terms of plastic wagon kits in 4mm scale, I have found Chivers Fineline to offer the best printed guidelines, as well as some of the best plastic mouldings. Some extra effort by the manufacturer in producing clear instructions really does give the modeller a head start.

The first chapter discussed the importance of prototype images from which to work, these being an additional aid in visualizing how a selection of plastic components can be put together to create an authentic 3-D object. An hour or two amassing such information and digesting the instructions before starting work helps the mind to organize the tasks ahead and some kits often recommend a certain means of progression. For example, it may be stated that the building of the bodyshell must be attacked first, with the underframe added later, or *vice versa*.

Many of these guidelines are drafted as the result of test-building experience by the maker, yet others are often drawn up according to the common convention of fitting solebars to the floor, adding wheels and sticking the body on top before the smaller details are fixed in place. However, with experience, you can soon divine which way is best for you.

Personally, I prefer to build up the bodyshell first, leaving the assembly to harden completely before adding the underfloor workings. Often, I will prime and paint the body before adding the underframe; as most chassis are formed of self-coloured black components, this approach removes the need to mask the body before painting the chassis back to its original colour. However, this is getting ahead of things a little. Firstly, we need to take a look at preparing the components before assembly can begin.

WASHING BEFORE USE

Due to the demands of the injection-moulding process, plastic components will probably contain traces of a chemical releasing agent. This is employed to ease the parts from the mould and in rare instances excessive amounts can hinder glues and paints from adhering to the surface. Better to err on the side of caution and adopt a standard ritual of washing the plastic sprues in clean, cool water before starting work. A spoonful of soda crystals, diluted in the water, will effectively remove any residues or greasy deposits and a rinse in clean water finishes the job. Dry the parts naturally and avoid using any other form of detergents, especially washing-up liquid, which will leave an even more troublesome residue on the surface.

Once you have formulated the order in which construction is to begin, the parts can be extracted from the sprues using a set of shears or a knife. Only remove the parts needed for the immediate job, rather than cutting them all away and loosing track of their purpose, especially if parts are numbered by

A knife will struggle to cut through bulky sprue connections. A mini-razor saw or a set of sprue cutters will do the job quickly and cleanly. Work well on the waste side to avoid damage. If the tool struggles to reach into tight corners, trim away the sprue to give the tool more room to manoeuvre.

their location on the sprue. Unlike mass-produced kits in the ranges of Airfix or Tamiya, model railway kit parts are seldom numbered on either themselves or the sprue. Instead, a diagram in the instructions is usually the only clue as to a part's identity.

For the purpose of our demonstration, I have deemed it helpful to start with a wagon's bodyshell,

Take care when cutting plastic parts from the sprue. For smaller items, use a fresh scalpel blade and work away from the edge of the component; any waste can be trimmed later. Delicate parts can easily break at this stage.

Take a flat file to the edge of the component and remove the excess material. Use light strokes to avoid cutting away too much plastic, ensuring the edges are maintained at the correct angle. A larger file makes it easier to treat longer edges.

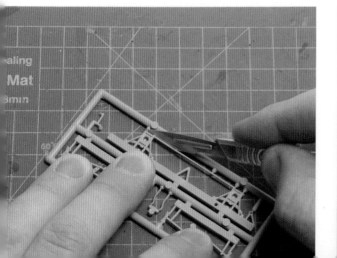

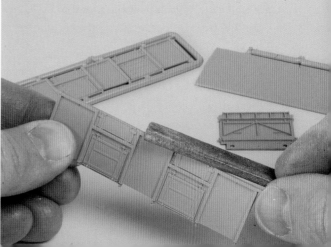

so the floor, ends and sides can be cut from the sprue. Whatever tool is being used, do not bother trying to get a perfectly clean cut at this stage. Instead, cut well on the waste side of the sprue 'pip' and use the file to dress the edge flush. It is all too easy to damage the component with overeagerness to save a few minutes' worth of cleaning up.

Dedicated pairs of plastic sprue cutters are a definite boon, but these can struggle with smaller or more delicate components. Moreover, the cutters may not reach into confined areas and it may be necessary to cut away the waste material surrounding the part before it can be released. Trying to force a knife or cutters into a tight space will only result in the soft plastic of the component (not the thicker sprue) coming off worse.

With all of the necessary parts removed, use a flat file gently to shave away the excess material, keeping the tool perpendicular to the face, checking with a mini-set square to ensure the correct 90-degree angle. Be aware that the corner joints of sides and ends may be designed to meet at a 45-degree angle, therefore must be dressed accordingly. Once the file has removed all of the waste, use a fine abrasive, such as a sanding stick, to remove the tool marks and leave a smooth finish.

Remove the bulk of the excess with files before a rub-down with sanding sticks or abrasive paper for a smoother finish. Work through a couple of grades, from coarse, medium to fine. Also, look out for any injection 'pips' on the inside faces of the components, lest they impede the fitting of any other parts. In this case, a pair of raised 'pips' sat just where the wagon's floor was meant to fit.

Now's the time to have a dry run and check that the parts meet correctly and can be aligned at the correct angle, making any adjustments with a file where necessary. Mitred butt joints are notoriously difficult to get right, especially in 4mm scale and below, so concentrate on getting the outside faces meeting tidily – the interior can be addressed later.

EARLY TROUBLES

Life often throws obstacles in our path and there is nothing more frustrating than being faced with hours of remedial work before parts can even begin to be assembled. Aside from the issue of 'flash' and moulding marks to be removed, plastic components can sometimes be damaged in transit. This depends very much on the quality of packaging and how the kit has been handled. For example, Dapol's plastic bags are notorious for indirectly causing damage to the components, although, to its credit, the Welsh company offers to replace any broken or missing parts.

Warped or distorted parts can be rectified with care. Indeed, many kits anticipate this happening to certain parts and offer tips on how to effect repairs. This, to me, is a bit like selling a car, then including a Haynes manual in the glovebox for advice when the timing belt snaps. Reshaping plastic parts is not

Kits supplied in plastic bags leave the components at risk of damage and it is not just small, fiddly bits of plastic that can become distorted, as this wagon side from a 7mm scale kit illustrates. If parts are assembled without addressing the problem, then the whole vehicle will be out of true.

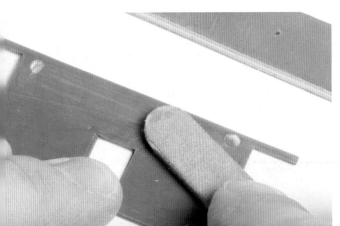

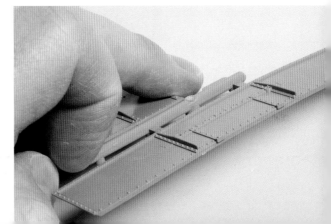

Test-fitting all parts is an essential task, showing up potential problem areas for treatment. It also reveals how the various bits go together.

While it is possible to rectify slight bowing or twisting with gentle hand pressure, it is safer to immerse the plastic in a jug of hot water for a few minutes to soften the material. Do not use boiling water – it should be at a temperature where you can dip in your hand without scalding yourself.

GETTING STUCK IN

a big deal, but should we be expected to do this after spending good money on a product? I suppose, given the inherent softness of the material, there will always be a risk, but careful packaging and considerate handling and storage by retailers makes it wholly avoidable. If a kit has to be offered in a plastic bag, at least those packed with a sheet of stout card (Parkside Dundas, for example) offer protection.

Getting the body assembled entirely square can be more challenging than one might assume and the success of the venture hinges on getting this basic bit of assembly right. When bonding polystyrene, the parts are chemically fusing together, so once the bond has been made, there is only a small window

Corner joints can prove troublesome, especially mitred joints. The thinness of the material provides very little surface area for the glue to work on and, unless both faces are dressed exactly to the correct angle, the joint will not be reliable. Recessed butt joints are more effective, in that they offer a similar gluing area, but it is a lot easier to get the bits fitting together cleanly. When in doubt, prioritize the appearance of the outside face – the joint can be reinforced from the inside later.

Either manipulate the component by hand, or, for best results, clamp it immediately against a flat surface, preferably a scrap of thick plywood.

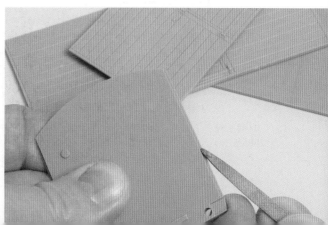

of opportunity to make corrections. Once the adhesive begins to dry, the parts may be impossible to break apart again, hence the repeated mention of test-fitting parts before committing them to the glue. For beginners, Roket Plastic Glue from Deluxe Materials is a very good choice of glue. Not only is it less smelly than stronger solvents, it also allows much more time to make adjustments before a bond becomes permanent.

A sheet of plate glass, a polished stone tile, or any other surface that is absolutely flat and inflexible will make assembly much easier. As a reference surface, it will help with getting the sides and ends perfectly square and, later, setting up the axles and wheels correctly.

When putting the sides and ends together, using the wagon's floor as a reference point to build them around is not always to be recommended, despite often being prescribed in a kit's instructions. I have almost come to expect floor units to be either undersize or out of true, such is the commonness of the phenomenon in 2mm and 4mm scale kits. Instead, try putting one end together with one side and repeating with the other two elements, checking that the joints are at right angles as the glue starts to 'grab'. After a few moments, the two sides of the puzzle can then be brought together and, using the glass surface and set square, they can be aligned perfectly in the horizontal and vertical planes as the adhesive is applied.

Ideally, the assembly should not be disturbed as the bonds harden. Then, the floor can be dropped in and any fettling affected, if necessary. The plastic is liable to flex, so keep checking that the assembly remains true. As the chassis members will be suspended from the floor, it must also sit squarely, so double check with the set square during bonding. If the floor is undersize, prioritize the glue bonds against the two ends if possible and do not worry about any gaps for now. In most instances, moulded ledges are provided on the inside faces of the ends on to which the floor will sit. As long as the floor is not more than a few millimetres short (which is very rare and renders the floor unusable), it can be perched on the ledges and glued firmly in place.

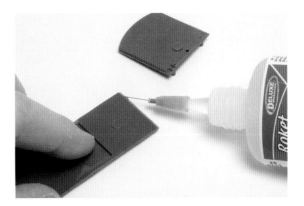

When you are happy that the parts fit correctly, it is time to add glue. For beginners, I would recommend Roket Plastic Glue, as the slower curing time allows for more adjustment. Using the supplied needle tip, run a thin bead of adhesive on to one side of the joint. Wipe away any spillage or excess immediately with a damp cloth.

Once this assembly has set hard, preferably being left overnight, interventions can be made to address any shortcomings in the kit's joints. With closed vehicles such as vans, some form of internal corner reinforcement is recommended, as the small surface area of mitred joints will always be a weak point;

With a set square on hand, bring the parts together, pressing against the joint lightly until they mate correctly. If any glue is squeezed out on to the outside face, remove with the damp cloth and hold the parts in place for a minute or two, checking the angle with a set square. Repeat this process with the other side and end.

Plastic Magic has a fast action, gripping the parts together within seconds. To keep the ends and sides perfectly aligned and square, apply a little weight while the solvent cures. All four corners of the wagon should be in contact with the glass.

Faster-acting liquid plastic glues, such as Deluxe's Plastic Magic or Slater's Mek-Pak, must be applied direct to the joint with a paintbrush, or, for neater results, a Pin Flow applicator. Simply upturn the glass tube in a bottle of liquid cement and watch the fluid draw itself upwards. Remove the tube, turn upright and the fluid will flow down to the tip. The amount of glue dispensed depends on the angle at which the tool is held.

With the two halves of the bodyshell brought together on a sheet of glass or other flat surface, apply a small amount of glue into the joint. The thin liquid will find its own way between the two faces, so do not be tempted to apply too much. Beware also of the liquid penetrating to the outer face, as it may seep under your fingers and leave a fingerprint 'welded' into the plastic.

plastic angle, as offered in the Evergreen or Plastruct ranges, provides the perfect solution. Additionally, if gaps have appeared between the floor and sides, use some plastic strip as a fillet, trimmed to length and pushed into the void before applying liquid poly. Once it has cured, use a file to dress it flush with the underside, if necessary.

Something to note when adding a fillet to under-size floors, is that there may be mounting guides for the solebars moulded to the underside. If the floor has been pressed up against one side, then you may eventually find the chassis being biased towards that

It may be helpful to clamp the corners of the body with low-tack masking tape to keep everything in place while the glue cures.

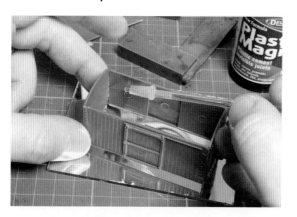

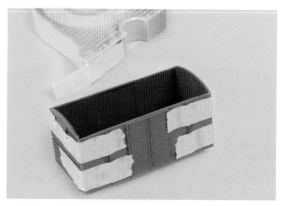

Test the fit of the floor once the sides have dried, fettling the moulding if necessary until it sits snugly without forcing the sides or ends to bulge. I have long since given up trying to construct bodyshells around a moulded floor as they are seldom of the right size. Instead, I find that getting the four 'walls' right from the outset saves a lot of messing around.

For closed vehicles, such as this van, I like to reinforce the inside of the corner joints, using plastic angle from the Evergreen range. This can also be done with open wagons, as long as a fixed cargo is added to hide the brackets.

As is often the case, the supplied floor may need the addition of plastic shims to fill a gap between the sides or ends. Evergreen plastic strip does the job, secured in place and trimmed flush on the underside when the glue has cured.

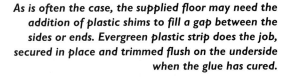

Building around a floor is possible, but only if the moulding is of the right size and each edge is dressed to an exact 90-degree angle. Fit one side at a time, checking that each is correctly aligned before adding the next.

The bulkier parts of an O gauge kit need a bit more adhesive to work on the plastic, applied with a brush from the inside. Check that all four corners of the body are in contact with the reference surface to ensure everything is straight and true.

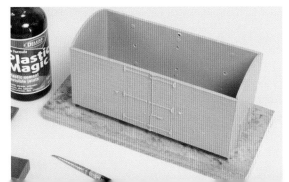

flank. With a little forward thinking, this is simply resolved by leaving an equal gap on either side and adding shims of equal width. Styrene strip by both Slater's and Evergreen is available in increments of 0.010in (0.25mm); it helps to have some stocks of varying sizes at hand for such eventualities.

Another factor worth flagging up is the risk of causing the sides to bow outwards by forcing too thick a fillet into the gaps. Choose a strip size that sits as comfortably as possible into the gap. A thick formula of cyano glue or epoxy can always be used instead of liquid poly-cement to make up for any slight shortfall.

A van's roof will give the body its full rigidity once it has been securely affixed. Again, test-fit the component and make any adjustments to the joint faces of body or roof wherever necessary. Be sure that all solvent fumes have evaporated from inside the body before it is sealed, especially if cyano glue has been used, as a concentration of vapours may cause distortion. If in doubt, a small ventilation hole (about 2mm in diameter) drilled in the base, somewhere out of view, will solve the problem.

Weight is an important issue for reliable running, with plastic kits needing a little help in this respect. It makes sense to put the weight out of sight; Liquid Gravity can simply be poured in and fixed with a thin, penetrating glue like Super 'Phatic!. Make sure there are no gaps around the floor, as the weight and glue will leak out. Leave overnight to set.

A WEIGHTY ISSUE

Before the roof is added, you may want to consider adding some ballast to aid smooth and reliable running. Scraps of metal, lumps of Plasticine, or even lead shot can be used. By far the most convenient and versatile solution is Liquid Gravity, a non-toxic alternative to lead pellets. It can be persuaded into the most awkward locations and a single jar provides enough material for a large fleet of vehicles.

By placing the model on to a set of kitchen weighing scales, Liquid Gravity can be decanted into the bodyshell until the desired weight is achieved. Standardizing weights makes for even performance across your fleet and avoids any risk of a heavier wagon at the end of a rake causing a derailment on tight corners. Using RTR wagons as a guide, a small four-wheel van in 4mm scale will run happily with a mass of around 25g (0.9oz). When adding weight before assembly is complete, simply fill the wagon to

It is hard to specify the optimum weight of rolling stock, as it depends on many different factors unique to your own layout and operating practices. However, standardizing your fleet is recommended using the best RTR models as a guide. Gauge the amount of weight being added with a set of kitchen scales.

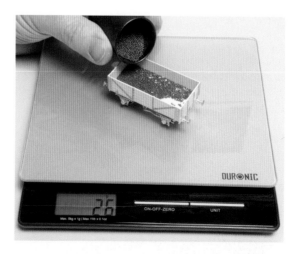

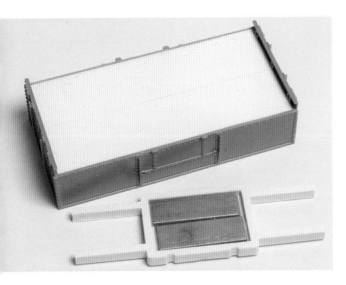

Coopercraft is one of only a handful of kit makers who supply suitable ballast weights with its 4mm and 7mm scale kits. Steel strips fit within the chassis frame overlay that is then glued to the wagon's floor.

just below the desired weight to compensate for the addition of metal wheels, couplings or buffers.

For N gauge subjects, similar-size wagons operate reliably with a mass of around 8g (0.3oz). Larger scale kits, in O gauge and above, tend to have enough bulk in themselves, due to the thicker and larger lumps of plastic involved. However, it is a good idea to add a little extra ballast to balance the plastic kits with metal rolling stock.

With the body assembled and weighted, the roof can be tested for a good fit, fettling the roof, sides or ends, as necessary, until the roof sits cleanly atop the body. When satisfied, tape it in position, ensuring an equal overhang on all four aspects and apply liquid poly-cement into the joint with the Pin Flow applicator or a fine brush. Let the glue cure fully before removing the tape.

PAUSE FOR THOUGHT

Getting the fundamentals right – cutting, trimming, testing and fitting – lays the foundations for success, as most of the ensuing techniques have these four skills at their core. Practice is the best teacher and, equipped with a handful of kits, repetition of these initial stages will stand the beginner in good stead.

CHAPTER FIVE

WHEELING AND DEALING

Wheels and axles are to a vehicle what the foundations are to a building. They must give the carriage a firm footing on the rails, providing a smooth ride and not be prone to derailments. They must also be correctly aligned and safely retained without risk of coming loose in the bearings. Conversely, the axles also require a degree of sideways movement to promote free running and the ability to cope with tight curves.

With the vehicle body assembled square and true, the all-important underframe is the next item on the agenda. Usually, this takes the form of a pair of solebars with integral axle guards (also referred to as W-irons), from which the axles are hung. We will come to the technicalities in due course, but first a quick look into the prototype is in order.

THE REAL THING

'There are wheels within wheels,' as P.G. Wodehouse's Monty Bodkin was oft to say and this is certainly the case in terms of railway rolling stock. Wheel design has been a constantly evolving process, since the days of hand- or horse-operated tramways. Materials and manufacturing processes have dictated patterns, while operating practices place their own demands upon the wheels and axles.

In the early days of locomotive-hauled railways, wheels were formed as single iron castings, complete with a flange to guide the vehicle around curves. As things progressed, so a more resilient solution was required, bringing about the separate steel tyre and a variety of wheel boss designs and manufacturing processes. Spoke wheels were the most common variety for many years, particularly for freight vehicles, with open (or split) spokes offering a greater loading potential than solid spokes.

Spoke wheels were easy and cheap to produce, although they had a finite lifespan, being prone to shifting on their axles after a certain period of time.

Disc wheels, of steel manufacture, only became popular in the UK in the 1910s, despite being widely used in the USA for some years previously. Wooden-centred wheels, pioneered by Mansell of the South Eastern Railway, had given significantly smoother and quieter riding qualities for passenger stock, yet these were expensive to manufacture and maintain.

Steel discs offer superior strength and also allow for greater heat dissipation during braking (something that wooden-centred wheels did not), especially those wheels with small holes let into the discs. Furthermore, discs do not stir up as much dust and dirt as spoke wheels and they are also easier to balance on the axles.

For the British-outline enthusiast, spoke or disc wheels of the correct diameter will have to be chosen according to the prototype in question. Some kits provide suitable sets, but these are in the minority, especially in 4mm scale, although most instructions should at least specify the type and size of wheels required.

In general, for freight vehicles, a prototypical diameter of 3ft 1.5in (952.5mm) abounded across all of the various railway companies from the late 1800s up to the end of the BR era. Variations do exist, however, with freight stock sometimes employing a wider variety of wheel sizes to suit the nature of the vehicle types. Low-floor wagons or modern intermodal 'flats' have often required smaller wheels, while larger diameters have been employed for 'express' goods stock.

Passenger carriages, on the other hand, have long been borne on slightly larger sets, with a typical diameter of 3ft 6in (1,066.8mm), the larger size being more appropriate for faster speeds. Modern coaching stock and some freight vehicles may have brake discs fitted to the outside face of the wheel, making for a dramatically shiny effect, and there are kits and aftermarket accessories that cater for these fittings (such as Intercity Models, PH Designs and

Passenger vehicles, or those designed for use at passenger train speeds, have long run on disc wheels of a larger diameter than those fitted to general freight stock. Yet, to relieve stresses, dissipate heat and aid in the balancing of the wheels, small holes are often a feature, as can be glimpsed on this LMS six-wheel van.

In contrast to the sleek-looking discs, this GWR Mink van sports an archaic set of plain spoke wheels. Wagons were still being fitted with spoke wheels well into BR days.

Cambrian Kits). Alternatively, the brakes may act on discs mounted on the axles.

With a choice of three-hole discs, plain discs, straight-spoke, split-spoke or curved-spoke, British-outline rolling stock could even appear with mis-

matched wheels – in terms of pattern rather than size – especially in the 1960s 'transition' era, all of which highlights the importance of careful research before starting on a kit project.

The three-hole disc wheel became the standard British fitting for freight vehicles in the 1950s, offering an ease of manufacture and higher level of reliability and payload capacity than its predecessors.

ABOVE: *The humble three-hole disc was eventually usurped with the growth of air-braked stock. Depending on the prototype, airbrakes operated on to the edge of the wheel (as had been the previous custom of vacuum brakes) or on steel discs fitted to the front and rear of each wheel, similar to those common on motorcars. This preserved van evidently hasn't seen much use in an air-braked formation, as the discs have rusted over. In service, these would have a bright metallic appearance.*

BELOW: *Up-to-date air-braked freight and passenger stock use plain disc wheels, as is the case with this DB Schenker-operated MBA aggregate wagon.*

WHEEL THEORY

On the prototype, a degree of side play in the axle journals is desired to help the vehicle cope with the transition from straight to curved rails and this same principle applies in model form. If we consider how a pair of wheels, attached to a fixed axle, behaves when tackling a tight curve, it is evident that the wheel on the outside of the bend will travel slightly further than the inner wheel.

This can be appreciated by bending a length of flexible track into a circle and noting how, despite both rails being of the same length, there is a vast discrepancy between the two once the curve is formed. Yet there is no 'give' in a railway axle, unlike a road vehicle where each steered wheel travels along different radiuses, albeit with the same centre. To compensate, there are some pretty complicated mathematical equations that govern the shape and inclination of the wheel-rail interface. It is not necessary to grapple with too much of this, but it does help to have a basic appreciation of what is going on. At the very least, it might help in understanding troublesome derailments that may have no visible explanation.

By looking head-on at a real train as it sits on the track – if it is safe to do so – it can be discerned that both wheel flanges will not be in contact with the inner faces of both rails. Indeed, there will be quite a gap – the space between the inner faces of the wheels of standard gauge vehicles is somewhere in the region of 1,372mm (4ft 6in), while the rails are spaced at 1,435mm (4ft 8.5in), giving 64mm (2.5in) of side play. If the flanges did press against both rails, then the vehicle would struggle with even the slightest degree of curvature.

It should also be clear that only a tiny surface area of each wheel is in contact with the head of the rails. The fact that the rails are both inclined towards the centre of the track may also be discerned, matching the angle of the wheel's tyres. This is known as 'coning' and allows the wheels to move from side to side within the limits of the gauge and their flanges, thus creating a smoother, safer ride around curves.

In model terms, not only is it important to have our rails set at a consistent gauge, but the wheels must also be accurately set up, most importantly by checking the back-to-back measurements. Additionally, with the issue of side play also being important, some degree of 'slop' in each axle is welcome to permit free running; if the axles are too rigidly retained, they will not turn freely. However, only a tiny amount of sideways movement is required – excessive 'slop' will be counterproductive.

Just as in real life, the wheels of model trains require a degree of side play between the flanges and the inner edges of the rails. The distance between the inner faces of the wheels is known as the back-to-back measurement and this can be crucial in ensuring reliable operation.

MODEL WHEELS

In the early days, wheel specifications differed drastically from company to company, but by the turn of the 1900s, the various railways agreed to a standard set of specifications (as laid down by the Railway Clearing House). Funnily enough, it has taken a similar situation before model wheels have been produced to a similarly consistent standard, thanks to the efforts of the NMRA (National Model Railroad Association) and NEM (Normen Europäischer Modellbahnen) organizations.

Wheel profile specifications can get complicated, especially as there are discrepancies between those stated by the NMRA and NEM across different scales and gauges, so there is little point reproducing all of the information here (it would take up a couple of chapters). Moreover, NMRA and NEM standards are modified from time to time, so it pays to keep up to date. All of the information is freely available on the Internet and a number of helpful websites are listed in the Appendix.

To summarize, it is desirous to the majority of modellers that the wheels of model trains are rendered as close to prototype as possible within the limits of the medium. That is, perfectly scaled-down wheels would require supremely finely crafted trackwork in order for the trains to stay on the tracks, so there is always an element of compromise and this is where the NMRA and NEM standards come into play. Derived from years of experimentation, they suggest the finest-looking wheels that can reliably be run on specific track types (also governed by separate NMRA/NEM standards) and RTR manufacturers are increasingly adapting these specifications to ensure that their products look good and run well.

Without getting bogged-down in too much technical jargon and specifications, it goes without saying that investment in high-quality wheels will be rewarded with better-running wagons. Choice can depend upon the track system that you have, as wheels with larger flanges can struggle on finescale rails. Again, this is where the NMRA and NEM standards prove useful, as cross-reference to the 'specs' for track and wheels will reveal what is compatible.

Of optimum relevance is the NMRA RP-25 recommended practice document that outlines the optimum dimensions for wheels to cope with different rail 'codes'. The code describes the height of the rail, expressed in thousandths of an inch. For instance, the popular OO gauge Code 75 boasts rails 0.075in high, whereas Code 55 (popular for N gauge) 0.055in and so on. The RP-25 specification governs wheel contour across all gauges and commonly appears in the marketing spiel for new locomotives and rolling stock. Indeed, when sourcing wheels for kits, it is worth checking that they conform to the same standards.

Alan Gibson and Romford have become something of the standard bearers over the years, offering high-quality wheels and axles in most gauges. Other recommended sources include Ultrascale, Markits (both 4mm scale), Slater's (7mm) and Peco (various gauges). Some are rendered entirely in metal, with insulated washers to prevent shorting-out the track power, while others consist of metal axles and tyres with plastic wheel bosses. Purists may prefer all-metal construction, but the plastic-centred Gibson wheels offer much quieter operation with no discernible loss in performance or appearance. A little

Model wheels come in many different patterns, gauges and standards. On the left is an OO set from Romford, conforming to RP-25 standards and supplied with many Parkside Dundas kits. On the right is a mass-produced version from Dapol, with a slightly overscale wheel diameter and a large flange. To its credit, Dapol has recently upgraded its wagon wheels to a much finer, RP-25 standard.

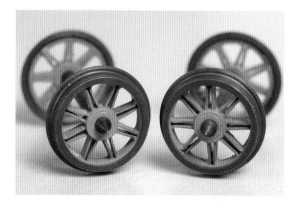

These EM gauge, split-spoke wheels are real beauties. Produced by Alan Gibson, the plastic wheel centres need painting, but their delicate outline gives a model a refined footing.

flash sometimes requires removing from the inner faces, but this is no hardship. Indeed, I find that the plastic bosses take paint far easier than metal wheels.

In OO gauge, Dapol, Hornby and Bachmann each offer packs of wagon and carriage wheels, packaged as spare parts and often available from local model shops. These are a fraction of the cost of bespoke products, although they are produced by the inferior die-stamping process rather than the lathe-turning

Standard N gauge wheels can be a little cruder where the flanges and wheel tread are concerned. Yet the rendition of these Farish sets is impressive. In larger scales, wheels invariably offer a greater degree of refinement. Slater's and Peco are two of the main sources for O gauge wheels.

favoured by Romford, Gibson and the like. The standard is usually good, although Hornby's wheels tend to have larger flanges that are not ideal for finer codes of rail.

In N gauge, Graham Farish wheel sets are also readily available, as well as being offered with a number of 2mm scale wagon kits from other makers, such as Parkside Dundas. While not the finest wheels in the world and certainly no match for Romford equivalents, they are fine for use on Peco 'Streamline' Code 80 and Code 55 rails.

GAUGING WHEELS

Virtually all rolling-stock wheels come pre-assembled to whatever specific gauge is requested. That is, the wheels have been set on to the axles by either a friction or screw fit. However, different manufacturer's specifications and the vagaries of packaging and storage may result in variations and it is important to check the back-to-back measurement before the wagon is wheeled-up.

The variance in back-to-back measurements – the distance between the inner faces of each wheel on the axle – can be substantial on RTR stock and separately supplied wheel sets are no different. A few fractions of a millimetre here and there can be accepted when running on proprietary, non-finescale track systems. However, fine rails and intricate layouts will prove troublesome to out-of-gauge wheels. Therefore, a modest investment in a back-to-back gauge will be rewarded by reliable rolling stock.

Furthermore, a kit that demands the use of inside bearings may necessitate one wheel to be removed from the axle to allow it to be threaded through the bearings. In such cases, refixing the wheel to the correct gauge will be impossible without some means of measurement. A set of calipers will help, but the beauty of a back-to-back gauge is that it will also help to ensure that the wheels are aligned squarely on the axle, removing the risk of 'wobbles' when on the track. A DIY solution is a realistic prospect, as most back-to-back gauges are simple affairs, but the cheapness of ready-made tools makes them an essential item for the toolbox.

Checking the back-to-back measurement of your wheel sets is important in preventing derailments or unreliable running. A simple gauge makes the job easier and allows minor adjustments to be made. In most cases, wheels are a friction-fit on to the axles and firm hand pressure will open or close the gap as necessary. This L-shaped gauge, from Alan Gibson, also helps to ensure that the wheels are square in relation to the axle.

Below is a list of back-to-back measurements for each of the most popular 'standard gauge' modelling scales. These are offered as a guideline only, as there are a number of minor variations for each scale according to different schools of thought or modelling societies. Readers are therefore advised to check the NMRA and NEM websites in the Appendix, plus the various other scale organizations for more information on this thorny issue.

BACK-TO-BACK MEASUREMENTS FOR THE POPULAR GAUGES

* N: 7.4mm
* HO: 14.5mm
* OO: 14.4mm (Standard OO) or 14.8mm (Double O Gauge Association finescale standard)
* EM: 16.5mm
* P4: 17.75mm
* O: 29mm

BEARINGS

A recent conversation with an experienced non-railway modeller moved on to the subject of bearings and he looked puzzled as I described how RTR rolling stock in most scales relied on metal pinpoint axles running directly into the plastic of the axle guards. 'But doesn't that just wear out the plastic until the wheels drop out?' he asked. Well, yes it does, but the rugged nature of RTR underframe materials means that the erosion is a slow process for all but the most intensively used vehicles.

Admittedly, it is not an ideal solution, propagated more on cost grounds than anything else, and should be avoided in kit-built stock wherever possible. Indeed, the majority of kits are tailored to the use of metal bearings to promote smooth running and longevity. Various types of bearing exist, but by far the most common is the flanged, or top-hat pattern to suit pinpoint axles. Turned from brass, the bearings slot into holes in the axle guards and promote ultra-free running when correctly set up and maintained with a little light lubrication from time to time.

In most cases, a friction fit is enough to retain the brass bearings and a test fit will reveal if a moulded hole requires opening out slightly with a drill bit. Be careful not to drill right through the axle guard and choose a bit fractionally smaller than the bearing. For example, Romford brass top hats in 4mm scale are 2mm in diameter, so a 1.9mm drill bit will achieve a snug friction fit.

Conversely, if the holes are too big, fix the bearing in place with a tiny amount of thick, slow-drying cyano glue, such as Roket Max. Apply the adhesive into the hole with a cocktail stick and be sure to fix the bearing into the centre of the hole. The extra few seconds of working time offered by the thick cyano will allow for adjustments. If the fit is only a little loose then glue may not be required, as the pinpoint axle will hold them in place once the chassis is wheeled-up. Moreover, gluing the bearings in place may not be a good idea until the fit of all the chassis parts has been tested.

The length of pinpoint axles varies according to scale, so fixing the bearing sets at the correct distance

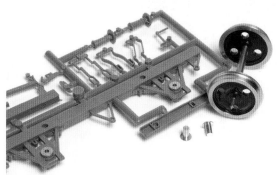

Pinpoint axles and top-hat bearings are a common combination for wagons and carriages in 4mm scale. The point of the axle bears against the inside of the bearing and the sympathetic coning of each allows a little side play in the axle, but only if the solebars are spaced accordingly.

Plain bearings, such as these O gauge units, allow for a greater degree of side play, as the tips of the axles are not in constant contact with the inner ends of the bearings – hence why the axle ends are longer, providing a greater horizontal bearing surface.

Plain and top-hat bearings are designed to be a snug friction fit into plastic solebars and can be pushed into position with a flat-bladed screwdriver or tail end of a set of tweezers. Check that the flange is sitting tight against the surface of the plastic.

If the holes are too tight, or the kit is not designed for this type of bearing, they will need opening out. Measure the bearing's outer diameter with calipers and choose a drill bit 0.1mm smaller, to obtain a tight fit. Masking tape on the bit serves as a depth gauge.

If the holes are a little sloppy, err on the side of caution and fix the bearings with a single drop of cyano glue, applied with a cocktail stick. Be sure to keep the glue out of the bearing's interior.

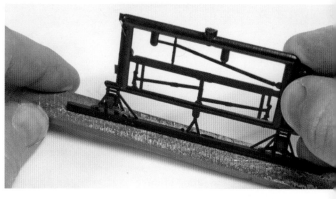

Flangeless bearings, as supplied with Peco's Wonderful Wagon kits, offer the same level of performance as top-hat bearings, although the lack of a flange makes extraction almost impossible.

Cleaning up the mating faces of the solebars is an important stage, as they need to sit at right angles to the vehicle's floor and be flat and true along their full length. Rubbing along a broad file, while the parts are still supported on the sprue is helpful.

is not always easy. Indeed, the moulded guides on a kit's underframe are rarely a guarantee of a perfect fit. There are ways and means of setting the wheels correctly, ignoring the kit's in-built alignment aids, as demonstrated below.

Without the side-acting retention forces of pin-point axles, plain bearings have deep slots to allow the axle to slide laterally without the risk of dropping out of the chassis. Plain bearings are common in larger scale kits and are especially suited to long wheelbase, non-bogie or six-axle vehicles, the extra 'play' easing the movement of the stock around short radius curves.

A similar advantage is possessed by inside bearings, although the amount of lateral movement is restricted. These are more commonly found on articulated bogies where the small amount of lateral 'play' in the axles is overcome by the freedom of the bogie to rotate around curved track. Brass predominates across most bearing types, being a soft, yet fairly durable metal, although some kits may include an internal bearing surface of whitemetal.

WHEELING UP

Plastic solebars invariably need careful handling before fitting and some degree of tidying up will be required to remove flash or moulding marks. Keeping

the long upper surface flat and true is important to ensure a tidy fit and correct axle alignment, so filing away excess material must be done with this in mind; a broad flat file is the ideal tool. As both axles must be parallel to each other, equal amounts of material must be removed from both solebars as any fluctuation will have the knock-on effect of misaligning the bearings.

A good tip is to check the upper face of the solebars on a sheet of glass against a set square. By placing both solebars back to back, it should be clear if one is standing a little taller than the other. Do not forget also to remove any raised injection marks on

It is also vital to get both solebars set up as matching pairs. In other words, the same amount of material should be shaved away from both. Placing them back-to-back on a sheet of glass is a good way of gauging them.

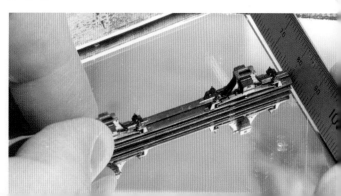

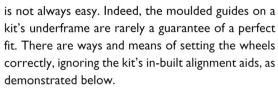

Remember to remove any raised injection marks on the floor and the inner faces of the solebars, before fitting them in place. I was a bit hasty with this O gauge van and missed these small discs, which then impeded the fitting of the brakes. With the framing and solebars already fixed, trying to flatten the surface is now difficult.

A flat-bottomed milling bit in a mini-drill made short work of the protrusions, without damaging any surrounding material. Set the tool to a slow speed and apply very light pressure to maintain full control over the drill.

the inside of the solebars and axle guards, as they will likely interfere with the siting of brake components.

As already mentioned, it is best not to assume that a kit can be built exactly according to any guides that may be moulded on to the underframe. A simple dry run, holding the wheels into the bearings by hand, will reveal whether this is the case. You may find that the solebars are being forced outwards at an awkward angle (they should be sitting vertically), but do not worry – the solebars can be fixed wherever they need to be. As long as they are spaced equidistantly from the longitudinal centre line of the floor and the wheels are turning freely and are correctly aligned, then any diversion from the instructions or any location guides will be forgiven. Indeed, it may be worth measuring and marking out the floor's centre line anyway, as it may help in aligning subsequent components.

Another important factor to check before adding glue concerns any moulded location guides for brake gear, especially if fitting finescale wheels, such as EM or P4 gauge. As it is desirous to get the brake shoes in line with the wheel tyres, the locations will have to be altered. Finding this out beforehand is preferable, especially if the underframe requires a little modification.

One other thing to note during the test fitting is whether the solebars need trimming in length to sit inside the buffer beams at each end, if these are already in place. If so, be sure to trim the same amount from the same end on both sides or, again, the axles will be put out of alignment.

When happy with how the parts and wheels fit during testing, assembly can begin. Fix one solebar in place and ensure it is sitting vertically and correctly aligned along the length of the underframe. If you are disregarding the moulded location guides, be sure to fit the solebar in such a way that the second one will be equidistantly spaced from the wagon's centre line.

Long wheelbase wagons can be tricky to get right, as the plastic has a tendency to flex during gluing and so should be checked against a straight edge. Once the adhesive has had a few minutes to 'grab' the solebar (but not cured completely), the axles can be added and the other solebar fitted to lock the wheels in place. Make any adjustments to positioning while the glue joint is still pliable and keep checking that the wheels are correctly aligned and turning freely.

After a dry run of checking the fit of both solebars and that the wheels have enough clearance to rotate freely, fix one solebar on to the floor. Check that it sits squarely and vertically. Allow a few minutes for the poly-cement to form a bond.

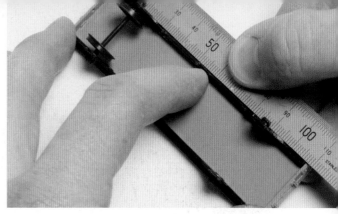

Place the second solebar into position and add the wheels, checking that everything fits correctly before applying adhesive. If the axles are too tight, nudge the solebars fractionally further apart before the glue sets. However, do not be tempted to flare them outwards, as they will move back as the glue sets – although these issues should have already been addressed during the dry run.

For long wheelbase vehicles, the solebars can prove a little unwieldy and difficult to fix exactly straight, especially if the floor has limited location aids. This old Ian Kirk wagon had few location tabs, so a straight edge is being used to get the parts aligned correctly while the glue is applied.

TESTING, TESTING

One of the best ways of testing whether a rigid wagon chassis has been wheeled correctly is to sit it on a sheet of glass and check that all four wheels are in contact with the surface. If it rocks like a table with a wonky leg, the axles are misaligned, probably due to the solebars being out of true, the floor distorted, or the bearings misaligned. By process of elimination, it should be possible to discern which. A look along the length of the chassis will show if the two axles are sitting parallel, or if the floor is not completely flat. Check also that the wheels are spinning absolutely freely and that the axles are perpendicular (at right angles) to the wagon's longitudinal centre line.

These problems are far easier to diagnose and correct before the glue begins to cure, as the parts should remain pliable for up to 10min. Ideally, there should be a small amount of side play in the axles for reasons outlined earlier. Too much slackness in the axles is counterproductive, as the ride will be unpredictable and the wheels at risk of dropping out. A maximum of 0.5mm lateral movement in the axles (in OO gauge) helps a vehicle to deal with tightly curved track, absorbing any sudden change in direction. For larger gauges, a couple of tenths of a millimetre could be added to that, or the same subtracted in the smaller scales.

A good way to check if the axles are correctly aligned is to turn it upside down and look along its length. The two axles should appear parallel to each other and the floor (or underside of the buffer beams if fitted. Check also that the wheels spin absolutely freely.

Another test is to place the wagon on a sheet of glass and check that all the wheel flanges are in contact with the surface. Any wobbling indicates one of the axles is out of true. The wheels should also be rotating freely, ideally with just a smidgen of side play.

A final test is to roll the chassis along a stretch of straight and curved track. I have a little test track on an offcut of timber, propped at a very slight gradient, and if the chassis rolls gently downhill without any prompting, then I know that all is well.

PROBLEMS?

The authentic appearance of the finished kit is still our priority, so if, during the test-fitting stage, it is impossible to get the solebars into a good position for the wheels to rotate easily, then try countersinking bearings into the axle guards, using a drill bit just larger than the diameter of the bearing's flange. The overall depth of the holes may need increasing slightly and, as before, add a depth gauge (of masking tape) to the drill bit to prevent passing through the moulded axle box.

With the heads of the bearings sitting flush with, or slightly beneath, the inner faces of the solebars, the axle will gain an extra millimetre or two in which to move about. Flangeless pinpoint bearings are a viable alternative to the top-hat variety, although these are a little awkward to handle and, once

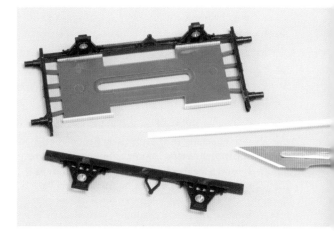

If the axles need more than a couple of millimetres extra leeway, the solebars may have to be pushed further apart. If possible, derive the shortfall in the spacing and divide it by two. The appropriate thickness of plastic strip can then be inserted on both sides. In the case of this Red Panda shock van chassis, the floor unit was discerned to be about 1.4mm too narrow, so 0.7mm thick shims were added on either side.

they're in, they're in. Trying to prise them out again to deepen the mounting holes is very difficult.

In the event of too much side play, instead of fitting the solebars too far inboard of the outside of the wagon – and sacrificing realism – the bearings can be 'jacked up' a little, fixing them proud of the inside faces of the axle guards. Collars from drilled plastic sheet will act as washers to help achieve a uniform

If, during dry runs, the axles refuse to rotate freely and the solebars cannot be edged a little further apart, the top-hat bearings can be countersunk into the axle guards. Drill the mounting hole a millimetre or two deeper, then use a bit of the same diameter as the bearings' flange to cut a recess for the whole unit to sit flush with, or just below, the surface. This technique is handy for kits not designed for use with brass bearings, such as Dapol's (ex-Airfix) OO wagon kits.

The extra material allowed the solebars to sit exactly vertical and gave the wheels enough room to move unhindered.

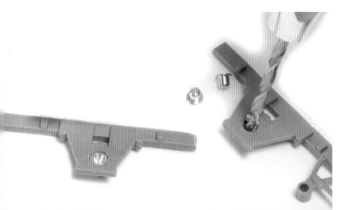

positioning. Failing that, a longer set of axles should do the trick.

Once satisfied that the parts are properly set up, leave the model aside to cure overnight, preferably laid on its back to take away any pressure from the axles and solebars. Make another quick check after half an hour to determine if anything has shifted. When parts have been 'fudged' about to free the wheels, plastic's elastic memory will see it creep back to its original position as the adhesive evaporates. The benefits of repeated dry fitting and fettling of parts so that they fit properly in the first place cannot be overstated, although it is bound to take a little practice to get things right.

SUMMING UP

Hopefully, all of the complicated theory at the head of this chapter has not proved too heavy going and an understanding of the various components has been gained. It is also hoped that the descriptions of the potential pitfalls of solebar alignment have not put you off, with such problems being fairly rare on good-quality plastic kits.

Some kits are better than others in this respect. Older products were probably designed with now obsolete wheels and axles in mind, while others, such as the ex-Airfix wagons in Dapol's range, were not intended for use with metal wheels and bearings at all. Similarly, aged moulds will have lost some of their sharp edges, leaving parts that fail to fit together as well as they might. That old chestnut of 'try it dry' crops up time and again, with so many problems being easily averted by assembling the various parts without glue.

Another statement that will be proved accurate after this stage is to choose your first plastic kits carefully. It is not just the quality of production that counts, but the nature of the components. Kits where the solebars are moulded integrally to the bodysides can prove troublesome, as there is little room for manoeuvre if the parts are not fitting together properly. Having said that, we tend to learn more from a challenging kit than from one that makes the job too easy.

With the bare bones of a wagon complete, including a rolling chassis, we can now start to consider adding the smaller details and tackling a few more demanding tasks. But already we have covered many of the fundamentals of rolling-stock construction. With an appreciation and understanding of what has been covered so far, you are now set up to tackle almost anything else that a plastic kit may throw at you.

This Brassmasters' axle spacing gauge is perfect for checking that both axles are parallel to each other and perpendicular to the solebars.

CHAPTER SIX

MAKING AMENDS

This is an opportune moment to consider how we can improve certain aspects of our assembled kits. Taking a look at the quality of our glued joints, do they need filling and sanding smooth? What kinds of materials can we use and what is the best way to apply them? In this chapter, we will discuss a few 'tricks of the trade' that allow better joints to be made first time, ideally without recourse to filler, as well as looking at how to cope with larger or more awkward parts. And, if things do not quite go to plan, there are a few hints and tips offered that should get you out of any tight spots.

BIGGER BITS

Working with larger components, when tackling bogie vehicles for example, requires a little extra forethought at the preparation stage. Whatever the scale, it takes care to dress long expanses of plastic (or other materials for that matter) without introducing a 'dishing' effect as the material flexes under pressure. Secure support of as much of the part as possible is essential, whether in a suitably padded vice or clamps. A long, broad, flat file is needed; a small needle file may not be enough.

Parts such as carriage or wagon sides, solebars and roof mating edges must be rendered absolutely straight and true if assembly is to proceed smoothly. Accurate and tidy joints will improve the model's appearance, but what is more crucial is the risk of building a distorted body or chassis due to ill-fitting parts. We discussed the risks of parts shifting during gluing in the previous chapter, but it is worth repeating that if structural joints are made in a sloppy fashion, the risk of distortion is increased and the vehicle is unlikely to run reliably.

An alternative to clamping a part in a vice is to swap over the role of abrasive tool and material. Fixing sheets of emery paper to a perfectly flat surface, such as a mirror or offcut of kitchen worktop, provides

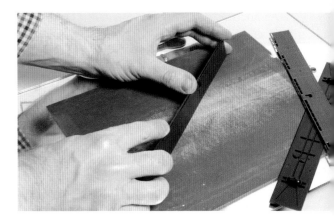

Filing straight and square faces over long stretches requires a broader file and constant checks with a set square to ensure consistent results. Instead of clamping the soft material in a vice, try fixing a sheet of emery paper to a mirror (with double-sided tape) and rubbing the part over the surface.

a simple flattening tool. Holding the part firmly in the hand (or both hands), it can be worked over the abrasive and repeatedly checked against a straight edge. Where accurate right-angle edges are important, a 'fence' of timber can be clamped over the surface and the part held against the edge as it is drawn over the abrasive.

Check the edges at regular intervals with a straight edge and set square. A wooden 'fence' can be improvised to aid the accurate dressing of 90-degree and 45-degree joint faces.

Bonding larger components requires a slightly different approach. Check at all points along the edge and fettle where necessary before committing to glue. Start at one end and add a small amount of poly-cement, just enough to 'spot weld' the parts together.

Fixing long parts together also demands a tailored approach as far as glue application is concerned. Trying to fix them in one go is not a good idea, as there will be much toing and froing to get the parts

As the parts start to 'grab', recheck the alignment about halfway along and add another small amount of adhesive. Repeat the process at the other end and, when happy that the parts are accurately placed at all points, brush on more adhesive to secure the joint. A few strips of masking tape here and there will hold everything still while you work.

correctly aligned along their entire length. It is far better to use a 'spot gluing' approach, akin to spot-soldering as described in Chapter 15. After checking that the parts fit properly, get one end set up correctly and add just a small drop of liquid poly-cement into the joint, holding the parts together until the plastics begin to grab each other. Recheck the alignment in the middle and add another drop of glue, then move to the opposite end. Further fine-tuning will then be possible, before the glue is added to the rest of the joint's length to finish the job.

GAP FILLING

Hopefully, a combination of perfectly executed mouldings and supreme craftsmanship on the modeller's part will have produced flawless joints. Alas, this is not the norm and we are likely to be faced with a little remedial work. Model fillers, or putties, are a great help to kit builders in sealing gaps or holes, as well as making repairs and disguising surface imperfections.

TYPES OF FILLER

Filler choice is important, as some are tailored for use on specific materials. Indeed, some formulas can attack certain plastics if used in large quantities, while others will struggle to adhere to some materials. Shrinkage is also important – some brands are only intended for use in very thin layers and trying to fill deeper gaps will prove hard work. Curing times also differ according to formula and while the colour of the putty may appear of trifling importance, its visibility on a grey or white plastic surface will determine how easy it is to smooth off before painting and finishing.

There are many different filler options, with some of the big plastic kit makers offering their own brands, such as Revell and Humbrol. Both of these are tailored for use on polystyrene kits, so are reliable and readily available from model shops. More specialist fillers are produced by Deluxe Materials, Squadron, Tamiya and Vallejo and are aimed at the more discerning user. With greater versatility and super-smooth finish, these are a tad more expensive but are worth the extra pennies.

Some brands even offer different grades of fillers to suit different types of situation. Squadron's Green Putty, for example, is a fairly coarse and rugged material that is ideal for correcting larger flaws or filling small holes. It is highly visible, which makes it easier to work with, and can be sanded to a fairly smooth finish. The same company's White Putty is much finer and is aimed at more modest repairs, or for following the Green Putty during the sanding stage to provide a glass-like finish. Squadron's tubes of putty contain some pretty strong chemical solvents, so should be used carefully and in well-ventilated areas. Acrylic-based formulas, as offered by Vallejo and Deluxe Materials, are less toxic, with little odour and easy workability. These are only suited to light-duty tasks, such as small gaps or minor surface flaws, and can be sanded easily.

For minor repairs to plastic kits, single-pack filler is more than adequate and those mentioned above come under this category, being ready for use straight from the tube. However, to make more substantial repairs, fill larger holes, or treat areas that must later be drilled or shaped, two-part putty is essential. Twin-pack putties are usually formulated from epoxy and consist of a separate resin and hardener, in a similar fashion to epoxy adhesives. The two components must be mixed together in equal quantities and working times vary according to brand. Once fully cured, they can be carved, drilled, tapped and turned if necessary and will adhere well to almost any material.

APPLYING FILLERS

Crucially, all bonds must be fully hardened before applying any fillers, as any residual solvent vapours may cause problems. This is especially important with strong solvent-based formulas such as Humbrol, Revell and Squadron.

Always read the label before applying any filler and preferably test some of it on a scrap of the same material beforehand, just in case. There is no golden rule as to the best tool for applying filler. Basically, as long as the putty is put where it is meant to go and can be spread evenly, essentially anything goes. Plastic spatulas are available, but these are usually far too big; I often find myself using a range of flat-bladed mini-screwdrivers, of differing sizes. Cocktail sticks can also be handy for small, hard-to-reach areas.

Try to avoid clogging-up areas of intricate surface relief, such as rows of rivet heads, as it will be hard to remove the excess once it has dried. A cotton swab dipped in a little white spirit will remove excess solvent filler while it is still wet. Avoid problems by applying only small amounts of filler at a time and replace the lid on the tube quickly, having wiped the threads clean. Fast-drying formulas, such as Squadron, have an annoying habit of drying around the nozzle and lid, making it hard to effect an airtight seal once the tube has been used a few times.

When building up more than one layer of putty, make sure that the previous application has cured completely. As well as feeling dry to the touch, there should not be any trace of the putty's smell, signifying that all traces of the solvent have evaporated. Rushing the job will simply melt the filler beneath, leading to even longer curing times.

It is tempting to try to get the filler smooth and flush with the model's surface from the offing, with the hope of lessening the amount of sanding to do later. However, we must take into account the filler's propensity to shrink as it dries. Instead, build

There are a number of different model fillers on the market. Some, like Milliput, are two-part epoxy putties that require mixing before use. These are great for filling large areas, or if the cured putty will require shaping or drilling. For small gaps and imperfections, a softer formula will suffice.

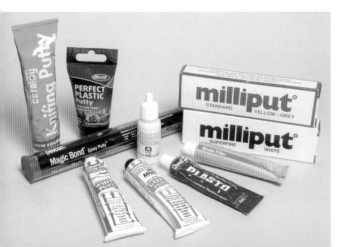

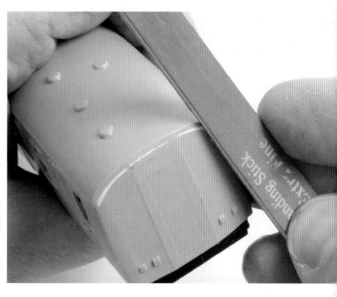

Soft putties, offered by Deluxe, Vallejo, Humbrol, Revell, Squadron and Tamiya, are simply spread over the affected area with a spatula or a small flat-bladed screwdriver. Build it up in thin layers and leave proud of the surface to allow for shrinkage as it cures.

Files and abrasive papers or sticks can be used to flatten the filler and blend it into the surrounding surface. Be sure that the filler is completely dry and avoid inhaling the dust.

Take the time to tidy seams that will be highly visible, such as tank barrels. It may take a few attempts of filling and sanding before the joint becomes invisible.

Try not to clog areas of fine detail with excess filler, as it can be hard to remove it when dry. A damp swab will clean up the material before it dries.

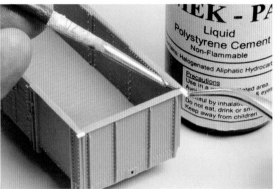

Care is necessary when filing and sanding around any raised rivets or other details. It helps to fill and abrade any gaps as you go, rather than leaving all remedial work until later, as some parts may become difficult to reach once extra parts have been fitted.

Fillers have their limitations and plastic strip may be a better bet for instances like this. The corners of this wagon did not meet properly, resulting in the raised beading looking unsightly. Filler, even epoxy putty, would struggle to do this job, so strips of 0.5mm thick plastic were glued into the gaps and left overnight to cure.

up the filler to sit about a millimetre proud of the surface. Being able to sand it down to meet the surrounding surface will result in a much superior – and hopefully invisible – finish.

No attempt should be made to abrade the filler until it is completely dry. Wet filler, even when appearing dry on the surface, will clog up files and sanding paper, making one heck of a mess. A bit of patience is never wasted and results in smoother progress. If there is a lot of filler to flatten, a file may

be handy to start with; ditto if the filler is located at a corner or other area where the shaping must be sharp and true to match the surroundings. With fine abrasive paper or sanding sticks, it is easy to round over edges, as the flexible material conforms to the surface. Wrapping abrasive sheets around small strips of wood or plastic produces more reliable sanding tools for work in awkward spaces.

A note of caution – sanding and filing plastic fillers will produce a very fine powder dust that is harmful

A little Squadron Green Putty filled any gaps and the bright colour made it easy to see against the grey of the plastic.

With the filler completely cured, the sharp edges of the beading were reinstated with a file and sanding sticks.

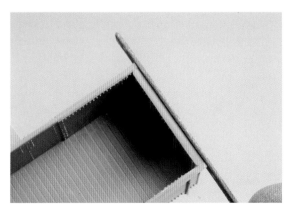

Here's a top tip – when assembling items like tank wagon barrels, clamp the parts together tightly and apply plenty of strong liquid poly-cement to the inside of the joints ...

... then squeeze the parts together until the molten plastic oozes up from the joint. Tighten the tape or clamps further and leave to harden completely. The following day, the squeezed-out plastic can be filed and sanded flush, negating the need for any filler.

if inhaled, so wear a facemask. Using abrasive sheets and sticks wet offers a safer way of working, as well as a smoother finish to the surface, because the water stops the sheets clogging up with dust and debris.

TROUBLESOME PARTS

For a number of reasons, some parts may simply refuse to mate properly at their joint faces. Poor moulds, damage, overenthusiastic flash removal, or simply bad kit design may be to blame, but there is usually a way of navigating most problems. Corner joints on wagon bodies are the most consistent culprits, with large gaps appearing and leaving precious little material with which to secure a decent bond. In other cases, it may be necessary drastically to trim some components to allow them to fit, or, conversely, to enlarge them with shims of plastic.

Of paramount importance when 'correcting' kit components, is the veracity of the vehicle's outer contours. It does not matter what is going on inside if the interior is hidden from view, but perfectly square corners and a correctly set roof are a priority. Therefore if, even after endless fettling, the joint faces still will not join correctly, they will have to be helped with some internal reinforcement, then tidied up with filler.

As illustrated in Chapter 4, adding plastic angle to strengthen internal corners also offers the benefit of compensating for barely matching joints. The plastic angle helps to form the exact 90-degree joint in accordance to the overall dimensions of the prototype rather than any compromise of scale, forced by the need to get the parts together any which way. This has happened to me a few times recently, both with aged OO freight van kits. In one case, there was but a couple of millimetres worth of material meeting at each corner joint of sides and ends. Instead of filing back those mitred joints to get true, flat faces (and losing a millimetre or two from the length and width of the model), I simply added 0.25in Evergreen plastic angle to the inside of each corner and fixed the four aspects together in line with the scale outer dimensions. The gaps at each corner were quite dramatic, but were later filled with epoxy putty and blended seamlessly into the surface.

Not quite so drastic, yet all too common, is the problem of rendering the top corners of steel-bodied mineral wagons. Large-scale kits seem to be immune from this, but 4mm and 2mm kits invariably see these crucial edges disappear during construction. The situation can often be rescued with a little filler alone, while at other times it may be necessary to insert small pieces of plastic strip to create the distinctive square-edged reinforcing plates.

It is frustrating when kits do not fit together as they should, especially if one is relying on moulded guides to help get important parts aligned. When building a Mailcoach kit of a Thompson brake van, the ends and floor unit formed the foundations of the bodyshell. Rather than lose the alignment steps on the inside of the ends, the upper face of the floor needed thinning considerably to fit into the corresponding slot in the ends. The job was speeded up with a sanding drum in a mini-drill.

The ends could then be affixed and set-up correctly with a set square, using the unmodified lower face of the floor to rest on the moulded guides on each end.

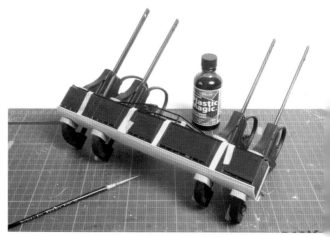

The roof still proved troublesome on the Thompson van, with plenty of fettling of the inside face. Firm clamping and minor adjustments to its position eventually saw it located correctly and the glue could be applied. The clamps were left in place for 24hr, just to make sure.

INNER STRENGTH

When handling an item of rolling stock, we all tend to pick it up by the sides of the vehicle's body, being careful to keep our hands away from the more delicate underframe. Kit-built chassis are particularly susceptible to damage, with brake gear, door springs and axle-guard tie-bars the most at risk from 12in:1ft fingers. So, instead, we grab the model in the centre of the body, yet there is a real danger of the sides being compressed a little too far, with the result that they will bow inwards, breaking the joint with the roof or even dislodging any glazing.

It differs from kit to kit and the sides may be given a degree of rigidity from the joints at the floor and corners, but the mating of side and roof usually consists of little more than a butt joint with very little in the way of internal bracing. Closed vehicles, such as vans with no interior detail, can be strengthened with a simple internal support cut from scraps of plastic. The humble 10ft wheelbase van will benefit and it is virtually imperative for anything longer. Keeping the walls of the wagon square and true helps all of the other components to fit properly and will make for a more realistic and purposeful-looking model.

Another awkward customer was this Parkside LNER brake van, in which few of the main body sections mated up perfectly. I have built a few of these and the kit makes a great model, but you really have to work at it. The four main walls, assembled on to the floor, will form the bedrock of the vehicle, so the parts have to be aligned exactly right.

Holding it together with masking tape while the glue was applied kept everything square.

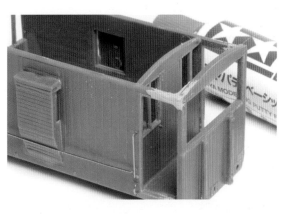

The main problem was the fit of the verandah ends against the sides and floor and copious amounts of filler was needed to bridge the gaps.

With the parts assembled, the top corner joints were left with little strength – if the parts met at all. Plastic shims were inserted, followed by more filler.

If corner joints have proved challenging, do not forget that internal reinforcements are possible. As well as angle section in the corners, a cross-brace also offers extra resilience to the sides of a vehicle.

Cross-braces are recommended for longer vehicles, especially where a kit's roof lacks any effective locating tabs that also serve as strengthening spars for the sides. As can be glimpsed on this Mailcoach kit, the roof sports only a handful of small tabs, few of which were of any use as they were misaligned.

WHAT IF IT GOES WRONG?

Mistakes will inevitably be made at some point and, as long as we learn a lesson and understand why something has gone wrong, it is never a wasted experience. Indeed, in the majority of cases, even a serious error can be remedied in one way or another. In the event that certain parts have been damaged beyond repair, fear not, as you will probably be able to obtain a spare sprue from the manufacturer rather than have to buy a whole new kit. Some firms generously offer to replace the odd part free of charge, but that is purely at their discretion and it helps to ask very nicely.

For less serious problems, such as misaligned components or the wrong part fitted in the wrong place, bonds can be broken with a sharp knife up to about thirty minutes after applying poly-cement (depending on the formula). However, as the plastic will have been chemically softened, the edges are likely to be a bit of a mess. If so, set all the parts aside overnight to harden before setting to with files to tidy up the mating faces once again. There will be a good chance that the model's dimensions will have been affected, but it should only be a question of fractions. If tidy or strong joints are now difficult, use the method outlined earlier in this chapter, making use of plastic angle as an internal reinforcement and alignment device.

Most importantly, do not lose heart. This is all part of the learning curve and, after the hassle of dismantling and effecting repairs, it is unlikely that you will make the same mistake again.

The most common mistake is to apply too much poly-cement and, as it seeps through the joint, it invariably finds its way under your fingers and leaves behind permanent fingerprints. If caught quickly, there is a chance that brushing on more solvent will soften the plastic further and remove the marks. But such good fortune is rare.

Allow the plastic to harden overnight, then try abrading the surface with a fibreglass scratch brush. Follow with successive grades of abrasives until the surface is smooth again and free of any scratches.

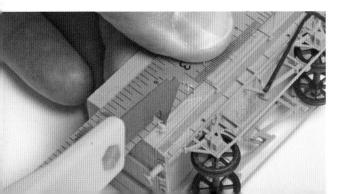

Planked wagons rely on their surface relief and all this intervention may have damaged the moulded recesses or panel lines. These can be reinstated with an Olfa profile-cutting tool. Draw the hooked blade towards you against a straight edge to cut narrow channels.

With careful remedial work, you might never know that there had been a problem with this wagon.

Breaking glue bonds is not easy if the parts have been in contact for more than thirty minutes, although a sharp, flat blade can often part the ways.

Even after ten minutes, the plastic components will have welded themselves together quite effectively. The parts will need to harden before being redressed with files.

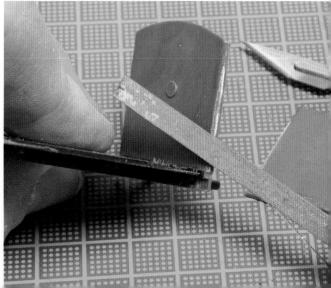

CHAPTER SEVEN

THE FINER POINTS

The ensuing pages are meant as an addendum to the previous two chapters, expanding on the plastic kit theme, so to speak. With a rolling chassis and body-shell complete and running reliably on a test track, we can now turn our attention to adding some of the finer details such as buffers and brake gear. We will also be looking at some alternative ways of adding weight, reinforcing joints and persuading stubborn parts to come together more effectively. And there is also the small matter of constructing articulated bogies.

WEIGHING UP YOUR OPTIONS

Back in Chapter 4, we briefly discussed adding weight to plastic kits during the early stages of construction. This is not always an appropriate time to address the ballast issue, as certain types of wagons or carriages dictate that adding weight must be left until later in the build. This is especially so when dealing with open wagons or hoppers intended for running with the payload area exposed.

Products like Liquid Gravity, from Deluxe Materials, offer the convenience of adding a pelleted, dense material into all manner of spots, such as the compartments created by a van's underfloor framing. Thin glues, such as Super 'Phatic!, are needed to penetrate the loose material and will need an overnight break to cure.

Even in larger scales, plastic kits offer little in the way of mass and need to gain a few pounds before being let loose on the tracks. However, finding room for extra ballast is not always easy and some improvisation is often necessary, such as adding strips of steel into a tank barrel before sealing up the ends.

Getting the weight evenly distributed is important. This hopper has had Liquid Gravity squeezed into as many spots as possible, secured with super-thin cyano glue. This formula penetrates the ballast and dries within a minute or so, but it must be used with extreme care.

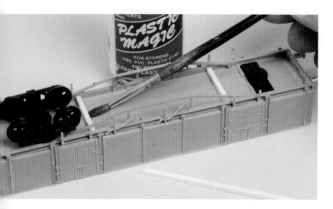

For plain underframes, add a simple barrier at each end to contain the loose weight. Make sure that the bogies and wheels are unhindered and that the plastic strip will not be visible when the vehicle is on the tracks.

With a needle-tip applicator, the penetrating glue can be applied over the ballast, allowing it to soak through the material. If using cyano, treat 6sq cm (1sq in) at a time and allow the fumes to evaporate for a few minutes before carrying on. A build-up of cyano vapours creates a lot of heat and can damage the plastic.

The fine tip of the Liquid Gravity pot makes pouring in the ballast easy. Tamp it down below the level of the solebars with a scrap of wood or plastic.

It is often difficult to find room for extra weight, yet getting enough mass into the right places is key for successful running. Liquid Gravity, Fluid Lead and other similar products ease the job considerably, as they allow small amounts of dense material to be lodged in a number of small voids or recesses in the underframe. Conversely, vehicles with plenty of underfloor space, such as bogie wagons or carriages, may need some means of containing this 'liquid' ballast, to keep it away from any moving parts and out of view.

Remember to weigh your vehicles before fixing the ballast in place, with an aim for a standardized weight for specific types of rolling stock. As a guide, matching, or slightly exceeding, the mass of similar RTR vehicles is a good guide, not least as the kits are likely to run with such stock, reducing the risks associated with heavier or lighter vehicles in the same rake.

BOGIES

Long-wheelbase freight and passenger stock make use of articulated bogies to cope better with curved rails and these involve a very similar assembly process to a rigid underframe, especially when pin-point bearings and axles are to be fitted. There are, however, a number of unique considerations to bear in mind. Adequate clearance between the wheel flanges and the vehicle's floor is essential, especially when the bogie swings around on its axis. The amount of rotation depends on the vehicle and the minimum radius curve that it will traverse (it does not have to perform a full 360-degree turn). Choice of wheels will be important and many freight vehicle

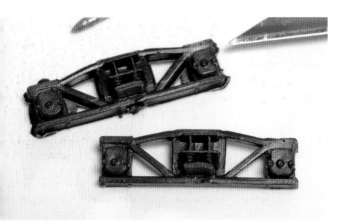

Plastic bogies have their advantages and disadvantages, although much of their success is down to the quality of the mouldings. These Parkside diamond frame units look a bit rough as supplied, but can be cleaned up to produce a pair of impressive bogies.

Fitting brass bearings and wheeling-up follows a similar method as fixed-wheel chassis. Hopefully, the centre spreader is rendered to the correct length to allow the axles to fit easily. If not, some plastic shims can be added (as described in the previous chapter). Test fitting and then assembling on a glass sheet will ensure that both axles are set correctly. The parts should be held together firmly for a few minutes until the glue has taken hold.

Bogie vehicles demand a number of additional considerations during assembly, free lateral and vertical rotation and correct ride height being the most important. Each of these factors is governed by how the pivoting bolster is designed. In this case, there is adequate bearing surface area on the bogie and separate bolster, each combining to keep the wheel flanges clear of the vehicle's chassis.

kits suggest using slightly underscale wheels (in OO and N gauge) to permit the bogies to rotate freely.

There should also be enough space to clear the coupling mount, if this is fitted to the vehicle's floor. If fitted to the bogie frame, the coupling must be able to move freely with the bogie and be aligned at the correct height. The method of attaching bogies to the chassis differs between kits, with a choice between permanent and removable fixings. The latter is preferable to ease maintenance and repair, although the fixings must be reliable and not become loose during operation.

Non-compensated bogies are inherently simple things, being a glorified cradle in which two or more axles are hung. The wheels and axles need to be aligned accurately, in parallel to each other and perpendicular to the bogie sides. The wheels must also turn freely in their bearings and sit level on the track, with no signs of twisting or distortion.

Self-tapping screws offer an effective bogie-mounting option. Indeed, many kits provide a pair of suitable screws. Before mounting the bogie, cut a matching thread in the plastic chassis by carefully screwing in the bolts. For every full turn clockwise, reverse the action half a turn and continue until the screw is almost home, keeping it vertical at all times.

When you come to fit the bogies, the screws will then have an easier passage into the bolsters. Don't over-tighten them or the bogie's movement will be impeded. They should be able to rotate freely as well as rock up and down a little. If you are worried about the screws coming undone in service, add a little Loctite 603 thread sealer during final assembly.

Coupling choice also plays a part in how bogies are fitted. Most plastic kits offer an integral tension lock mount on the bogie itself, as long-wheelbase vehicles benefit from having the coupling swing along with the bogie (see following chapter). Note the use of a set of Bachmann RTR Gresley bogies under this van. These are a perfect fit and solve the issue of adding couplings to match the rest of my RTR stock.

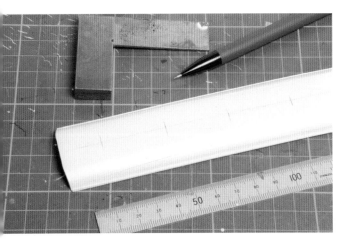

greater array of components, it is fast becoming the norm. Aside from purely opening out pre-moulded apertures, a number of kits invite the modeller to mark out and drill holes 'blind', requiring a good degree of accuracy if the parts are to fit properly.

Getting the drill to cut a hole exactly where it is needed is not a task to take lightly, especially when precision down to fractions of a millimetre is concerned, and it helps to have a good set of drill bits, pin vices and measuring tools at hand. Mini-power drills can speed up repetitive drilling tasks, or those using a larger size bit, but accuracy can suffer if working with small-diameter bits that will flex readily and move off course. The danger of excessive heat generated by the bit is also relevant when dealing with plastic kits.

Take your time marking out positions, checking the measurements a couple of times to ensure that they are in the right place. A sharp needle will act as an effective centre punch, marking the location of the hole more accurately than a pencil. The depression caused by the punch also guides the drill bit and helps it to start its cut into the material.

Parts being drilled should be adequately supported to prevent breakages or distortion and only very slight pressure should be exerted on the tool, patiently letting the bit do its work. If it is struggling

Many kits require the modeller to drill out holes for mounting certain pieces of equipment, such as handrails or brake-operating rods. Some form of moulded guide is usually provided, but this coach kit offered no such help. The cast ventilators needed holes drilling into the roof, so set square, straight edge and sharp pencil were employed for accurate measuring and marking, following the rough guide supplied in the instructions.

DRILLING

The need to drill holes for locating structural or detailing parts is an increasingly common task in kit building. As more and more kits are offering a

The marks created by the needle punch act as a guide for the drill bit, preventing it from wandering off course. Only light pressure is needed as the hand vice is turned, allowing the sharp bit to work through the plastic in its own time. A sheet of plywood beneath prevents damage to the work surface.

After checking and double-checking the measurements, the centre of each hole was punched with a needle in a hand vice.

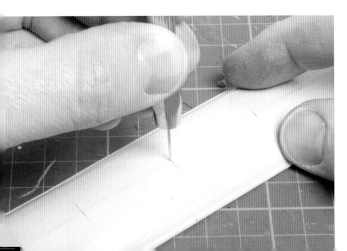

If the drill does slope off from its intended course, fill with Milliput or other epoxy putty and leave to cure completely. After sanding flush, mark out and punch the location and try drilling again. It helps to use a smaller bit for the first cut, moving up to the final size in increments.

to drill, remove from the hole and clear away the swarf from the bit's channels and try again. If it is still not cutting through, the bit may be blunt and should be replaced. A scrap of plywood provides a good, sturdy base on which to drill, with the bit simply going into the wood as it passes through the plastic.

Choose the right drill bit for the job, starting with a bit much smaller than the final size of the hole when working on delicate parts. Beginning with too big a drill bit can damage the soft plastic, while the smaller hole can be increased in increments for absolute accuracy and control.

BUFFERS

The solid wood, or 'dumb', buffers fitted to the earliest British freight vehicles persisted for longer than many enthusiasts realize, despite sprung units being fitted to passenger vehicles as early as 1834. Indeed, their use on new mainline wagons was not outlawed until 1889 and not banned altogether until 1913, although some lasted in service in Scotland until the early 1920s.

Many different buffers have appeared over the intervening years, designed to suit the specific needs of a range of vehicles. Shape and size is dependent on many factors, such as vehicle length and whether continuous brakes are fitted or not. As unfitted wagons were prone to more bumping around in loose-coupled formations, shorter buffers were generally used compared to those on fitted stock, which tended to be coupled more tightly together. Passenger stock with knuckle couplings also carried short buffers, although they could be extended for use when coupled with conventional draw gear. The weight of the vehicle also played a part, with some very heavy-duty designs emerging. The size and shape of the buffer head determined how well a vehicle could cope with propelling moves across very shallow curve radii without the risk of the buffers locking.

All kits come with at least some representation of buffing gear – if appropriate to the prototype – but quality and fidelity are variable. The majority of plastic kits come with plastic buffers formed on the sprues along with the rest of the components and, in some cases, they can be difficult to extract. Some can be beautifully rendered and thoughtfully positioned in the mould to make tidying and fitting a real breeze, while others may be so crudely rendered as to be barely usable.

A spot of prototype research will declare if the buffers provided are the right pattern. A good many kits simply offer fairly generic underframe components to suit different sorts of vehicle and, therefore, the buffers may not be exactly right. If this is bothersome to you, there are plenty of suppliers of alternative buffers with a greater degree of fidelity.

Depending on the kit, the buffer beam may have the buffer mounting holes already in place because the plastic originals will be a push fit, as is the case with many larger scale products. However, the common practice in OO and N is to mould the lower part of the buffer shank integral to the beams, so new holes will need to be drilled. A good tip is to use the moulded holes in the shank centres as a guide and, before cutting away the unwanted material, drill a pilot hole through the shank right through

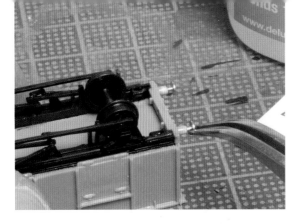

In an ideal world, all plastic kits would provide turned metal buffer heads. All the modeller has to do is open up the holes in the shanks and glue the heads in place with a tiny drop of cyano, applied with a cocktail stick.

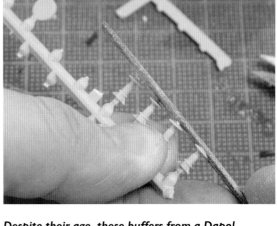

Despite their age, these buffers from a Dapol Prestwin are rendered beautifully. Dressing the heads while the shanks are still attached to the sprue makes them easier to handle.

the buffer beam. Once the shank has been removed, there will be a hole ready for opening out and fitting of replacements. Do check, though, that the buffers will be correctly spaced (usually around 173cm (5ft 8in) on standard gauge prototypes) and at the right height to match the rest of your stock, especially if working with scale couplings. For example, in OO the centre of each buffer scales out to 23mm apart (0.9in) (11.5mm [0.5in] either side of the centre line) and 14.3mm (0.6in) above the top of the rails.

Metal buffers can be found in some kits, in the form of entire units or just the buffer heads, and these are often a welcome addition. Protruding from each corner of a vehicle leaves the buffers open to damage and a more resilient material than plastic helps them to withstand the odd prang. Modellers

employing scale couplings will be reliant on the buffers to operate in the same way as the real thing, absorbing the shocks and taking the pressure of propelling moves without becoming locked on curves or points. Some prescribe miniature sprung buffers (see Chapter 14) as a must with scale couplings, but it is certainly possible to manage without them.

Round-head buffers demand careful cleaning after cutting them from the sprue. Such visible components deserve to be treated properly, as any elliptical or square heads will stand out like a sore thumb. If you are feeling brave, you can mount the shank in a powered mini-drill and 'turn' the edge and face with a flat file and abrasives.

Buffers must be accurately aligned and mounted straight and true in the buffer beams. Mounting holes

Unfortunately, most kits in each scale make use of plastic buffer shanks and heads. Invariably, these need much in the way of cleaning up before they can be fitted.

Unless the mouldings are perfect, creating truly round objects is not easy, although tidying up the buffer heads can be aided by mounting them in a hand drill vice.

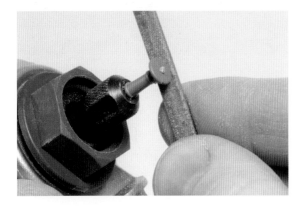 

For the brave, mounting the buffers in a mini-drill and turning them against a file is an option. The drill needs fixing into a press, or, as with this Dremel tool, into a vice-mounted attachment. Work at a slow speed setting and wear eye protection.

Finish by burnishing the buffers with sanding sticks. These Coopercraft O gauge buffers were a bit of a mess when cut from the sprue, a result of the mould's halves being misaligned. Although the finished buffers are smaller than intended, they are at least round.

If the supplied buffers are not up to scratch, or simply the wrong pattern to suit your prototype, there are plenty of options for replacements, in turned brass, nickel silver, or cast whitemetal. RTR makers also offer bulk packs of buffers, in sprung or fixed format.

Cut away the moulded shanks with a sharp blade and file the buffer beam flush. Carefully mark the centre of the mounting holes for the new buffers, using a needle punch for accuracy. Start drilling with a small diameter bit, working up to the final size in increments to avoid splitting the buffer beam edges.

Dress the surface to remove any burrs created by the drills and test-fit the new buffers. Add a little cyano to the shanks with a cocktail stick and push them home. Make sure they are the right way up, especially if they incorporate footsteps.

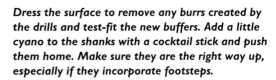
 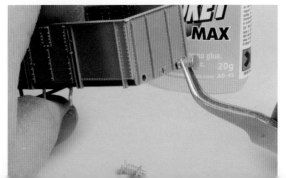

may need opening out slightly with a drill and, if plastic heads are provided to sit into moulded shanks, it is a good idea to leave these off until after painting and final assembly, to avoid accidental breakage.

A minor detail to watch out for with ribbed-shank buffers is to ensure that they are fixed the right way up. A close look at those with cast ribs reveals that one will be slightly shorter than the others – this is the face that sits uppermost.

BRAKE GEAR

The rendition of carriage and wagon brake gear, in 4mm scale and smaller kits, is probably the area where most kits disappoint. The situation has improved in recent years, but there are still many kits on the market with slightly crude renditions of brake shoes, actuating arms and linkages. Larger scale kits, with more space to fill, tend to do a better job.

As with buffers, there are plenty of aftermarket alternatives to provide a more authentic array of components or a different kind of gear altogether to correct a kit's generic contents. It is really a case of 'horses for courses', as a lot of supplied plastic brake gear can be upgraded to a certain extent purely by

Brake shoes should be placed as close to the wheel treads as possible, while still allowing free rotation. Any side play in the axle must also be taken into account and test-fitting is recommended, trimming material from the face of the shoes if necessary.

fettling with a knife and needle files. Drilling out small holes and adding brass wire to mimic linkages and cross-shafts also makes a massive difference with little financial outlay.

Working with what we have in the kit, it is important to read the instructions carefully and study prototype images to ensure that the right parts go in the right place. Carriage and wagon underframes

Once the brakes are in position, the attendant rodding and other fittings can be added, following the kit's instructions closely. Many will provide moulded locating holes or brackets in the floor for vacuum cylinders and 'V' hangers, as many vehicles are 'handed' as far as placement of particular equipment is concerned. Also, if any wire rod is provided, mounting holes may need drilling out.

Brake gear may need fettling before fitting, making sure that the parts are free of unsightly flash. After checking which parts go where – and that they are oriented correctly – fix them in position. Test-fitting will reveal whether the brake shoe faces need filing back to give adequate clearance.

Do not forget to thread any actuating arms on to the rods before fixing the wire in position with a drop of cyano. Once the wire is secure, the final positioning of the various arms and levers can be set, with more cyano added where necessary.

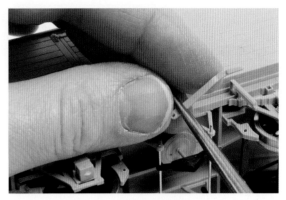

Drill out the 'big end' of the brake handle to accommodate the protruding wire, as this acts as a metal dowel, strengthening the joint. Handles usually need bending to shape and the plastic may be at risk of snapping unless bathed in warm water beforehand to soften it slightly. Alternatively, a few drops of poly-cement will also make the material more amenable to shaping.

can be murky places and photographs rarely show everything clearly, so you may have to rely on any illustrations or written descriptions supplied with the kit.

Morton-type brake gear can catch out the unwary as the brake pushrods must be fitted in a certain way. Being arranged so that the brake rods are pushed towards the wheels when the hand lever is moved downwards, if the kit parts are fitted the wrong way around, it will present one of those 'impossible 3-D puzzles'. A clutch arrangement was fitted to one side in some cases, often with an extra V-shaped

After snipping off the waste wire with a set of end cutters, gently tidy up the edges with a flat needle file. Leave the wire a couple of millimetres proud of the main V hangers where the brake handles are to be fitted.

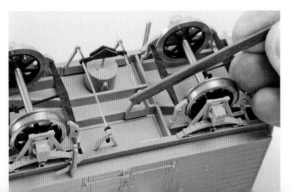

hanger and with the pushrods working in a different arrangement than the other side. Again, check the instructions and cross-reference prototype images to familiarize yourself with the layout of the parts.

Whatever type of brake gear is fitted, getting the brake shoes in line with the wheels is important and having the shoes as close to the tyres as possible also boosts realism. The real things only need a clearance of a fraction of an inch when the brakes are 'off', so huge gaps on our models always spoil the effect. Naturally, the wheels still need to rotate unhindered, so careful placement and dressing of the shoe faces with a round file should do the trick. Siting and orientation of vacuum or air-brake cylinders also carries a high priority as locations varied across different fleets, with some 'vac' cylinders inclined to achieve more efficient operation.

WHAT'S NEXT?

Although our kit project should be looking almost complete at this stage, there are still many crucial elements that have not been discussed, most notably the subject of choosing and fitting couplings.

CHAPTER EIGHT

COUPLINGS

In reality, it is advisable to address the issue of coupling choice at the earliest opportunity, not least as it might affect the assembly process and any physical modifications to chassis or bodywork will doubtless be easier beforehand. However, for the purposes of this book, it seemed more important to get down to the act of sticking bits together sooner, rather than fill so many early chapters with a lot of theory.

As things stand, the vast majority of N gauge modellers utilize the 'standard' Rapido coupling, as found on all British-outline RTR models. Similarly, most OO gauge enthusiasts favour the tried-and-trusted tension-lock device and there are few signs that either *status quo* is likely to change at any point soon. As a result, kit manufacturers cater for this demand by adding suitable mounting pockets to the list of components supplied; some even offer the couplings as well. This not only allows full compatibility with RTR rolling stock, but also simplifies construction

for the customer, as much of the hassle of alignment will be avoided.

First introduced in the early 1960s by Tri-ang, the tension lock was eventually adopted across all manufacturers of OO gauge models for the UK market. Prior to its invention, mixing models from different manufacturers was a difficult business, with converter wagons being offered to link Hornby Dublo and Tri-ang stock. Indeed, the first semblance of standardization only occurred when these two leading brands came under the ownership of one parent company. Thus, the sideways-acting Hornby Dublo couplings became a thing of the past. Refined over the years in terms of performance and appearance, the tension lock has held sway ever since.

The N gauge Rapido also dates back to the 1960s, rooted in a design introduced by Arnold in the USA. Graham Farish, Peco and Dapol fit these as standard, although the latter had just released an impressive

Few rolling-stock kits come supplied with any form of working couplings, although there is plenty of choice amongst proprietary units to match RTR stock. The humble tension lock still rules supreme in OO gauge, albeit in a narrower profile than the older style. The Rapido remains similarly universal in N.

range of magnetically operated knuckle couplings as this book neared completion.

What we in Britain quaintly refer to as Continental brands (in other words, anything foreign!) have been fitting superior automatic couplings for many years. A variety of mechanisms exist, many of which are not compatible with other brands, but may be interchanged using the NEM (Normen Europäischer Modellbahnen) coupling system.

ENTER THE NEM

In an effort to achieve standardization across all manufacturers, the NEM specification was developed to govern the desired height and positioning of couplings on locomotives and rolling stock. Specifications were drawn up for all popular scales, but the system has not proved entirely successful. Despite many RTR products claiming to be NEM-compliant, coupling heights remain inconsistent, preventing complete reliability.

It is, however, a starting point and the fitting of NEM-style interchangeable coupling pockets offers the user a choice of slimline tension locks, working

buckeye-style knuckle couplers and a whole host of Continental designs, many of which allow unsightly gaps between vehicles to be shortened while also imparting a more pleasing visual appearance. All you need to do is simply pull out one coupling type and push in another. Furthermore, the NEM system allows the user to tailor his or her coupling choice to suit the radius of a layout's curves, the type of vehicle, or how the stock is to be used. Long or short wheelbase, bogie or fixed axle, passenger or freight, fixed rakes or stock for shunting; all are deciding factors.

Happily, kit makers are slowly cottoning on to NEM, with brands like Parkside and Chivers including a choice of coupling pockets, including NEM-compatible sockets, with all of its wagon kits. Until such time as it becomes universal, there are also a number of components and kits available separately, such as the Symoba NEM system, which can be fitted to virtually any 4mm scale vehicle and is fully adjustable. Offering close coupling, with lateral movement to cope with curves, they are more reliable than fixed mount couplings, especially on longer wheelbase fixed-axle vehicles.

The arrival of the NEM specification has brought some sense of standardization to OO and N models, and the interchangeable pocket allows different couplers to be clipped into position. Indeed, the NEM pocket offers the modeller greater choice, with each of these couplers being freely available from RTR makers.

Amongst the most popular alternative working couplers in 4mm and 7mm scale are those in the American Kadee range. Although knuckle couplers are not widely adopted in Britain, Kadees offer great performance, with magnetic operation allowing for remotely controlled uncoupling. A similar coupler is offered in N by Micro Trains.

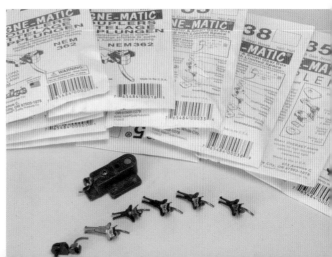

Most working coupler systems rely on magnets for remote operation, some of which require burying beneath the track, so choice needs to be made at an early stage of a layout's development. Kadees can also be operated with hand-held decoupling magnets, however. Tension locks and other RTR systems make use of sprung ramps between the rails.

Many kits do supply mounting brackets for off-the-shelf couplers, such as these standard mouldings offered by Parkside to suit the old style of Hornby tension locks. Alternative brackets are available for a variety of NEM and non-NEM-style couplers from Bachmann, Dapol and Hornby.

Kits move with the times and mounting brackets for NEM couplers are turning up on the sprues of plastic kits. This Chivers mineral wagon comes with sockets to match Bachmann or Hornby NEM couplings. Part of the NEM specification governs a common height above the rails and straight- or cranked-shafted couplers are available to suit different vehicle types. The kit's instructions will advise the best type to use.

The Symoba NEM362 conversion kit includes enough parts to convert three kit-built or RTR vehicles to NEM compatibility. A choice of NEM pockets is supplied (straight or cranked), along with a height-setting gauge. The coupling mount consists of a swivelling bracket, giving plenty of lateral movement that is great for layouts with sharp curves or for long-wheelbase vehicles.

All that is needed is enough space behind the buffer beam and a flat surface on which to fix the coupler mount. As many kits feature moulded location points for their own coupling mounts, these will have to be flattened, along with any injection marks or pips. If the model has already been assembled, reaching these with a knife or file will be difficult, so use a flat-bottomed milling bit in a mini-drill.

Clean away all dust and debris and mark out the centre of the wagon, fixing the Symoba mounting brackets exactly in the middle of the floor, close to the rear of the buffer beam. Strong poly-cement will do the job, but keep the adhesive away from the moving parts.

Slot on the straight or cranked NEM pocket and use the height gauge to set it correctly. Add a drop of poly-cement to the joint and allow it to dry, checking the height again for good measure.

COUPLING CHOICE

There are a number of coupling options open to us, especially in the ever-popular 4mm scale. Some, like the Kadee knuckle coupler (available for HO/OO and O gauge), offer unrivalled performance and value for money. However, they still bear little resemblance to traditional UK practice, although 'knuckles' can now be found on much contemporary freight traffic.

Close-coupling designs, such as Keen Systems' range of OO kits, are perfect for fitting to fixed

Clip in your desired NEM-compatible coupler and test with your other rolling stock. When satisfied, the stem of the Symoba mounting bracket can be trimmed. Kadees are available with NEM tails, in a variety of lengths and either straight or cranked shafts, allowing greater flexibility in height settings. Choose the length to suit the radius of your layout's curves, as the vehicle's buffers must be kept apart to prevent locking.

Kadees are also available with their own mounting system (known as 'draftboxes'), yet with a great degree of flexibility in height and length to suit almost any vehicle. As with the Symoba NEM kit, a height gauge is essential when fitting Kadees, as it allows all stock to be set up identically, guaranteeing optimum performance.

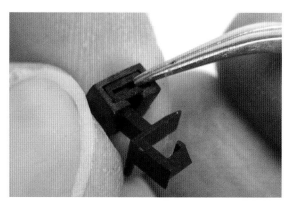

The Farish Rapido coupler has been the standard fitment on British N stock for years and many 2mm kits are designed with this system in mind. Some even include the couplers too, as is the case with this Parkside kit.

The Rapido is placed into the coupling pocket and a small retaining fillet pushed into the top. Do not bother gluing this, as the coupler head needs to remain free to pivot up and down.

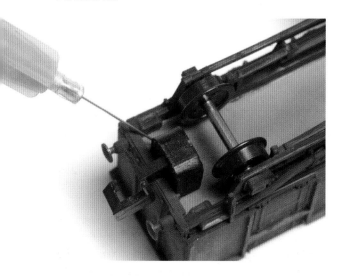

This kit features raised pips on the inner face of the buffer beam, allowing instant alignment of the coupler pockets. Use a pinpoint applicator to get just the right amount of liquid poly-cement into the joint without flooding and seizing the coupler.

Not all kits provide mounting brackets and this C-Rail PFA required an improvised solution. Blu-Tack was used as a temporary adhesive while the floor was shimmed and the coupler tested with a nominated RTR gauging wagon.

In the absence of a bespoke height gauge, choose an item of RTR rolling stock with its couplers set at the NEM-specified height above the rails as a test bed.

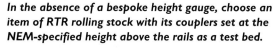

When happy with its position, the coupler was fixed in place with cyano. Although the vertical pivoting action has been lost, the model still operates reliably. It is the ease of uncoupling that has been compromised, but this is acceptable as these wagons were built to run in a fixed rake on the layout. For stock intended for shunting, the Parkside moulded pockets can be obtained as spare parts.

The wonderfully named Spratt & Winkle coupling system offers a more refined appearance and remote operation is possible through the use of hidden magnets. Available in kit form, each coupler has to be assembled from etched-brass components, so they require a little experience to get right.

rakes of coaching stock or multiple units and allow for a choice of semi-fixed or easy-to-detach couplers at the end of the swinging arms, which keep cars close together on straight rails and push them apart on curves. These and other similarly innovative systems can prove costly in terms of price and time spent in assembly and installation. Often, it is not just the couplers that need to be obtained, but also adapting brackets to cope with particular vehicles. Add in uncoupling magnets or tools and the cost rises even further, especially when treating a large fleet.

In contrast, homemade solutions that follow freely available specifications, such as the Alex Jackson system, cost very little, although do require a respectable degree of modelling skill and accuracy to get them set up and working correctly. Such couplers are not designed to cope with tight radius curves, although a handful of compromise solutions exist that offer near-scale appearance, yet with a more practical twist. In this bracket can be mentioned the Spratt & Winkle and DG systems for 3, 3.5 and 4mm scales.

Tension lock, hook and loop, knuckle couplers and other similar auto-couplers rely on an outside force to allow them to detach themselves without the physical intervention of the Great Hand from the Sky. Fitted with a vertical arm trailing beneath, the coupling is lifted by a magnet hidden beneath the baseboard or a sprung ramp between the rails. Once the tension between the two couplings has been eased, the hooks rise, allowing the vehicles to move apart.

Magnetically operated systems, such as Spratt & Winkle and Kadees, need a bit of forethought as the hidden magnets are much easier to install as the railway is being built, rather than trying to retro-fit them to ballasted track.

Despite NEM specifications also being drafted for N gauge, there is much less in the way of ready-made alternatives. Micro Trains' range of knuckle couplings is highly regarded, especially overseas, which is understandable as they look good and perform admirably. Similar in appearance and operation to the Kadee HO/OO 'knuckles', they can also be remotely controlled by hidden magnets beneath the rails, or with a handheld device. Proprietary automatic couplers are also thin on the ground in 7mm scale, although O gauge Kadees are well suited to modern-day subjects.

The hook of the Spratt & Winkle system is fairly unobtrusive, especially as it allows scale chain or screw-link couplings to be added for cosmetic purposes. The reciprocal angle of the hooks allows vehicles to couple together, while motive power requires only a simple wire bar between the buffers. When the couplings are relaxed, the magnet beneath the rails causes the brass plate to rock on its pivot wire, thus uncoupling the vehicles.

Standardizing the couplers across your entire fleet makes sense if all of the stock is intended to be compatible. Fixed coaching rakes, for example, need only be fitted with working couplings at the outer ends for easy motive power changes. Intermediate links between carriages could make use of semi-fixed, close-coupling units for heightened realism and less risk of unwanted detachments. The same principle can apply to block freight trains, while

Micro Trains N gauge knuckle couplings offer improved performance and the potential of magnetic, hands-free operation. Various lengths and mounting options are available, the easiest of which can simply be glued to the vehicle's underframe or bogies, after gauging the correct height.

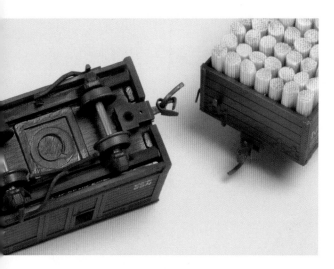

Perfect for modern N gauge rolling stock, or for OO9 narrow gauge, the Micro Trains knuckle couplings look highly authentic.

Conductive couplers, such as offered by Brelec and T4T, are great for DCC-operated layouts, offering full control of interior and exterior lights without the need for separate decoders and power collection aboard every vehicle. Now available with NEM tails, they are simple to fit, with only the routing and soldering of the electrical connections offering any challenges.

slow pick-up goods would benefit from automatic couplings between each vehicle to ease shunting, especially in hard to reach areas of the layout.

Coupling choice is primarily a matter of personal taste, informed by specific operating requirements of a layout. However, certain factors need to be borne in mind, such as the radius of curves and turnouts on the layout, with many coupling systems coping only with gently meandering track. Helpfully, a number of these coupling options are available in cheap trial packs and it pays to experiment to find the system that suits you best.

CONDUCTIVE COUPLINGS

With the increasing popularity of Digital Command Control (DCC), more and more layouts are being illuminated with miniature lighting of buildings, loco-motives and rolling stock. As a result, a number of innovative electrical accessories have appeared recently, aimed at this lucrative sector of the market. Relevant to this chapter is the availability of elec-trically conductive couplings, some of which boast up to four separate poles for the transmission of DCC signals governing interior and exterior light-ing throughout an entire rake of coaching stock,

without the need for separate decoders in the trailing vehicles.

According to the brand and specification, these couplings can be a little bulky, although they do look very convincing when fitted to modern coaching stock and multiple units. They require some careful wiring up and are designed for use in semi-perma-nently coupled rakes, as they are not so easy to uncouple while the vehicles are on the rails. With NEM-compatible mounting tails, though, they are easy to fit.

SCALE COUPLINGS

For the purist, there is nothing quite like the working 'scale' couplings of the three-link, screw-link or Instanter variety. These look wonderful and can be a joy to operate as long as you have good eyesight, a steady hand and a long reach. If your layout is exten-sive, with far-flung sidings, then scale couplings will prove challenging, to say the least. They are great for micro-layouts, though, especially where the slow shunting and marshalling of rolling stock are all part of the plan. Scale couplings are virtually stand-ard in O gauge, being a much more viable option in a larger scale, with many wagon and carriage kits

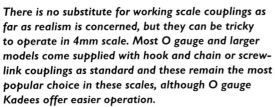

There is no substitute for working scale couplings as far as realism is concerned, but they can be tricky to operate in 4mm scale. Most O gauge and larger models come supplied with hook and chain or screw-link couplings as standard and these remain the most popular choice in these scales, although O gauge Kadees offer easier operation.

As per the prototype, there is a choice between the traditional three-link couplings (for non-continuous braked vehicles), screw-links (for continuous-braked freight and passenger vehicles) and Instanter couplings (for post-1960s air-braked freight stock).

Fitting scale couplings to kits is often simple, as the hole for the draw hook is usually moulded into the buffer beam. In some cases, however, it may need opening out slightly with a small drill bit. The hook should be able to slide easily within the slot.

Just like the real thing, the hook is sprung from the inside, retained with a split pin that should have its tails bent over to keep it in place.

Because of the need for a sprung draw hook – to absorb the shocks during haulage and allow the vehicles to cope with tight curves without derailing or locking buffers – adequate space is needed behind the buffer beam. Some kits are not designed with scale couplings in mind, so some modification will be necessary, as illustrated with this Peco Wonderful Wagon kit. The large expanse of solid plastic has been cut back with a mini-drill and milling bit.

It is important not to remove too much material, as the spring will exert some force on to the back of the buffer beam, which will also be weakened by having a slot cut into the centre for the hook. About 3mm thickness was left in this instance.

If you do not fancy cutting away all that plastic, or if it would be extremely difficult to do so – as is the case with this Dapol tank wagon chassis – the sprung action can be foregone, although the level of performance will be compromised.

Instead of drilling or cutting a deep slot in the solid plastic, heat the shank of the draw hook over a candle flame for a few minutes, until it glows red hot.

Push the hot metal into the centre of the buffer beam and it will melt its way through. If it stops short of the required depth, remove it, reheat and try again. Once it sits correctly, pull it out again and let it cool, before fixing permanently with a drop of cyano in the slot.

As long as couplings with long links, such as these Smiths Instanters, are used, the lack of springing can be ameliorated, especially if the wagon in question is marshalled between two vehicles with working sprung couplings. Operation of scale links is best with a homemade tool, fashioned from a length of stiff wire with a hook at the end. Fitting this to a mini-pen-style torch greatly improves sighting in confined spaces.

coming supplied with suitable draw hooks and couplings. While not an impossible prospect in N gauge, installation and operation are very demanding.

Working scale couplings are offered pre- or unassembled, with a substantial cost saving if you are prepared to put them together yourself (which is a simple task). Consisting of draw hooks, springs, split pins and chain links, they mirror the prototype in almost every way. Quality offerings can be found in the ranges of Smiths, Jackson/Romford, Slater's and Alan Gibson.

A slot for the draw hook must be cut in the buffer beam to allow it to slide freely (but not sloppily) back and forth. The spring and retaining pin provide the couplings with a degree of compensation, absorbing any 'snatching' of the couplings as the train moves along, thus reducing the risk of buffers locking and causing derailments.

BOGIE VEHICLES

Fitting couplings to rigid axle vehicles is simple enough – just find the centre of the underframe and fit whatever coupler you choose at the correct height and protrusion from the buffer beam to keep the buffers from locking up (if fitted). For longer vehicles or those mounted on bogies, the amount of lateral swing – caused as the car traverses a curve – makes fixing couplings to the underframe difficult, unless they too can swing from side to side.

They say that necessity is the mother of invention and this is often true in kit building. This bogie van had no provision for couplings, so some rudimentary mounts were fabricated from plastic section and sheet. Firstly, angle section was fixed firmly (with cyano) behind the bogie stretcher, leaving a flat surface along the lower edge.

NEM coupling pockets were fixed to 1mm thick plastic sheet, trimmed to form low-profile mounts.

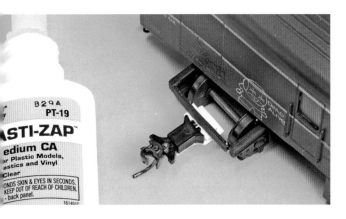

These were then fixed to the plastic angle on the bogie stretcher.

All of the assembly was tested without glue to ensure the correct height of the couplers, using a Kadee gauge. Double-sided tape is a great medium for temporary joints, being removed with a little white spirit before the glue bonds were made.

This is the system commonly found on recent RTR stock; a sprung arm rotates either with the help of the bogie as it enters a curve, or in reaction to the swing of the adjacent vehicle's coupling. The vehicles are pushed apart before returning to the original distance as the coupling swings back to the centre. Keen Systems coupling units follow a similar principle, although they lack the self-centring springs fitted to RTR models. They can be a straightforward fit to plastic or resin coaching-stock underframes; easier, in fact, than fitting to many RTR models, for which they are primarily aimed. However, metal underframes may present problems, depending on the design of the chassis. In some cases, though, the thin, flat nature of a brass underframe may negate the need for cutting a large hole in the carriage floor to accommodate the coupling unit, as is the case with plastic stock.

If difficulties arise with a chassis-mounted coupling, the unit will be better placed on the bogie. This removes the problem of coping with even the tightest of curves and the coupling will swing with the movement of the wheels. As long as the couplings are arranged at the correct height and are not fouled in their movement by any buffer beam or solebar fittings (brake pipes or footsteps, for instance), operation should be reliable. However, it will invariably lead to larger gaps between vehicles to allow clearance for buffers around curves.

The above demonstrates that there are plenty of coupling options available, with new designs continuing to appear. Indeed, just as I was completing this manuscript, I received a number of new prod-ucts to trial from manufacturers big and small. One product even boasted miniature electric motors fitted to the hooks of tension-lock couplings, operated by a DCC signal, allowing remote-controlled shunting. Clearly, this is a facet of the hobby that is due to see some belated innovation over the next few years.

A more effective solution for coaching stock is to fit Keen Systems' close coupling units. Similar to the coupling systems now ubiquitous among RTR carriages, the pivoting coupler pushes the cars apart on curves, while bringing them closer together on the straights. Depending on the kit, a hole may be required in the floor. If so, use the coupler base as a guide to mark out the area to be removed and drill a series of holes on the waste side of the line. Cut away the material with a stout blade and use files to trim back to the final size, checking with the coupler until a snug fit is achieved.

Thoroughly mix equal amounts of epoxy adhesive on a scrap of card and apply to the inner edge of the cavity with a cocktail stick. Slot in the coupler, keeping the glue away from the moving parts. Check that it is sitting level with the floor's upper surface and leave aside to cure fully. Wipe away excess glue with a damp cloth.

The Keen units benefit from a little lubrication after the kit has been painted and finished, although a dry lubricant, such as Labelle PTFE powder, is preferable. This also works wonders for the Symoba coupling units. Make sure working couplings are protected (or temporarily removed) during the priming, painting and varnishing stages, as they are sensitive to blocking with paints and adhesives.

The pockets will accept Keen's own range of fixed couplers or NEM-style units that may need gluing in place. Gauge the height of the couplers carefully, adding shims inside the pockets if necessary.

CHAPTER NINE

FURTHER ADVENTURES IN PLASTIC

At this stage, preparing and fixing plastic parts together should now hold no fears, so this is a good time to look at assembling vehicles that are not formed of simple box-like shapes, such as vans or open mineral wagons. Intricately shaped hoppers are a great way of refining your building techniques, especially those kits where the underframe is built around the body, as precision and correct alignment of all parts is essential.

This may sound daunting, but it is really just a continuation of the techniques already covered. Thorough preparation of parts before assembly, with mating faces dressed carefully and an understanding of what goes where (by reading the instructions and studying photographs), will make the job much easier. Testing all the parts in a dry run before assembly will also help.

I have chosen one of Parkside Dundas' recent coal hopper kits (available in OO and O) as a perfect demonstration piece, as it depends on all of the above-mentioned factors for successful results. The

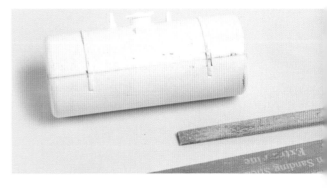

With tank barrels, take the time to fill any seams with putty and abrade carefully to achieve a flawless finish. Even small gaps will be unsightly on such prominent surfaces.

body is made up of a number of subassemblies and the fit of each of these must be tidy and square in order for them to build up to the overall shape. The underframe is then built around these assemblies and it is all too easy to end up with a wonky chassis if the initial stages are not carried out properly.

So far, we have concentrated on rolling stock with fairly rudimentary outlines, but there are plenty of vehicles with complex body shapes, such as hoppers, tanks and silo wagons. Each of these offers its own challenges, although the ease of construction depends largely on the quality of the kit.

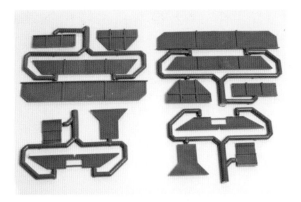

Hopper wagons can appear daunting when the parts are first taken from the box, yet assembly is actually straightforward when broken down into separate stages.

Construction of this Parkside kit begins with the upper section of the hopper, cleaning up the parts carefully before assembling on a sheet of glass, checking all angles with a set square. When all four corners are joined, check the angles once more and leave to cure.

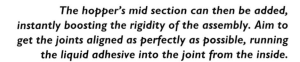

The hopper's mid section can then be added, instantly boosting the rigidity of the assembly. Aim to get the joints aligned as perfectly as possible, running the liquid adhesive into the joint from the inside.

Even the best kits will need filling around the joints, especially a complex object like this.

Taking care of the gaps and surface imperfections now, rather than later in the assembly process, means the hopper can be filed and sanded more easily. If any of the seams still look rough, add more filler and try again.

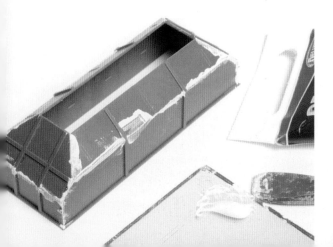

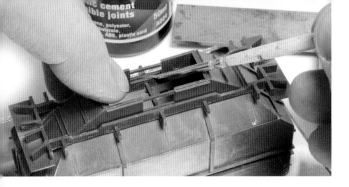

The lower section of the hopper is assembled in much the same way. The chassis frame is then attached, before joining to the rest of the hopper. This is the critical stage, as any distortion or poor alignment will affect the appearance and performance of the wagon.

Constant checking and adjusting sees the parts set correctly and left in a safe place to harden. The solebars are then added, along with the wheels, and further checks are carried out to see if the axles are aligned.

When the rolling chassis is complete, the inner sections of the hopper are added and any gaps treated. This sounds like a complicated procedure, but, once you have tackled one successfully, any further builds will be easier.

out and drilling holes for the replacements does need to be accurately done. Further study of prototype images will reveal other details on or about the buffer beams that you may like to add, such as footsteps, lamp brackets or brake pipes. Indeed, the latter are not universally supplied with wagon kits in OO and N, even for those vehicles that should have them; this is probably due to their fitment impeding all but scale couplings. Each of these can be knocked up from scrap materials, or from the various detailing parts available off the shelf. Coaching stock with jumper cables and plenty of handrails and filler pipes greatly benefit from removal of plastic mouldings in favour of finer metal versions.

Handrail wire is available in various thicknesses to suit different tasks and scales and is supplied in

A look at this rather forlorn mineral wagon reveals an odd set of axle boxes. This was a common occurrence towards the end of the lives of hardworking freight vehicles in BR or private ownership.

EASY ENHANCEMENTS

Plastic has its limitations and there are instances where substituting superior components is important in improving a model's appearance, or correcting any prototype inaccuracies. Furthermore, adding some variety to a fleet of similar vehicles by fitting different patterns of axle boxes, buffers or brake gear produces a pleasing overall effect. After all, once railway wagons and coaches have been in service for a few years, small (or major) modifications invariably appear during routine maintenance or overhauls.

Cutting away plastic moulded buffers is not difficult, as shown briefly in Chapter 7, although marking

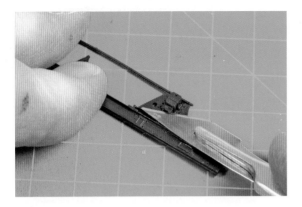

Some kits offer a choice of axle-box patterns to suit different periods or modified versions. Other kits simply offer generic underframes, which may include the wrong style of axle box and spring arrangement. Therefore, making modifications may be necessary, although it helps to make this decision from the outset. Before assembly, use a sharp knife to cut away the moulded axle boxes, following with a file to flatten the face of the axle guard.

Fit the brass bearings into the holes, fixing them with a drop of cyano. The wagon can then be assembled as usual.

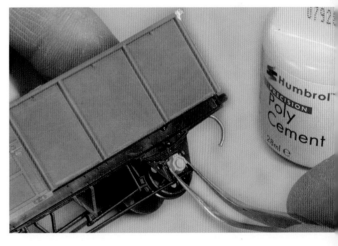

Open up the holes in the rear of the axle boxes and glue them in place. Liquid poly-cement will work for plastic units, but cast metal versions will require cyano. It pays never to throw anything away, as these roller bearing axle boxes were left over from a Chivers kit. They are perfect for this Parkside kit of a modified 21t mineral wagon.

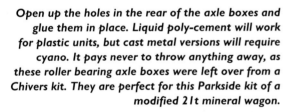

There is a wide choice of replacement axle boxes available from the likes of MJT and Wizard Models, along with different patterns of leaf springs. Study the prototype carefully to see if the kit has the right style of suspension. In this case, these mineral wagons were upgraded in the 1970s with heavier springs and roller bearings. Note also the replacement tie-bar between the axle guards, cut from 10thou (1mm) wide brass strip.

Vacuum pipes and steam-heating hoses, with
their distinctive ribbed appearance, can be easily
portrayed using steel-wound guitar strings. Choose
a gauge to suit your scale and prototype, this 0.46
'E' string being ideal for 1970s vacuum-fitted freight
stock. Round-nose pliers are ideal for shaping
the hoses. Form a mounting lug of about 4mm
of wire and drill a suitable mounting hole in the
buffer beam.

Pay attention to where the brake and steam pipes
were fitted on your prototype. These whitemetal
castings were supplied with this Parkside kit and
the lower hose required a mounting hole drilling
alongside the coupling, while the raised steam pipe
emerges from under the buffer beam, rather than
through it.

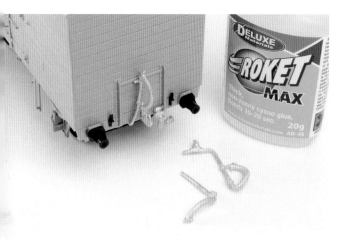

Lamp brackets can be quickly formed from the same
1mm wide brass strip used for the tie-bars, shaped
with pliers and the upper edge filed over to a slight
curve. Only guards vans, passenger stock or 'fitted'
freight wagons carried lamp brackets and their
positions varied.

straight lengths, most commonly rendered from
brass wire. Gibson is one of the best suppliers, with
packs in 0.33, 0.45, 0.7 and 0.9mm diameters. Having
a pack of each at hand is not too frivolous, as the
different sizes will come in handy for many different tasks, whatever the scale you are working in.
Handrail bending jigs are also available, allowing consistently sized replacements to be fashioned simply
by bending with a set of fine-nose pliers. What is
most important when adding new wire handrails is
to make a clean job of removing the old mouldings
and marking out and drilling the mounting holes
accurately.

Brass, copper and nickel wire, aimed at jewellery-
making, can be found in craft stores and can be
cheaper than many model railway sources. Available
in many different diameters and supplied in spools, it
can be very difficult to straighten out and is, therefore, not suited to handrails or pipes that ought to
be ramrod straight. Some kits supplied with wire fittings insist on including reels of wire, simply so that
they will fit within the packaging. These are invariably
useless for the intended purpose and should be con-
signed to the spares box in favour of packs of straight
brass wire, from the likes of Alan Gibson.

Returning to the Parkside hopper wagon, the door-operating mechanism is rendered with plastic brackets and brass wire. Before fitting the various brackets, open out the holes with a drill bit.

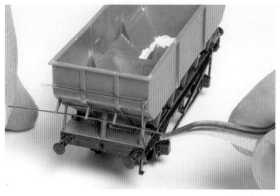

Fix the brackets in place and allow them to dry before threading the supplied brass wire through the holes.

The handles have to be bent to shape *in situ*, using round-nose pliers. The ends are then trimmed to length with sharp cutters. Secure the wire with tiny drops of cyano.

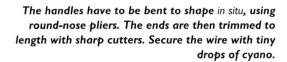

Replacing moulded handrails with wire adds a great amount of realism for very little effort. Scrape away the unwanted plastic, following with a file and abrasives if necessary, until the surface is absolutely smooth and carefully mark out the position of the new handrails.

Drill out the mounting holes, using a pin as a centre punch (described in Chapter 7), for added accuracy.

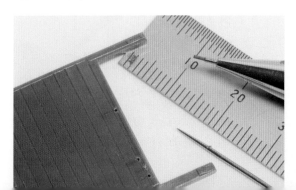

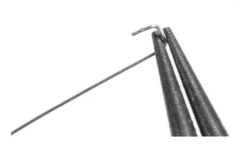

Forming the new handrails is simple: take some straight brass wire (0.33mm wire is used on this OO model) and form into a 'staple' shape with pliers, measuring the width between the mounting lugs to match the holes in the model.

A Bill Bedford handrail-bending jig makes the task of forming accurate shapes easier and quicker. Just measure the required length and thread the wire through the corresponding point on the jig, using pliers to form the shape.

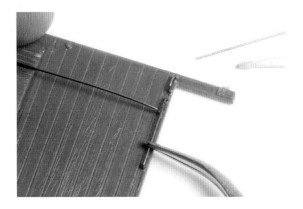

Having drilled mounting holes of the same diameter as the wire, a snug fit into the plastic will be assured. Use a scrap of plastic as a shim to get the rails set at the desired height above the surface and add a drop of cyano to each lug from the inside.

Only ever use straight wire for handrails, operating rods, turnbuckles or other similar fittings. Some kits supply spools of brass wire for the purpose, but this can never be straightened out. This Peco milk tank is a typical culprit.

The wire retaining rods have to be perfectly straight, or the wagon will look awful. So, Gibson 0.9mm wire was substituted for the horizontal rods and 0.7mm for the shorter diagonal ties.

Kits featuring wheel-operated handbrakes, as opposed to lever-operated, can be quickly upgraded by swapping the bulky plastic mouldings with etched-metal replacements, these being generally more resilient than plastic, as well as looking more attractive. Brake linkages and cross-shafts are also available as part of wagon detailing kits, although cluttering up the underframes is not always suitable, depending on the need for bulky coupling mounts behind the wheels. However, having as full a representation as possible of the underfloor workings of carriages and wagons does have a pleasing effect on the eye, especially if they are rendered finely. Plastic underframe details can be attractively reproduced, but will always remain vulnerable to breakage, whereas metal parts have a built-in resilience, up to a point.

One thing to remember when fitting lots of metal bits and bobs around the wheels is the risk of short-circuiting the track's power supply. Metal brake shoes and linkages are the biggest offenders, even when painted. To avoid problems, keep the parts a safe distance away from wheels and flanges, remembering to take into account any side play of the axles.

There are countless small detail enhancements that can be made to any kit and part of the joy is in finding where and how. Indeed, much of the detailing can be carried out before the model is assembled, often making the task of removing original moulded parts and accurately marking and drilling for replacements more convenient. Moreover, some details may be best left until after the painting process to preserve the bare metal's appearance (especially with brass handrails), or to make masking up or rubbing down prior to painting that bit easier.

Illustrated throughout this chapter are a number of suggested upgrades that are not too taxing in terms of time, ability and financial outlay, offering a chance to develop further our modelling skills and gain some experience in tasks demanding a good degree of accuracy and precision. More involved detailing projects are reserved for Chapters 14 and 15.

Cast roof ventilators are invariably far better than most moulded originals, especially in OO gauge kits. Either cut and file away those moulded integrally to the roof, or simply slot in metal replacements to drilled locating holes. These lovely castings are from Comet Models, who offer a range of different patterns.

Comet also produces much in the way of carriage underframe details, such as cast vacuum cylinders, battery boxes, dynamos and buffers. These not only look more purposeful than many kit-supplied fittings, but the heavy whitemetal also adds some extra weight to the plastic model. Tidy up the new parts with a file before fixing with cyano glue.

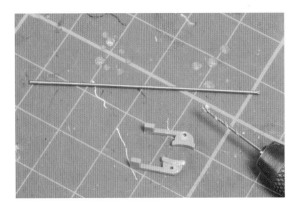

A quick upgrade to a vehicle's clasp brake gear involves drilling the centre of the shoe to take a rod of stiff brass wire (0.7mm). Fit the brakes to the underframe and thread the rod through before the glue dries. Get the parts aligned neatly and leave to dry before trimming the wire back flush with the brake shoes. Secure with cyano.

The same wire is perfect for forming cross-shafts for the handbrake and vacuum-cylinder actuating arms, in the absence of any representation supplied with this kit. Also note the length of white plastic rod filling in the gap on the transverse unloading pipe.

For even greater fidelity, form safety loops from thin wire (0.3mm or 0.45mm) and fit them into drilled holes in the chassis. These were intended to stop any broken linkages from falling into the ballast and causing derailments. They take time to assemble and fit, but the results are worth the effort.

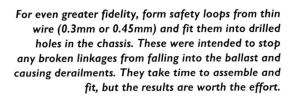

Although not immediately obvious, the extra brake gear detail offers a subtle but effective upgrade to the chassis.

Another quick fix is to replace moulded plastic hand wheels with etched-brass versions. The immediate improvement is obvious.

OTHER PLASTIC KITS

Aside from the popular injection-moulded plastic kit, there are an increasing number of packages emerging that make use of more cutting-edge production methods. Advances in technology and the attendant fall in cost of specialist equipment has opened up the laser-cutting process to model kit manufacture. While a number of laser-cut wood building and scenic kits have been around for some time, plastic rolling stock created from the same process is a more recent phenomenon. Still quite a rare species, laser-cut plastic kits, from the likes of York Modelmaking, are produced from computer-generated artwork, plus bespoke design and production services are also offered for a surprisingly low cost.

To withstand the laser-cutting process, a tough plastic compound is used and the flat components can be slightly more challenging to fix together. The use of strong solvent cement is essential, such as Slater's Mek Pak or Deluxe Materials' new formula of Plastic Magic. Careful preparation of the parts before cutting from the frets and assembly is paramount, not least

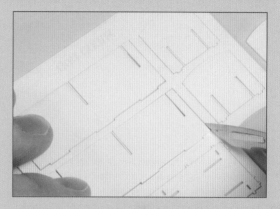

The sheet material relies on tab-and-slot assembly methods, so the parts need to be cut and trimmed carefully to allow them all to slot seamlessly together.

as the production method leaves a raised burr around the edges of all parts. A rub-down with a sanding pad is enough to deburr the parts and the abrading also gives the adhesive a helping hand.

Laser-cut components have their limitations, most notably in the inherent flatness of continued overleaf

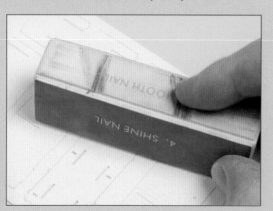

Laser-cut plastic offers a different experience to injection-moulded kits, with everything rendered in sheet form. Before assembly begins, the sheets will need rubbing over with abrasives to remove the raised burrs around every component.

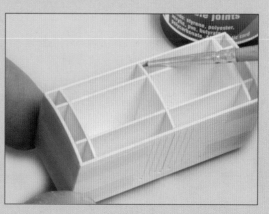

It is amazing how quick the parts fit together to produce 3-D objects; a strong solvent is needed to bond the tough plastic together. The latest formula of Deluxe's Plastic Magic works very well.

This OO9 narrow gauge vehicle relies on a set of Farish N gauge wheels and the chassis is made up from numerous layers to produce some pleasing relief in the form of axle boxes, springs and brakes. Take care to get the chassis set up correctly, using the same techniques described in Chapter 5.

The chassis needs to cure overnight to prevent any distortion through handling. Then, it can be fixed to the underside of the wagons.

As everything is supplied flat, the roofs need forming to shape. Place the roof on the rear of a computer mouse mat and roll with a metal rod over the top. The plastic soon starts to take on a bowed form. Continue until the desired radius is achieved, softening the plastic in hot water if necessary.

Several layers are built up to give the wagons the desired surface relief. In this case, the strapping for this open wagon is rendered in laser-cut, self-adhesive sheets.

The plastic has a tendency to remember its original flat shape, so tape the roof down over the van tightly and apply the adhesive into the joint. Leave to cure overnight before removing the tape.

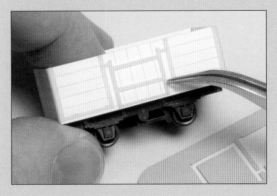

With extra brass details added from various wagon detailing packs, plus a few homemade features, the flat-pack origins of the kit are quickly forgotten.

the material. However, clever design allows the layering of separate tiers in order to introduce some convincing relief. The ability to render very intricate shapes raises the possibility of producing highly authentic models.

Other recent developments are the techniques of stereo lithography and 3-D printing, where computer artwork guides a cutting machine in rendering 3-D objects in plastic. Shapeways is an interesting, US-based company who will print virtually anything in 3-D; all you need to do is send them your CAD artwork. Existing products can also be purchased via the Shapeways service, such as Wild Boar Models, a military railway wagon specialist offering single-piece models in OO gauge.

I suppose you can still call it kit building, as although the body is ready made, it is lacking small details such as brake handles and load-securing shackles, plus there is a need to provide your own wheels and bogies. Painting and finishing is then all that is needed to complete the model. Another 3-D Printing kit maker is Chris J. Ward Railway Parts, who offers single-piece renderings of narrow gauge locomotive and rolling-stock kits for fitting on to RTR chassis.

This new medium is an exciting prospect, as it opens up the chance of manufacturing any type or size of model vehicle that you can come up with. As long as it can be designed, either by yourself or a third party, you can become your own kit manufacturer.

Is this the future of plastic kits? This 3-D 'printed' wagon bodyshell was received just as I was finishing this book. Designed by Wild Boar Models, the laser-cut material is produced by Shapeways at an automated factory in Eindhoven. It is a bit rough, but should make a decent model after quite a bit of work. Bogies and all other fittings have to be sourced separately.

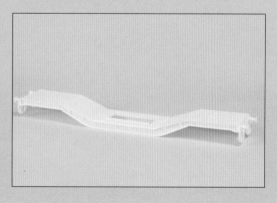

RESIN KITS

If I was writing this chapter ten years ago, I would be intimating that resin kits should be avoided wherever possible, as a good deal of the products on the market were of dubious quality. However, in that time there has been a massive improvement in resin locomotive and rolling-stock kits and components. The step change in quality has not been universal, however, so it pays to be choosy when considering purchasing a resin kit and it is a good idea to have a look at the contents in person before handing over any cash.

As outlined in Chapter 3, resin is a lightweight, fairly soft material that can be moulded into very fine detail. The most crucial factor in the success of a resin kit is in the quality of the moulds and manufacture. I have had the pleasure of struggling with some truly awful resin products in my time, with ill-fitting parts, incomplete mouldings and irreparably warped chassis units. With the benefit of experience, I tend to steer clear of anything with a resin-cast underframe, especially long-wheelbase

vehicles. Because of the material's weakness, it has to be cast in very thick sections to remain rigid. An alternative is to cast metal wire within the components, but this seldom cures the problem of twisting and distortion.

As always, there are exceptions to the rule, as will be illustrated in this chapter, but it depends on the skill of the person designing the kit. Indeed, a good manufacturer will identify the limitations of the medium and offer certain key components in other materials. Due no doubt to his long experience in the trade, Charlie Petty of DC Kits usually offers his resin kits with metal or plastic chassis and bogies, with the result that his kits have been much easier to build and more reliable in service than a lot of other resin products.

Perhaps the main benefit of resin is its cheapness, allowing some very comprehensive kits to be offered at a fraction of the cost of metal kits. It is also quite easy to work with, providing care is taken and the right tools and adhesives are employed.

The great potential of resin is illustrated in this view of an LBSCR van, built from the Smallbrook Studio kit by Chris Nevard. Photo by Chris Nevard

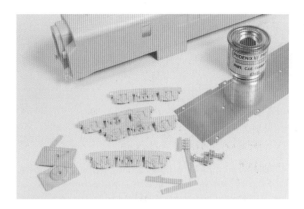

A typical resin kit package from one of the best sources: a DC Kits CIE generator van. A single-piece body, etched floor and exquisite whitemetal bogies (by Dave Alexander) offer a sturdy and rapid assembly, with little remedial work required to the resin casting. Furthermore, the metal components add precious weight to the assembly.

As well as complete kits, some manufacturers offer resin bodyshells designed to fit on to underframes from RTR models or other kits. This Keen Systems Pullman car is an example of the former, intended to sit on a Hornby chassis, while the O gauge mineral wagon body is produced by HMRS, to be mounted on a Slater's, Peco or Parkside chassis.

Another great kit with an Irish theme is this cement wagon from Model Irish Railways. I had my reservations about the resin chassis at first, but it was easy to build and has proved reliable over the past couple of years. Again, other materials are included: brass wire and whitemetal castings.

PREPARATION

Even the best resin castings will require a certain amount of excess material to be cut away. Window apertures and intricate raised details like buffer-beam fittings or lamp brackets are particularly prone to build-ups of 'flash'. Because of the softness of the material, all cutting, drilling, filing and sanding tasks must be undertaken with utmost care, as an alarming amount of resin can be removed with only the slightest pressure from a hand tool. Certainly, powered mini-drills and sanding attachments are used at your peril.

On the subject of drills, if replacing moulded handrails or other similar details, mark out the positions of new holes very carefully. Use a fine centre punch, or a pin held in a hand vice, to mark the exact centre and act as a guide for the drill bits, which will be prone to wandering off-course in the soft resin.

Watch out for the fine dust that is created when working with polyurethane resin. Always wear a mask when sanding or drilling resin and wash down work surfaces and clean your hands thoroughly after each session, as the material is toxic. Some may find the resin dust or debris irritating to the skin, so wear gloves when handling if necessary.

Mould-releasing agents ease the casting process, but traces of these chemicals give the resin components a greasy coating that must be removed before glues or paints will adhere to the surface. As has been suggested for kits in other materials, a thorough wash and degreasing of all kit components

The first thing to do with any resin kit or components is to give the castings a thorough scrub. This will remove any traces of the silicon used during the casting process.

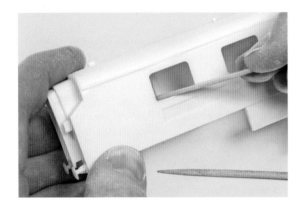

After washing, the parts can be cleaned up of any excess material. According to the kit's quality, this can take anything from a few minutes to a couple of days; it pays to inspect the kit's contents before purchase. The DC Kits casting was a quick job, with just the window apertures demanding care, as it is easy to remove too much of the soft material.

This Ayjay Models EMU car, on the other hand, took quite some cleaning up as every window and door opening had a film of excess resin to be removed. Being a compartment car, there were a lot of windows to treat.

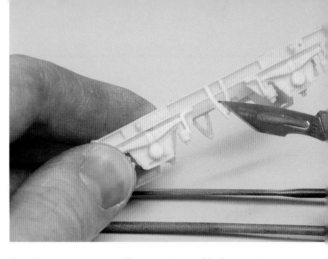

A knife can be more effective than a file for working into tight spots and for leaving a smoother finish. Just be careful not to slice away too much material.

before assembly is highly recommended. A soak in a bath of diluted soda crystals and lukewarm water will shift most unwanted residues, along with any dust and debris.

There are a number of liquid cleaning solutions especially formulated for use with resin kits, some of which contain micro-abrasive compounds to give the material a thorough scrubbing. Finescale Model World is one source of such cleaning products (see Appendix for details).

WHAT TO KEEP?

Small, delicate components are not best suited to resin manufacture, due to the risk of breakage and the fact that most raised features may be cast as fairly solid-looking blobs as opposed to delicate fittings. It is no hardship to slice these away and replace with homemade or off-the-shelf detailing components. Indeed, resin buffers and other delicate protuberances are seldom a good idea, being best removed in favour of more hardwearing brass or whitemetal (or even plastic) parts.

Take the time to look over the resin parts before commencing assembly, as it will probably be easier to make any detail upgrades now, before the parts are stuck together. There have been kits that I have assembled over the years that have needed so much pre-assembly remedial work as to make scratch-building a quicker option! As with any kit-building project, it is up to you how far you want to go in the detail stakes.

Depending on your own tastes, removing and replacing cast details such as handrails and pipes can make quite an improvement to a resin kit. This Pullman body has been produced to a high standard, but the distinctive rooftop tank-filler pipes and handrails will look better rendered in fine brass wire. The softness of resin makes for easy slicing away of any unwanted detail.

Fix brass wire and other details with good-quality cyano glue. A slower-setting formula allows a few extra seconds of adjustment before curing.

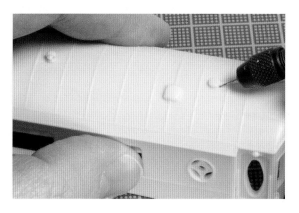

Mark out and drill new mounting holes carefully. Do not use a power drill when working in resin – the material is too soft.

ASSEMBLY

Epoxy and cyanoacrylate adhesives are best suited to the assembly of resin kits and components. In particular, cyano is ideal for fixing smaller parts as well as any etched-brass overlays or detailing accessories, while epoxy is recommended for joining the main resin sections together, or adding any heavy metal castings, such as buffers or brake cylinders.

Often, alignment issues between resin parts cause the most difficulty, with the material lacking the positive mating action that injection-moulded plastic or etched-metal kits possess. Fettling is par for the course and filing joint surfaces completely flat and square will result in considerably stronger joints. With thick adhesives – like epoxy – you can fudge the joints to a degree, but a sloppy approach is only likely to bring about a sloppy end result.

There is also the need to align the parts and keep them in position while they set, which is critical when assembling a bodyshell. Using similar methods as those outlined in previous chapters, a glass or wood reference surface and a few clamps will do the trick. The thick and uneven inner faces of resin parts can make it difficult to make internal angle checks with a set square. Similarly, external measurements can be complicated by the presence of raised detail or contoured bodylines, so extra effort is required to get things right.

Luckily, the majority of good-quality resin kits offer wagon or carriage bodyshells as single-piece castings, in 4mm scale at least. Larger scales inevitably require separate assemblies to be built up and, unless the materials are prepared meticulously, a decidedly wobbly looking construction can arise.

There are kits where the body has to be assembled from individual sections, such as this LSWR brake van from Smallbrook Studio. Cyano or epoxy adhesives are recommended. *Photo by Chris Nevard*

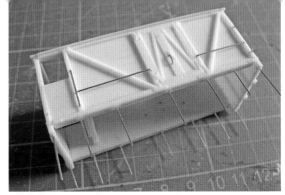

Guides are provided in the castings for holes to be drilled to accommodate the wire handrails. Thicker wire is employed as 'dropper' brackets for the footsteps. Fix the wire with cyano glue.
Photo by Chris Nevard

With the footsteps in place, the van is beginning to take shape. Note the whitemetal buffers.
Photo by Chris Nevard

In this instance, a plastic roof is supplied that is a direct fit on to the resin body. To add a bit of texture, crêpe paper is bonded to the plastic with liquid poly-cement. Once dry, it can be trimmed back to the edges. *Photo by Chris Nevard*

Mounted on a Dapol RTR chassis, the finished Smallbrook Studio brake van really looks the part. The brass handrails and enhanced roof make a big difference. *Photo by Chris Nevard*

This one-piece wagon chassis takes away the need for setting up pairs of solebars and the resin is surprisingly resistant to distortion, especially when the body is affixed. Brass top-hat bearings were glued into the cast holes and the wheels simply popped into position. After testing, the brakes and other details were fixed. The metal buffers were my addition, as resin units are prone to breakage.

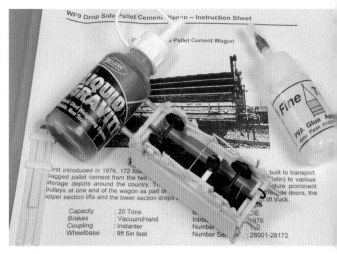

Resin has very little mass unless it is cast in a solid lump, so adding extra ballast is essential.

WEIGHT

Adding additional ballast is vital with most resin projects and it must be distributed evenly to promote a low centre of gravity between the axles wherever possible. Locating the weight centrally is preferable, although the shape and design of the kit may not leave the modeller with much choice.

Witness the Irish cement wagon featured here, where the large hollow bodyshell and open chassis frame left no option but to fix the ballast to the inside of the roof. Being a short-wheelbase, four-wheel vehicle, this offered no problems as far as performance was concerned, However, the same treatment on a larger, bogie-mounted vehicle would make it top heavy and potentially unstable. A false floor, crafted from plastic or metal sheet, is the simplest answer to this kind of conundrum. Conversely, multi-media kits, with brass floors, whitemetal bogies and plenty of metal detail castings may not need much in the way of extra weight.

MOVING PARTS

Now and again I have come across kits designed for moving parts to be fitted directly into resin components. This is fine insomuch as polyurethane resin possesses a high resistance to light lubricating oils and, in fact, has a self-lubricating quality built in. However, as we have mentioned numerous times already, resin is a soft material with a low level of durability, so expecting it to withstand wear and tear from metal axles is unrealistic. Always fit separate brass bearings into resin bogie frames or axle boxes and secure them firmly with cyano glue. Unlike injection-moulded underframes where a friction fit will suffice, resin does not have the same elastic properties, so a strong adhesive is essential. Also crucial is correct alignment of each axle bearing. Remember that drilling or opening out mounting holes is fraught with the danger of the drill losing its bearings, so be thorough with your marking out and gentle with your hand drill.

Metal axles running in inside bearings are a different matter and, with a little light lubrication, performance and reliability can be more than satisfactory. If in any doubt as to whether the material in a particular kit will be resistant to oil, there is always a 'dry' lubricant such as Labelle's '134' formula; a

Painted and weathered, the Irish cement wagon looks pretty good. The resin chassis is a little chunky in places, lacking the refinement of plastic or metal kits, but the body has a real sense of bulk, just like the prototype.

PTFE (polytetrafluoroethylene) powder lubricant that will not seep out of the bearings or damage painted surfaces.

Brass floorpans require folding to shape, preferably with a Hold & Fold tool to ensure good, clean lines without risk of distortion (see Chapter 11 for more details). The two folded sides give the floor rigidity and convenient gluing faces to sit inside the resin bodyshell. Preformed holes accept the supplied bogie retention nuts. If fixing the chassis permanently, it may be a good idea to attach the nuts to the floor with a soldered joint (see Chapter 13).

The only other piece of advice I can give to anyone interested in resin kits is to start with a good example of the genre. Choose a dud and it will put you off for life, yet a well designed and executed package will provide an economical and hugely rewarding experience.

Extra time spent on 'beefing up' the underframe will be rewarded with heightened realism. These fuel tanks have been given greater depth with plastic sheet.

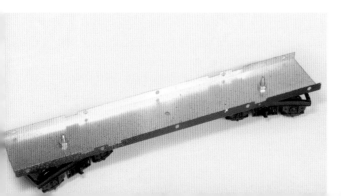

Resin, being of a pale cream appearance, can make treating surface imperfections difficult. Indeed, most minor scratches or rough areas only appear once the painting starts. It can therefore be helpful to spray a light coat of grey primer over the model during assembly.

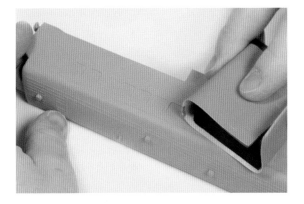

The dull matt grey instantly reveals areas that require a little filler and sanding to gain a smooth surface and this is best carried out before lots of delicate details are added.

Extra details, such wire handrails, jumper cables, brake hoses and buckeye coupling greatly enhance any resin model.

A combination of quality cast body and bogies combine to portray plenty of surface relief as well as an overall air of solidity that betrays the fairly flimsy nature of the resin material.

Resin lends itself to conversion tasks well, being easy to work. However, it also produces lots of dust and debris that is harmful if inhaled or ingested. Keep a vacuum cleaner at hand and wear a facemask at all times.

Cutting, drilling and shaping takes very little effort.

Be prepared to use a lot of filler if making any structural alterations. There may be air pockets or other imperfections within the resin that will be revealed when cutting into the material.

Filling large areas will require some extra help; plastic strip or sheet, fixed into a cavity, offers a sounder base for the filler. Milliput epoxy putty is recommended for large tasks like this, with a fillet of plastic sheet fixed to the inside of the aperture.

When thoroughly cured, the Milliput can be filed and sanded smooth, but remember that all surrounding detail will be more susceptible to damage than is the case with plastic kits.

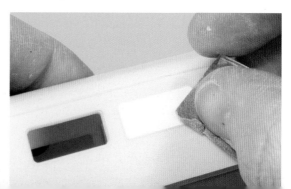

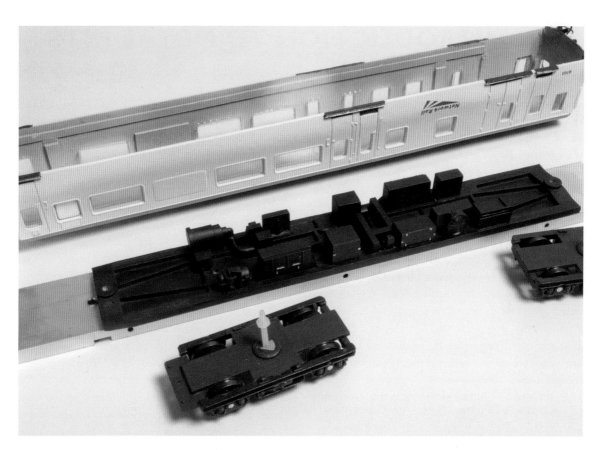

ABOVE: *Final assembly can be very rapid, following painting, especially when single-piece underframe castings are included.*

BELOW: *Resin still retains something of a homemade nature about it, but it can produce some great results.*

CHAPTER ELEVEN

AN INTRODUCTION TO METAL KITS

What benefits does a metal kit offer over one rendered in plastic? As outlined back in Chapter 3, etched brass or nickel silver offers the benefit of a material with a more prototypical thickness without any sacrifice in strength or durability. Plastic has to be rendered overscale, at least in OO and smaller, in order to maintain its integrity. Resin, too, must be cast in thick sections for the same reason. Metal kits also have a satisfying sense of bulk about them, needing little in the way of extra ballast, and displaying an authentic solidity that is difficult to define in words – it just looks more purposeful somehow. Problems can arise from this extra mass, however, although metal underframes, when built properly, can offer smoother running and higher levels of reliability.

Cast metal kits, in whitemetal, offer similar advantages to etched brass or nickel silver, although a lot depends on the quality of the production and assembly. The best kits offer a mix of materials, chosen to suit specific tasks, so we can have etched-brass sides for a carriage, with cast whitemetal underframe components, for instance.

Again, it depends on the manufacturer, but rendering super-fine detail in metal offers crisp relief that only a few plastic kits can rival, especially in the smaller scales. Conversely, limitations in the etching process dictate that details must sometimes be formed by the modeller, using a punching tool to shape raised rivets or bolts, for example.

Metals are becoming increasingly expensive, especially copper-based materials like brass, but the ease and speed with which they can be assembled with solder, combined with supreme strength, still makes them a very attractive proposition. Indeed, metal kit construction offers many rewards, not least in the application of a very different skillset than we have hitherto employed. Working in metal also has more of a feeling of miniature engineering than plastic kit building, although that is not to do the latter down

Metal kits offer many benefits over plastic: for example, authentic thickness of material; a more purposeful appearance; resilience; and a greater level of detail. This complex iron ore wagon is built from an OO Dave Bradwell kit and features brass and whitemetal components.

Different metals suit different tasks and kits may come with a range of brass, nickel silver and whitemetal components, in cast and etched form. Brass is easier to shape than nickel silver, with the rigidity of the latter being ideal for chassis frames or structural components.

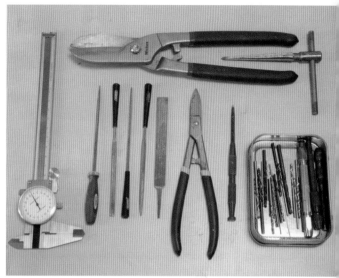

A handful of specialist tools is required for working in metal, most notably in the cutting, marking, drilling and joining processes. Good-quality snips, centre punch and scriber tools will return the investment with superior results. Files, pliers, a tapered reamer and a decent set of miniature drill bits are also essential. If you have yet to encounter any need for precision measuring devices, then they will be needed now; a set of dial or digital calipers is a must.

in any way. There is equal enjoyment and validity in all modelling, despite what some people say.

WHAT YOU NEED

There are undoubtedly a number of specialist tools that are vital to successful work in metal. Primarily, we need implements to cut, trim, abrade, shape, scribe, drill and join the parts together and, metals being a lot harder than plastics, more resilient tools are needed. We do not need to break the bank, however, and most tools are available cheaply from craft and hobbyist outlets.

A set of metal fret cutters and/or a set of decent tin snips are vital, for cutting the metal parts from their frets in the first instance. Mess around with a Stanley knife or scissors and you are likely to damage the delicate components. Xuron offers some great value metal cutting shears and, if looked after, will last a modeller's lifetime. A small centre punch, scribing tool, a set of files, various pliers and a tapered reamer are also handy, along with a set of

Equally vital is a slab of thick plywood, plus some lengths of copper pipe (various diameters – ask your plumber for any scrap) and steel rod. A computer mouse mat is a less obvious toolbox essential and a Hold & Fold or two is a justifiable luxury if a lot of work in this medium is envisaged.

decent miniature drill bits that can cope with hard materials (tungsten-tipped bits are recommended). An engineer's bench vice will also prove useful.

Less obvious, but no less important, is a sturdy piece of 9 or 12mm thick plywood, plus some lengths of copper pipe or steel rod and a computer mouse mat. Luxuries include a Hold & Fold device and a good-quality soldering iron and accessories, but more of the latter in the next chapter.

PREPARING THE PARTS

Cleaning the etched-metal parts is always the first task that should be tackled. Removing chemical residues from the production process is of paramount concern and a wash-down with a degreasing agent, such as isopropyl alcohol (IPA), is recommended. IPA can be obtained from good hardware stores, aimed primarily at cleaning electrical components. As brass develops a natural tarnish upon exposure to the atmosphere and is exacerbated by handling, a light rub-down with 1,000 grade wet/dry paper (used dry) before cutting the parts from the fret will help adhesives or solders to adhere. Whitemetal and cast-brass parts will have traces of unwanted

As with other materials, an initial bath for the components is heartily recommended. Failure to clean the metal of chemical residues and tarnishing will hinder both glue and solder joints. A can of isopropyl alcohol (IPA) is a convenient option, as it can be sprayed on, then the surfaces rubbed with a clean cloth. Alternatively, a bath in diluted soda crystals will suffice.

chemicals on the surface and these should also be cleaned thoroughly before use. Whitemetal, in particular, benefits from a little abrasion of jointing faces before soldering or gluing, as a dull tarnish invariably appears on the surface after a while.

Cutting etched parts from the fret carries the risk of distorting the delicate parts; making use of metal cutters greatly reduces this risk. Access to the 'tangs' that hold the parts to the outer fret is sometimes awkward, so take your time and try to remove waste material to give the tool a better angle of attack. Often, it simply will not be possible to get at the tangs with cutters and a punch can be a better option, although the parts must be supported on a sheet of plywood to prevent any flexing.

Having struggled with many kit parts over the years, I have had the cleanest results from a few homemade punches, created from scrap jigsaw blades. After removing the teeth on a bench grinder, the tip of the blade was ground to a sharp edge and honed on an oilstone. With a light tap from a hammer, these punches will cut through brass and nickel silver tangs with little effort.

Do not try to cut or punch the parts out perfectly first time. Rather, leave a short stub of tang material that can then be filed away; working too close to the part's edge encourages distortion. If the metal becomes twisted, straighten it as much as possible on a flat metal surface, running a piece of steel bar or other heavy object over the surface. You are unlikely to get it perfect, but a dressing with a flat file should tidy it up and any recessed areas can be filled with epoxy putty later.

Whitemetal castings can usually be released from their sprues with a set of end-cutting pliers or a stout blade, leaving plenty of waste on the component for dressing flush with files. Larger parts may need the help of a razor saw, while lost-wax components are incredibly tough and may be best cut with a saw or a heavy-duty slitting disc mounted in a mini-electric drill.

Removal of excess material is part and parcel of working with cast-metal parts, especially whitemetal, where casting marks and flash will need trimming away with files and abrasives. It is important to be thorough, as any remaining marks will show through the paintwork, so be sure to follow the files with a range of abrasive papers (250, 400, 600 and 1,000grade wet or dry papers are ideal).

This chore is not limited to castings, however, as etched parts will doubtless need some remedial work too. The etching process, especially when carried out over several separate 'baths' in the etchant, will leave a small ridge around the edge of the parts, which will interfere with the alignment of other parts if not removed at the beginning.

HAZARDS

Working with metal offers a number of specific hazards. Firstly, etched parts and their frets can be very sharp, catching out the unwary with nasty cuts to hands and fingers. Offcuts and filings should also be carefully handled and kept away from any electrical components, locomotive mechanisms or other moving parts, such as wheel bearings. As well as the risk of causing short circuits, metal scraps can also cause serious wear to mechanical components.

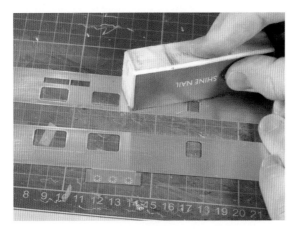

It doesn't hurt to be thorough: either before or after cutting etched parts from the fret, a rub-down with 1,000grade wet/dry paper (used dry) or a sanding stick will shift any remaining contaminants.

Take care when cutting thin metal components from the fret. Do not force the snips into tight corners or the parts will be damaged.

Make the job easier by clearing away the waste material, or other parts, to give the snips a clear shot at the tangs.

Specialist fret-cutting shears exist, such as this Xuron tool, which copes far better with the confined areas of a busy etched fret.

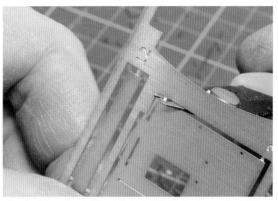

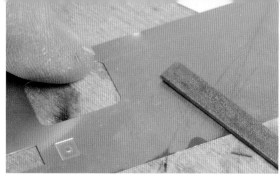

There will doubtless be instances where even the finest cutters will struggle to operate and a viable alternative is a punching tool. This device started life as a jigsaw blade, having its teeth removed and a sharp tip formed on a bench grinder. With the parts supported on a sheet of thick plywood, a swift tap with a hammer sees the tool cut through brass and nickel silver with little fuss. Work on the waste side of the tang, relying on files to dress the working edge flat.

If the parts are malformed in any way, lay them on a flat metal surface, such as the base of a pillar drill or engineer's vice. A few taps with a hammer should take away the worst of the distortion, followed by work with a flat file. It is unlikely that the surface will be perfect and some depressions may need filling later.

The etching process inevitably leaves a small ridge around the edge of each part. If not removed, the parts may not slot together properly.

Whitemetal parts can be cut from a sprue with end cutters, a stout blade or a razor saw. Again, cut well away from the component and rely on files and abrasives for final dressing and smoothing.

Lost-wax brass castings are incredibly tough, so a razor saw, stout end cutters or a slitting disc in a mini-drill will be needed to cut them from a sprue. In all cases, wear eye protection to guard against flying debris.

Tidy up round or cylindrical whitemetal or lost-wax brass components by mounting them in a mini-drill and turning against a file. Wear eye protection and avoid overheating whitemetal parts by using a slow speed setting.

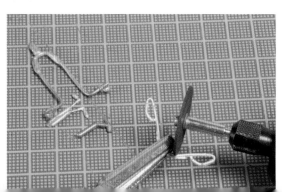

CUTTING

There should not be too much need for cutting large pieces of sheet metal, unless the kit is being modified in some way. Nonetheless, it helps to know how to do it effectively. Foremost is the need for good-quality metal snips so as to gain clean and straight cuts. Inevitably, the shearing action of the snips will cause the waste side to be deformed slightly, so always bear this in mind, especially if you are left-handed. The larger the snips, the easier it will be to maintain a long straight line, plus the added leverage of longer handles takes away much of the strain.

Again, there may not be much call for cutting whitemetal castings during assembly, but a stout knife and straight edge can deal with material up to a few millimetres thick, if required. Make several light passes with the blade, as it will be impossible to cut straight through. Once the cut is deep enough, it should be possible to snap the waste away and clean up the rough edge with a flat file. Alternatively, a razor saw will make a tidier job, but be warned that the teeth will clog up from time to time unless cleaned at regular intervals with a stiff brush.

To cut metal sheet, use good-quality snips and be prepared for the material on the waste side to become deformed. To get a square edge, use a set square as a physical guide for the jaws of the snips.

DRILLING

Always use the best-quality drill bits that you can afford, for more reliable cutting, longer life and accuracy. Choose high-speed steel or tungsten-tipped bits that are designed for use with metals, ideally with a shallow angle ground into the tip. General-use 'jobber' bits are all right, but a flatter tip of around 110 degrees reduces the risk of the tool getting stuck

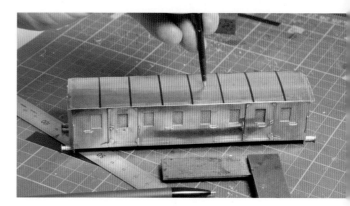

Drilling metal requires a high level of precision in marking out, as the harder material makes it more likely that a bit will wander off course. A sharp scriber makes marking-out easier and a fine centre punch will give the drill instant purchase into the metal.

If employing a power drill, use a slow setting and work up to the final diameter in increments to retain full control over the bit. Do not forget to wear eye protection and watch out for sharp swarf. If drilling through flat metal, lay it on a slab of plywood and clamp or hold it tightly, as the bit may 'snatch' as it passes through.

and causing injury or damage, especially if working with a mini-power drill.

It is also crucial to give a drill bit a helping hand in starting to form the hole. Careful marking out, scribing and punching will produce a reliable centre for the bit to work from and, if using a power drill, always set it to the lowest speed. Apply only light pressure to avoid overheating or breaking the bit.

When working in thin or delicately shaped metals, never try to drill a hole of more than 1mm diameter in one pass. Instead, start with a 0.5mm bit and move up in increments of around 0.2mm until the final size is reached. This way, accuracy can be ensured and the risk of any material distortion is greatly reduced.

RIVET PUNCHING

The etching process can produce an amazing array of surface relief, but it may be necessary in some instances to leave the modeller with the job of adding the raised rivet detail along panel seams or chassis frames. Half-etched depressions in the metal signify the rivets' location on the underside of the sheet and a suitable tool is required to push the metal outwards to form the rivet. Anything with a resilient point of the right size will do the trick, such as a fine scriber, centre punch or even a spare pinpoint axle.

Proprietary rivet punching tools are available, offering variable pressure settings to ensure that every rivet is formed identically. These tools are expensive, although they do speed up the process and promote a flawless appearance. Working with a punch and a light hammer does not guarantee the same levels of perfection, but this is not necessarily the desired result and with a little experience, the job soon becomes second nature. To keep the material from distorting, mount it securely on to a sheet of plywood and try to maintain a consistent pressure on the punch with each stroke. The job can get tedious if there are a lot of rivets to punch but, if accompanied by some suitably 'banging' music, the job can actually be fun.

Doing a bit of riveting in small bursts certainly breaks the monotony, but always try to finish a set of rivets in one area in the same sitting, as it is hard

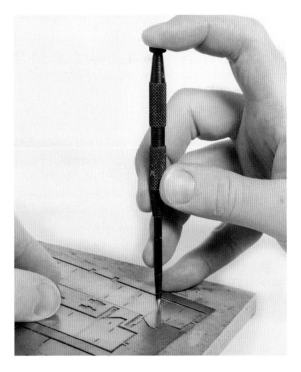

Many brass and nickel silver kits include half-etched rivet markings, needing to be pushed out from behind to form the raised rivet head on the outer surface. A scribing tool can be employed as a punch, although the tip may need blunting slightly if it is not to cut through the material rather than shape it. Hand pressure is often enough, although a tap with a toffee hammer is easier on the wrists. Work on a sheet of plywood to keep the metal from distorting.

The main difficulty of rivet-punching is maintaining an even pressure and avoiding breaking through the material. Rivet-punching machines are available, but they are not cheap. Practice, however, is free and it is amazing how soon you can do this sort of thing without giving it much thought.

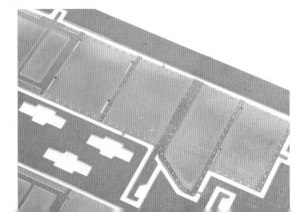

to recreate the same hammer pressure once the repetition has been interrupted. It does not matter if there is a bit of variety across different panels. Indeed, it can add a bit of extra realism.

SHAPING

Etched-metal parts invariably require folding or rolling to create the necessary three-dimensional shapes. This is another instance where careful study of the parts and the kit's instructions pays dividends, as the fold lines should be incorporated into the components by way of half-etched lines. Sometimes, these are hard to differentiate from decorative panel or seam lines, so you must be sure before making any folds. Moreover, brass and nickel silver, once shaped, are almost impossible to return to a perfectly flat surface.

Half-etched lines are usually formed on the inside of the intended fold, allowing the material space in which to bend in on itself. If the kit is poorly produced, the fold lines are often the first to suffer as they rely on accuracy and knife-sharp edges. They can be improved by scoring with a Stanley knife blade, but this is not something that the modeller should be left with – you may as well be scratch-building!

Folds need to be cleanly executed and the parts brought to the desired angle, using a set square or similar instrument as a guide. Smooth-nose pliers (without serrated teeth on the inside of the jaws) can affect folds in small parts, but the risk of getting a rounded corner, rather than the preferred knife-edge, is high. Bending bars and vices have been popular with metal kit builders for years, but the technique smacks of being a little crude in this day and age. Instead, the amazing Hold & Fold tool is a precision instrument that offers the chance of achieving perfect folds every time, with very little effort.

Consisting of two metal jaws that act as a vice when the thumbscrews are tightened, the sheet metal is inserted and aligned to the edge of the upper jaw. When secured, a flat blade or straight edge can be slid underneath and used to lever the metal upwards, forming a knife-edge fold perfectly along the entire length of the part. The jaws are revers-

Parts requiring folding are provided with half-etched lines on the inside of each fold.

ible, with a straight edge on one side and a series of finger-shapes on the other, allowing for intricate bends to be performed in various directions. These tools are available in many different sizes and prices, the larger devices being quite expensive. However, if you want to build long vehicles in brass, in OO scale and above, you will find it hard to get the same results without one.

Forming sheet metal into curves is slightly more difficult, often relying on a bit of improvisation to get the required shape. Compound curves are the worst, especially when working with larger or long components like carriage roofs. Most kits come with preformed roofs these days, which is a real blessing, but this is not always the case. However, by rolling a rod or pipe over the metal, just like making pastry with a rolling pin, the sheet material will start to take on a curved profile.

The pressure exerted on the sheet metal needs to be absorbed in some way, in order for the material to form itself around the rod or pipe. Anything, from layers of tissue paper, leather, or the rear face of a foam computer mouse mat, is perfect. Rolling brass over a hard surface can also be effective, but only for shallow curves and any detail relief may be damaged or lost.

The smaller the radius of the curvature, the harder it can be to form, especially on larger parts, such as carriage roofs or sides. Furthermore, the rolling process is eased when there is more material

Hold & Fold tools are unrivalled for their ability to produce consistent folds in sheet metal. Simply slot in the material, align the half-etched line upwards immediately in front of the upper jaw and tighten the thumbscrews.

Using the supplied flat blade, slide it under the metal and lift upwards. A knife-edge fold will be created with almost no effort.

Check the desired angle with a set square or protractor, release the screws and reposition the part for further folds.

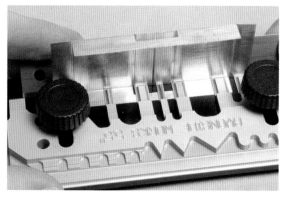

The reversible head offers a straight edge or a series of 'fingers' to permit intricate shapes to be formed, especially closed box-like structures.

It takes a bit of thought to work out the order of the folds, but that can be part of the fun. Structures like this can be assembled within minutes, with perfect edges all around.

Choose the appropriate part of the jaws to allow the material to be folded into enclosed shapes.

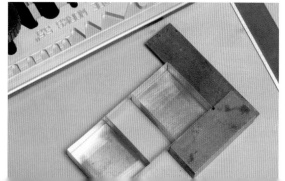

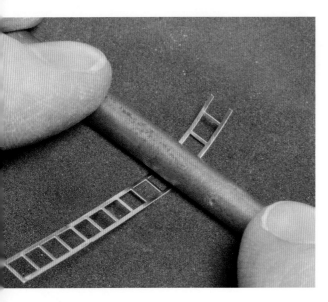

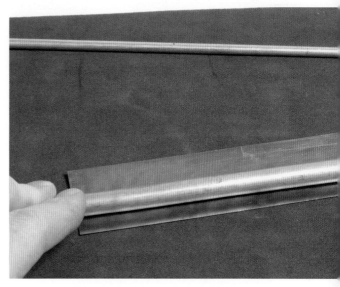

Forming curved parts is one of the discouraging factors that prevent many people from attempting etched-metal kits, but it is easier than it looks. Place the metal face down on the back of a computer mouse mat or other firm, but spongy, material. Then, simply by rolling a steel rod or pipe to and fro – just like a rolling pin – the sheet metal will take on a curved shape.

The radius of the curve is governed by the size of the rod and the amount of pressure exerted: larger rod = larger radius curve; more pressure = tighter radius. Concentrating the rolling action in one place will confine the shaping to that area.

Constant test fitting against the rest of the assembly will reveal whether more or less curvature is needed.

If the curvature is too great, just place the part on a hard, flat surface and apply light pressure in the centre with a steel rule. Test again and re-roll if necessary until a perfect match is achieved.

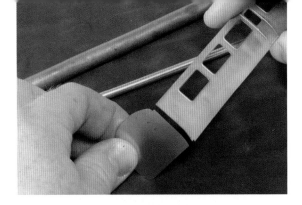

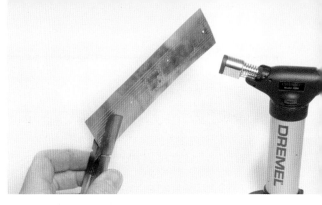

Carriage sides can be challenging, due to their length and the fact that the curve is often limited to the lower edges. The rolling process is the same, but with longer rods and a larger foam pad. Again, regular reference to the profile of the carriage ends reveals when the correct shape has been achieved. It is vital to keep the rolling rod parallel to the side at all times to get the curve exactly in the horizontal plane.

If the brass parts are not cooperating, annealing with a mini-blowtorch will soften the material and make it vastly more pliable. Hold the metal with a wooden clothes peg (to avoid the heat being absorbed by a metal clamp) and gently heat it in the flame until the entire surface turns a uniform shade of orange. Allow it to cool naturally – do not quench it in water.

Annealing also helps when forming tricky, compound curves such as this roof. After forming the general curve by rolling on the foam mat with a length of copper pipe, the shallow radius of the edges were produced by clamping the extreme edges in a Hold & Fold tool and forming it over a small-diameter steel rod.

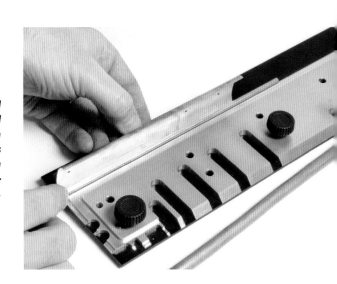

To ease the transition between radii, the copper pipe is then used as a former. The edge of the Hold & Fold's jaw is machined to a concave shape, allowing the pipe to sit tightly in place, while pressure is exerted on the outside of the brass.

This is the end result. Forming complex shapes like this is not common in today's brass kits, being more of a scratch-building exercise. But the technique is a very useful one to have in reserve.

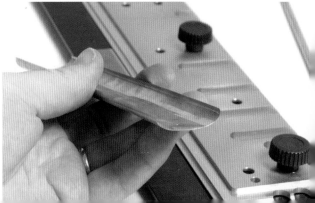

to work with. Forming tight radii curves on small parts or at the edge of a component, such as the tumble-home along the lower edge of a carriage, can be very tricky. Difficulty increases further with thicker material and it helps to have a variety of sizes of metal rod or pipe at hand. In troubled times, I turn to my trusty blowtorch. Annealing softens the metal enough to ease shaping without taking away any of the important properties of the material. After a few minutes of heating, the metal can be left to cool naturally before working on it in the usual way.

A mini-blowtorch provides the perfect annealing tool. Usually powered by aerosol-based butane gas, choose a device with automatic ignition, a sturdy base and a locking throttle for hands-free operation, such as the Dremel Versaflame. These tools need to be handled with respect and the work carried out in a suitable environment, free from any flammable materials. Wear a leather gauntlet and hold the metal in a secure hand clamp or vice during heating and, when setting aside to cool, place the metal on a heatproof mat (sold in the plumbing section of DIY stores), and leave well alone for about fifteen minutes or so; do not quench it in water.

Annealing is not a crude process; rather, it is something that needs doing carefully, raising the temperature of the metal gradually and evenly over the surface. Set the torch on a medium setting and hold the metal a few inches away from the base of the flame, watching closely as the brass starts to change appearance, with patches of orange-red blooming across the surface. The same technique can be useful for metal parts of any size, whenever rolling, bending or folding is found to be difficult.

JOINING THE PARTS

Like many aspects of this hobby, the ease with which a metal kit can be assembled depends largely on the design of the components. It would be great if all manufacturers adopted the helpful tab-and-slot system of construction, although other methods of positive component location can be equally as effective. Creating butt joints between structural components, especially in sheet metals, offers the

Soldering is the most rewarding method for metal kit construction, but adhesives can also be employed in some cases, depending how the kit is designed. Tab-and-slot assembly lends itself to the use of epoxy adhesives, although the parts will need clamping in their exact position while the glue sets, making the job quite laborious.

most difficulty and also the weakest bonds, unless some reinforcement is added. Cast components, being that bit thicker, can be joined more positively without the need for tabs or slots, offering a larger surface area for glues or solders to penetrate.

If soldering does not appeal, structural joints, or those with large areas, will benefit from bonding with epoxy adhesive, offering time to align the parts and providing a strong and resilient joint. Smaller components can also be applied with epoxy, but the hassle

Whitemetal kits can be better suited to glue assembly, the thicker components offering an increased surface area with which to make the joints.

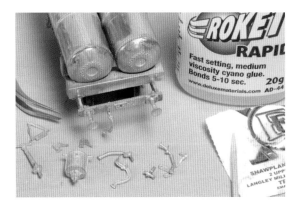

While epoxy is recommended for structural joints, cyano is the glue of choice for adding detail parts, being of a thinner viscosity. Apply only a small amount with a cocktail stick.

of mixing and the rather thick nature limits its use with very small details, which is where cyano finds its niche. Whatever formula is employed, the metal must be spotlessly clean before making glue joints, as any greasy residues or tarnish will compromise the integrity of the bond.

OTHER FACTORS TO CONSIDER

Relying on a twin-track arrangement of electrical power transmission makes the construction of railway vehicles entirely out of metal a potentially risky business. Unless the wheels are insulated from the axles and, thus, the metal chassis, there will be a risk of shorting out the power. Ensuring that all underframe components are kept clear of the wheels and rails is also important.

Weight is another factor, as alluded to at the beginning of this chapter. A rake of metal goods vehicles can form a taxing load, with even a powerful locomotive struggling for adhesion. The odd metal wagon or coach in a mixed rake will do no harm, but any major weight imbalance between vehicles can lead to derailments, especially if the heavier stock is riding at the end of the train. The problem is exacerbated on tight curves or during propelling movements, yet, if the bulkier vehicles are marshalled immediately aft of the locomotive, the negative effects can often be minimized.

Not all metal kits lend themselves to construction with adhesives and this fact should be ascertained before purchase if you are not a confident wielder of a soldering iron. But I always think it is a shame to use anything other than solder on brass, nickel silver and whitemetal. The idea of soldering seems to put more people off than perhaps it should. Hopefully, the following chapter should dispel a good many myths.

Surrounding the wheels with metal components runs the risk of causing short circuits to the track's power supply. Make sure there is a gap between the wheel treads, flanges, brake shoes and rodding, taking into account any degrees of side play in the axles.

CHAPTER TWELVE

THE ART OF SOLDERING

For anyone with any serious aspirations of working in metal, soldering is an essential skill. Many modellers are fearful of trying to master the techniques involved, but, like anything else in life, of a practical nature at least, all that is necessary is to learn a few ground rules and put in a bit of practice. Not surprisingly, it also helps if you have a range of decent tools at your disposal. Like airbrushing, trying to master a new skill with inferior equipment is enough to put anyone off for good and I have tried some truly awful budget soldering irons in my time.

So, if you have tried it in the past with limited success, or are facing soldering for the first time, save yourself hours of frustration and disillusionment and ignore the cheap soldering irons offered as free gifts and invest in a decent tool. As will be explained, for those working in OO gauge and below, this may only amount to around £20 (at 2013 prices) for an 18watt iron. With solders, flux, a stand and heat-resistant mat, a high-performance set-up can be had for less than £50. Put into context, a number of RTR carriages now retail at around £50, so spending the same amount on good-quality soldering equipment will be well worth the money, especially when you think of the many possibilities that soldering can offer.

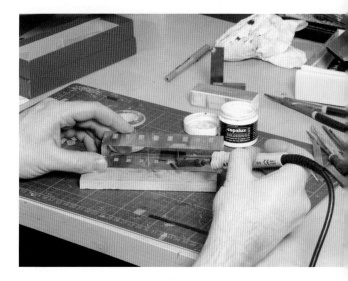

Soldering maintains a mystique amongst many modellers who may have struggled to get good results. However, it is really not that difficult, provided your tools are set up correctly and a few basic rules are followed.

WHAT IS SOLDERING?

In the simplest terms, soldering is a means of joining two metals together, using a third metal – the solder – as an adhesive. Solder itself is an alloy designed to melt at a much lower temperature than the metals being mated. However, unlike glue, when a decent smearing of the stuff will usually do the trick, soldering requires a number of factors to be in place before the process can work effectively.

Creating the right temperature across the workpiece is crucial, as is choosing the right type of solder to match the temperature and types of metal being joined. A suitable flux is also required, this being a chemical that assists the solder to flow exactly where it is needed. Moreover, the parts must be held absolutely still during the process, as any disturbance while the solder cools will compromise the joint's integrity. With so many things to consider, it is no wonder that soldering produces feelings of trepidation, but it is actually considerably simpler in practice than it sounds in theory.

SOLDERING IRONS

Generally classified by their power output, expressed in watts, soldering irons can be obtained in mains, battery or even gas-powered form. For general-purpose work, an iron of 25watts will be more than sufficient for the majority of modellers in 4mm scale and below. For those with a predilection for larger

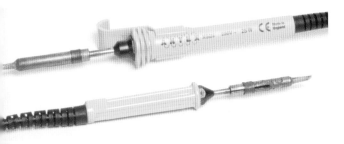

The reliable, British-built Antex range offers some of the best hobby soldering irons around, with power options to suit different materials and applications. For most, an iron in the 18–30watt range will suffice, while large-scale modellers might want something more powerful, such as a 50watt tool.

models, it will be worth upping the power to around 50–75watts. It should be explained that the wattage bears no relation to the temperature range of the tool's tip or the speed at which the tip will reach

A soldering station, complete with adjustable power control and a digital temperature read-out, is a real luxury. For a good-quality unit, expect to pay between £100–200, making it more of a tool for the serious metal kit builder. Most units have a minimum temperature setting of 150°C, which is fine for most jobs. However, for delicate work in whitemetal, look out for a tool that can be adjusted down to around 80°C.

operating temperature. Rather, higher wattage irons will maintain their optimum performance for longer, without the heat being drained away by the metals being joined.

Temperature-controlled irons, though more expensive, offer greater versatility. As will be explained, different materials benefit from being treated at varying heats, with special solder formulas designed to melt within specific temperature ranges. Working at lower temperatures also allows previously soldered areas to be joined without disturbing the earlier bonds. Most temperature-controlled irons have a minimum setting of 150°C, but for really delicate work in whitemetal, a setting of 80°C is preferable. However, tools with this amount of controllability tend to be more expensive, although Antex offers a very good unit, with a temperature range of 65–450°C, for under £150.

A cheaper alternative is to make use of an adjustable power regulator, also offered by Antex, which takes the place of the mains plug on any 240V-powered iron. A dial control governs the amount of power sent to the iron's tip and, despite being nowhere near as accurate as a soldering station with digital

A cheaper temperature-control option is this Energy Regulator from Antex, which takes the place of the mains plug on any regular iron. Although there is no temperature indication, a simple rotary control governs the power output. With a bit of guesswork, the output temperature can be judged fairly accurately.

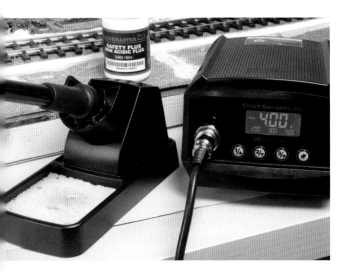

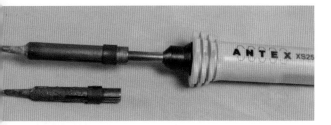

Irons with interchangeable tips are recommended, as simply swapping the bit will prove far cheaper than buying a whole new tool when a tip wears out.

Dremel's cordless Versa Tip iron is powered by butane gas and the tool comes supplied with large and small interchangeable tips, along with a range of other useful fittings. A sliding valve controls the power output and an integrated ignition system is fitted to the 'start' button. The Versa Flame mini-blowtorch can also be used for soldering large brass joints, as well as other tasks like annealing (see Chapter 11).

read-out, acceptable results can be achieved, albeit with a degree of guesswork as to how hot the iron's tip will be.

Irons with interchangeable tips are heartily recommended as they allow for cheaper replacement of worn or damaged parts. The essential use of chemical fluxes during soldering leaves the iron's tip vulnerable to corrosion and, while regular cleaning will minimize damage, no tip will last forever. Also, tips of varying sizes and shapes can be employed to cope with specific tasks, such as working in confined areas, or joining wide, flat shapes.

Readers may have heard of the term 'resistance soldering', which is a process in which the iron works on a different principle altogether. In contrast to conventional irons, which are simply switched on at the beginning of a session and remain at a set temperature until turned off, resistance soldering creates heat for only as long as an electric current is passed through the joint. Vaguely similar in principle to arc-welding techniques, the workpiece is energized by the iron, then a separate contact is attached to the metal by means of a spring clamp to complete the circuit.

Not only is this a more energy-efficient way of working, but it is also safer for previously soldered bonds, as only the local area is heated. Operation is usually by means of a foot switch, leaving one hand free to place the solder exactly where it is needed. Resistance-soldering units are not cheap, nor are they easy to obtain in the UK, being highly specialized pieces of kit. I have to admit that I have never really seen the point in investing in something like

this, when using a regular iron does the job perfectly well. And I am even less inclined to risk buying one of the many archaic-looking second-hand contraptions that regularly turn up at exhibitions or on the Internet – it is preferable to have the assurance of a valid warranty before plugging anything into the mains supply.

Making an informed choice when buying a soldering iron can be eased by first considering the type and amount of work that is envisaged. As already mentioned, work in larger scales requires a powerful iron of between 50–100watts. Smaller-scale work, in OO and N, demands a tool of between 15–25watts. A cheaper, hobby-rated iron will suffice for occasional use only, but I would suggest choosing a respected brand, such as the aforementioned Antex.

For the more committed, opting for a higher-quality tool designed for continuous use and with the capacity for controlling the temperature will repay the investment with reliable service and, if used correctly, with more successful results. Indeed, if you have ambitions to construct locomotive and rolling-stock kits containing whitemetal parts, the temperature-control feature will be a must and paying that little extra for a unit with a temperature read-out will take all of the guesswork out of the equation.

Cordless, gas-powered irons have their uses, aided by the facility to govern the tip's temperature by way of a sliding 'throttle'. While great for working unfettered by unwieldy mains leads, care must be taken in confined areas or with materials with a low melting point, as the tips feature a heat-venting valve on one side. It is all too easy unwittingly to melt the surrounding solder joints (or the material itself), unless this vent is angled away from the workpiece.

PAMPER YOUR IRON

Having invested your hard-earned cash in a tool, it is worth taking a few simple precautions to prolong its working life. Of primary importance is the need to prepare the tip before the iron is used for the first time. Heat is transferred to the joint via the tip and, the cleaner it is, the more effective it will be. By 'tinning' the tip, optimal heat transfer can be achieved, while also protecting it against attack from corrosive fluxes and solders. Failure to tin the tip from the outset will result in a stubborn layer

Where many soldering novices fail is in the preparation of their iron. The very first time that the tool is energized, the tip must be tinned with solder in order to provide a suitable platform for transmitting heat from the iron to the workpiece. Before plugging the tool into the mains, ensure that a damp sponge and a reel of resin-cored 60/40 solder are on hand.

of oxidization building up, making it frustratingly difficult to transfer the heat to the workpiece.

Therefore, when heating the iron for the first time, hold some resin-cored 60/40 solder against the tip and, when it finally starts to melt, smear it all around the working surface. Wiping the hot iron on a damp sponge will remove the excess solder, while leaving a shiny coating. Indeed, this shiny coating should be maintained at all times by wiping the tip before and after every soldered joint. A final wipe at the end of every session, as it cools, is also recommended. Most iron stands come complete with a space for a cleaning sponge, which should be removed and dipped in clean water at the start of every session.

Tip-cleaning compounds are also available, as are abrasive cleaners, but the latter are best avoided as they can do more harm than good unless your iron's instructions specifically call for their use. Iron tips are plated to maintain performance and prolong life, so using an abrasive will simply destroy this coating. Similarly, never feel tempted to take a file to an iron's tip. If it starts to take on an overly dull appearance, even after wiping on the damp sponge while hot, then the tip may need 're-tinning'.

The life of your tool can be extended by switching it off when not in use and, as it only takes a few moments to reach operating temperature, there is no real hardship in waiting. Keeping it energized for hours on end will drastically reduce the lifespan of both the tip and the heating element.

As the iron begins to warm up, hold the end of the solder reel against the tip and wait for it to start melting. It may take a few minutes, but, once it does, move the solder around the edge and faces of the tip. Do not use flux – the resin core of the solder will provide enough assistance.

Now wipe the hot tip across the damp sponge, drawing the tool towards you, while rotating the iron to treat all sides of the tip.

The tip should be left with a shiny layer of solder that will help the tool achieve optimum heat transfer, while also serving as a protective coating. Repeat the process, if necessary, to fill in any gaps around the tip's edge. Tinning compounds are also helpful in preparing the tip and for regular cleaning, the iron being dipped into the material while hot.

SURFACE PREPARATION

No matter what type of solder or flux is to be used, the joint surfaces must be absolutely clean before soldering. Traces of oil, dirt, debris, or even remnants of the etch-resisting chemicals, will hinder the molten solder from fusing with the surface. Brass and nickel silver tarnish naturally upon exposure to the air and it is good practice to begin all projects by rubbing the metal with fine abrasives, such as wet/dry paper or a glass-fibre pen before assembly begins. Many parts will inevitably be easier to abrade while flat and still attached to the main fret.

For heavily discoloured materials, a more thorough clean will be necessary – a wash in diluted soda crystals and warm water usually does the trick, especially if scrubbed with a toothbrush or other stiff-bristled brush. Surface-conditioning fluids are available from specialist suppliers and a rinse with one of these will leave the metal sparklingly clean and ready for soldering.

Abrading the joint faces with a glass-fibre brush prior to soldering is not a bad habit to get into, thereby cleaning away any greasy deposits and tarnishing that inevitably build up as the parts are handled. Coarse sanding sticks and brass wire brushes are also handy.

SOLDERS AND FLUXES

Solder

Solder formulas are tailored for work with different materials at different temperatures. They contain a combination of metals, most notably tin and lead, while certain formulas also contain cadmium or bismuth, according to their intended use. The addition of silver, for example, greatly improves electrical conductivity, as it allows the molten material to flow more smoothly.

The most common form of solder is known as 60/40grade, consisting of 60 per cent tin and 40 per cent lead. Good for a great many soldering tasks, including brass kit building and electrical work, 60/40 solder melts at around 190°C, solidifying again when the temperature drops below 180°C; this 10°C window signifies a solder's working range. Such a narrow window can prove a great help, as the parts need only be clamped and soldered for a few moments; once the surface temperature drops below the threshold, the joint will solidify. The solder's ingredients dictate the working range, with some silver-rich solders boasting a range of only about 2°C.

As a result of recent health regulations, lead-free solders have become more prevalent. Containing a high proportion of tin, flow characteristics are improved with the addition of copper or silver. There does not, as yet, appear to be a danger of leaded solder being outlawed, but the cost of it has been rising steadily.

In a similar manner to choosing the right adhesive to suit both the materials and the situation, so it is just as vital to employ the most appropriate solder. The type of metal is important, as is the size of the joint to be made and whether there are other soldered joints nearby that might be disturbed. Electrical connections may suffer from excess heat and a free-flowing formula will allow the molten material to penetrate the joint.

Resin-cored solders are impregnated with a resin flux, intended to help the solder flow around small electrical connections. Once the solder begins to cool, the flux is automatically neutralized without the need for any subsequent cleaning. However, some resin-cored solders contain an acidic ingredient, so always check before use. General-purpose 60/40 solders are designed to work at around 180°C, which is fine for joining brass, copper and nickel silver.

For more specialized tasks, such as bonding whitemetal, choosing the right solder becomes more important. Carr's offers a range of specialist solders aimed at particular materials and tasks. The labels spell out the melting point of each solder, with Carr's 70 being for ultra-low temperature work, while the heavy grade Carr's 224 is for larger joints in brass and similar metals.

Solders containing silver are a little more expensive, but their excellent flow characteristics are worth the extra cost. Brilliant for electrical connections, they are also a great boon to the kit builder, as the molten material will find its way into the most awkward joints.

Plenty of specialist solders exist and most are branded with their melting point (expressed in degrees Celsius), such as Carr's 70 or DCC Concepts Sapphire 179. From these names, we can discern that Carr's 70 is ideal for low-temperature use on whitemetal and similar materials, while Sapphire 179 is designed to be a general-purpose formula that is great for work on brass, copper and nickel silver. A similar formula is produced by Carr's (Carr's 179) and both contain silver for improved flow.

A heavier grade comes in the form of Carr's 224. This can be helpful when joining ill-fitting parts, as it has great gap-filling properties. The increased bulk also adds strength to a joint without the need to apply too much of it. A high heat is required, so a powerful iron is necessary, as it is with other high-temperature formulas such as Carr's 243. Such solders, in model kit-building scenarios, are intended for use when making preliminary 'core' joints, such as the main framework of a wagon's bodyshell. Once this phase of construction is complete, the heat of the iron can be reduced and a lower-temperature solder used to add smaller details without the risk of the

original bonds being affected. For detail work on brass or nickel silver, solders in the 140–150°C range are perfect.

Another 'low-melt' solder of note is DCC Concepts Sapphire 100, supplied in bar form rather than wire. Once fused with whitemetal, a higher temperature is required before it can be remelted; again this gives previous joints a degree of protection.

Flux

When metal is heated, a layer of oxidization is formed that will hinder the adhesion of solder unless an outside agent is introduced. Active fluxes work to clean the surface of the metal, even as the temperature rises. Due to their corrosive nature, all traces of active liquid and paste fluxes must be cleaned away once the joint has been made.

continued overleaf

Choosing the right flux is just as crucial as using the correct solder. Carr's Yellow Label liquid flux is a maid-of-all-work, being fine for use with brass, nickel silver and whitemetal. The Red Label, however, is tailored purely towards use at lower temperatures. Both are acid-based and must be used with care. For those with sensitive constitutions, try acid-free, non-corrosive fluxes, such as offered by Gaugemaster and DCC Concepts. I do find them less effective than acid-based formulas (much more flux is needed), but they certainly create a more pleasant working environment.

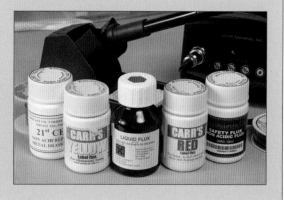

Fluxes also offer the benefit of transferring heat from the iron and drawing the molten solder deep into the heart of the joint. Acid-based, active fluxes are the most popular amongst modellers and can be neutralized by water or specially formulated neutralizing washes. There always remains the risk of acidic traces remaining in awkward places, so cleaning has to be absolutely thorough if future problems are to be averted.

For modellers, acid fluxes are offered in formulas tailored to work on particular materials. A few examples include the highly versatile Carr's Yellow Label, a great liquid flux for brass, nickel silver, copper and whitemetal; it is easily neutralized and removed by rinsing in water. Carr's Red Label, meanwhile, is optimized for work at lower temperatures, suiting it particularly to whitemetal. It is less corrosive than other acid-based formulas, although joints should still be cleaned thoroughly with water.

Be careful when using highly corrosive fluxes, such as Carr's Green, Grey or Brown Labels. Although they are helpful for use on hard-to-solder materials, such as aluminium or stainless steel, these metals are seldom found on rolling-stock kits these days and the hassle and added expense of using special neutralizing washes can be tiresome. They are also potentially very bad for your health, giving off noxious fumes during soldering.

In contrast to active, acid-based formulas, passive fluxes prevent oxidization occurring in the first place, by excluding oxygen from the metal's surface. Generally non-corrosive, passive fluxes are ideal for electrical work, or where parts are unable to be rinsed afterwards. Many resin-core solders aimed at electrical soldering already contain a passive flux and they are also available separately in paste or liquid form. Due to the milder action of passive fluxes, it is vital that the joint surfaces are cleaned beforehand, as all joints should be whatever the type of flux employed.

Non-corrosive fluxes, such as DCC Concepts Sapphire or Carr's Orange, are available in liquid or paste and are suited for use with brass, whitemetal, nickel silver or steel. Good for electrical work, any residues can be cleaned with water or methylated spirit. Acid-free fluxes also offer the benefit of a more pleasant working environment, as fewer harmful fumes are emitted.

Please remember that all solders and fluxes contain toxic ingredients and must be used with great care. Wash your hands thoroughly after use and avoid inhaling any fumes released during the soldering process. Always work in a well-ventilated area; mini-fume-extraction units are available for those who spend a lot of time soldering, or working in confined areas. Also, take care with hot irons, keeping the tool in a suitable holder that is secured to the workbench.

For many tasks, I have been using some standard plumber's flux obtained from a DIY store. Being a paste, it is easier to apply in many instances, as it does not run away with gravity like a liquid does. Although specified for use on copper pipe, I have found it to work just as well on brass, nickel silver and whitemetal. Purporting to be self-cleaning, it is much less corrosive than some of the Carr's liquids, but I prefer to take no chances and give all soldered joints a thorough clean afterwards.

Staying on the subject of cleanliness, failure to clean up the surface after making soldered joints results in this sort of thing. The residues of acid-based fluxes have oxidized, creating unsightly green deposits. A good wash at the end of every soldering session, followed by a deep clean before finishing, is a must.

After a wash, allow the metal to dry thoroughly and avoid handling the parts to be joined with your bare hands. A pair of cotton or latex gloves will prevent any further unwanted deposits appearing. If the parts are not to be soldered for a day or two, place them in a covered container; prior to assembly, a light wipe with a cotton swab soaked in an alcohol-based cleaning fluid will remove any subsequent tarnishing. Again, let the fluid evaporate before making the soldered joint.

If making any repairs to preassembled or pre-painted kits, the area will need stripping back to bare metal. Furthermore, any adhesives or plastics in close proximity will also be affected. Aside from the risk of damage, highly toxic fumes may be released, especially if cyanoacrylate glues have been used. As the name suggests, these adhesives contain cyanide and, if heated, can be dangerous.

GETTING STARTED

The first step to take before making a soldered joint is to arrange the parts on a heat-resistant surface and to ensure that they are held securely. The last thing we want is for the metal to be disturbed while the molten solder is being applied, as this will result in

what is known as a 'dry' joint. This is usually evident by the appearance of the cooled solder. Instead of being bright and shiny, it has a dull grey appearance and will not provide a reliable bond.

The heat produced by a soldering iron can make holding metal parts with the fingers an uncomfortable affair. Indeed, it can be amazing how quickly – and how far – metal transmits heat, even when soldering at a so-called low-temperature, which will still be around 100°C. It is often tempting to try to hold the bits together for just as long as it takes to run a small fillet of solder into a joint, but the heat will build up quickly and, worse, the metal will retain the heat for longer than may be supposed, catching out the unwary who rushes to handle the parts as soon as the solder has settled.

Clamping the parts offers the best solution, helping to keep everything aligned correctly and going some way to ensuring the best possible soldered bond. We have already mentioned the importance of not disturbing the solder as it cools, so being able to make the bond, then leaving it unmolested for a few minutes, is highly desirable. However, clamping up complex 3-D shapes is not always straightforward and a variety of tools and improvised implements will become invaluable.

Metal clamps, especially screw or spring-loaded clamps, are great for exerting a strong retentive force, although they may damage soft metals like brass and whitemetal unless the jaws are padded with leather or cork. The inherent mass of metal clamps lends them some inertia, although they do have the habit of absorbing heat from the work-piece. Sometimes this 'heat sink' effect is welcome, protecting previously soldered joints from being remelted. However, it also leads to the joint having to be heated for longer than usual, although the aforementioned jaw-padding of cork lessens the effect considerably.

The Hold & Fold tool also doubles up as a versatile clamp, being especially useful for holding small parts. Bulldog stationery clips, and anything else that is heat-resistant, may be useful. Indeed, the humble wooden sprung clothes peg makes a great alternative light-duty clamp. For the more

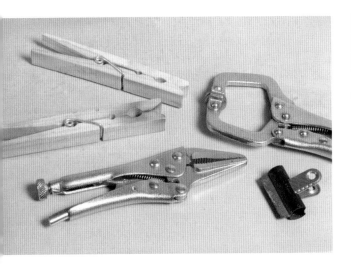

Essential workshop aids: clothes pegs; bulldog clips; and sprung mole clamps. Wooden pegs avoid the problem of heat loss through metal clamps, while working on a scrap of plywood is also recommended.

A homemade timber mitre block helps to create accurate right-angle joints. It is well worth the effort to get the parts set up and clamped properly before making the solder joints. Check and recheck that they fit correctly and are accurately aligned.

precise modeller, constructing simple plywood jigs can make aligning angled joints quicker, simpler and more consistent. Moreover, a block of hardboard or plywood is preferable as a working surface, as it does not draw away heat from the workpiece, unlike a metal surface.

When you are sure that the parts are set up correctly and securely held in place, power up the iron and wait for it to reach working temperature. Ensure that the cleaning sponge is damp and give the iron's tip a couple of wipes as it warms up. With your chosen solder, tin the tip to check that it is melting correctly (and the iron is at the right temperature), again wiping the tip on the damp sponge. This should leave the tip bright and clean.

Applying liquid or paste flux to the joint can be done with an old paintbrush, being sure to spread the chemical across both mating faces. Cocktail sticks are also handy for use with pastes in awkward spots. Take the iron, wipe it again on the sponge and melt another small amount of solder on to the iron's tip. Then place the tip on to the joint face and observe how the flux begins to bubble. After a moment, the solder should flow readily from the tip into the joint. More solder can be added by

touching the end of a reel on to the hot metal beside the tip, using the iron to spread it evenly over the surface.

Do not linger too long with the iron, as overheating can cause distortion to thin materials. As soon as the solder has entered the joint, remove the tip from the surface, wipe it on the sponge and return it to the tool's stand. Repeat the process, if necessary, to ensure that solder has entered the whole joint, adding a little more flux and remembering to wipe the tip on the sponge before and after each application.

If the solder is not flowing or is sticking to the surface in blobs, then the metal either needs cleaning or the tip is not heating the surface sufficiently and may itself need cleaning or 're-tinning'. Clean the parts thoroughly, ensure the iron is getting up to the right temperature and try again, applying a little more flux.

Always allow the joint to cool naturally without disturbing it; quenching in water is not necessary or recommended. Also, avoid applying too much solder to a joint, especially a structural bond on a chassis or bodyshell, as excess solder can weaken a joint rather than strengthen it, as might be presumed.

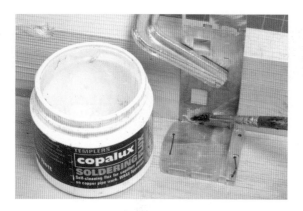

As the soldering iron heats up, apply a generous amount of flux paste or liquid directly into and around the joint with an old paintbrush.

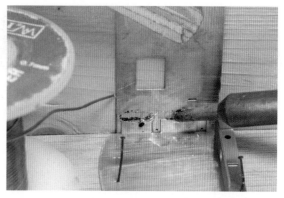

With the iron up to working temperature, melt a little solder on to the tip and introduce it to the joint, moving it a little in either direction to spread the heat across the surface. Do not be alarmed by the fizzing and spitting of the flux.

As the metal heats, the solder will begin to flow freely and the tool can now be used to spread the molten material evenly across the entire joint. A little more solder can be introduced from the spool, if required, but do not overdo it. In fact, it is preferable to remove the iron and repeat the process of melting the solder on to the tip and reintroducing it to the joint.

The outside face of the joint should ideally be as clean as this, without any solder having oozed through from the inside. The pinkish hue is the tarnish caused by the heat of the iron and the chemical action of the flux. This can be scrubbed and abraded away later.

A good habit to adopt is to have a bowl of water on hand and to give each freshly soldered joint a dip or a wipe with a dampened swab. A thorough clean at the end of every session is still essential, but this quick wash prevents any flux being spread around the work area and on to your tools.

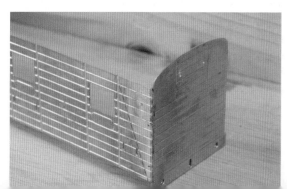

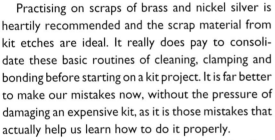

Try to avoid lumpy, unsightly joints, especially in corners where the solder has not been spread evenly across the joint, as the fitting of subsequent parts can be hindered.

If you end up with blobs of solder like this, then the problem is down to one or all of the following: the metal may not be clean; the iron is not hot enough (or the metal has not been heated for long enough); or too little flux (or the wrong type) has been applied.

Practising on scraps of brass and nickel silver is heartily recommended and the scrap material from kit etches are ideal. It really does pay to consolidate these basic routines of cleaning, clamping and bonding before starting on a kit project. It is far better to make our mistakes now, without the pressure of damaging an expensive kit, as it is those mistakes that actually help us learn how to do it properly.

Whitemetal soldering, incidentally, involves almost the exact same processes, save for the need for low-temperature solder and flux. Once again, the metal must be scrupulously cleaned beforehand and a temperature-controlled iron is essential. As will be described in more detail in Chapter 13, the iron should be set to around 80–100°C in order to heat the material sufficiently and melt the solder. The hot iron should be in contact with the metal for as short a time as possible to avoid damage, making the use of good-quality flux important. Plenty of practice on scrap material is recommended, as, although the process is not complicated, the technique takes a little getting used to.

TINNING

When joining like materials, such as brass to nickel silver or copper, tinning the parts in advance is not usually necessary. However, in situations where different metals are being joined or the parts can only withstand a lower temperature than normal, tinning is essential. For example, where plastics, electrical components or pre-soldered joints are in close proximity, or when bonding brass or nickel silver to whitemetal, an intermediate layer of solder will help immeasurably.

With both surfaces clean and fluxed, a thin layer of solder can be applied. When each part has cooled, bring the joint faces together and apply more flux. Proceed to heat the joint with the iron and, as it reaches the required heat, the flux will start to fizz and the previously applied solder deposits should fuse together. Add a little extra solder if required.

Pre-tinning surfaces really comes in useful when adding small detail components, such as lamp brackets or raised beading on carriage sides, where the conventional approach would leave unsightly mounds of excess solder and with less assuredness that the solder has penetrated the joint sufficiently. Similarly, the technique can be employed when laminating sheets of metal or making joints in hard-to-reach areas, where the act of 'sweating' the two parts together makes for very discreet and reliable bonds – but more of this in the next chapter.

Pre-tinning both faces of a joint before they are brought together offers many benefits, especially when adding smaller components or working in confined areas. Brush flux around the joint face of both parts and apply solder in the same way as before, using the iron to spread the molten material evenly.

Treat the other component similarly, in this case the rear of the detail overlay. Treating this delicate part while still on the fret avoids any risk of distortion.

When the parts have cooled, lightly file down any lumps in the solder to ensure that the two parts meet neatly. Go easy though, so as not to remove more solder than necessary.

Pop the overlay in place and clamp with wooden pegs if necessary. Spread flux over both surfaces and apply heat. When both parts reach operating temperature, the pre-applied solder will start to melt and flow through the joint (known as 'sweating'). Move the iron along the joint to distribute the heat evenly. It should not be necessary to add any more solder.

Tidy up the joint with a scratch brush once the metal has cooled, removing any excess solder for a tidy finish.

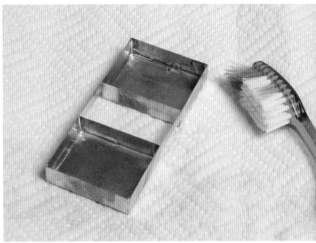

Pre-tinning is also useful for structural parts, especially if butt corner joints are required. Ensuring even coverage of both surfaces, the joint can be made quicker and more effectively. As before, after tinning both faces, dress the edges back with a file to ensure the parts can be aligned precisely.

Give the assembly a bath at the end of every soldering session, scrubbing with a toothbrush and detergent (or proprietary neutralizing wash). It is a good idea also to clean up any metal tools that have been used, such as tweezers, set squares or straight edges, lest any flux residues cause corrosion.

TAKING IT FURTHER

We have now covered the basic principles behind soldering and, hopefully it has proved, with some practice, not to be too difficult. There are certainly more advanced ways and means of soldering and some of these will be covered in the ensuing chapters, but these simply build on what we have learnt so far.

Being confident with a soldering iron certainly opens up new avenues for modellers and kit builders, with a wide array of rolling stock, locomotive and building subjects offered in kit form. There is no reason why etched kits need to be viewed as the preserve of the elite hobbyist and, with metal parts being found in many multi-media kits, soldering will prove a useful skill to have up your sleeve.

CHAPTER THIRTEEN

MORE METAL

Continuing the theme of metal kits and metalworking, this chapter introduces a number of further techniques that will prove invaluable to any kit builder. Soldering whitemetal requires specialist equipment and a unique approach, while opening up a wide avenue of potential modelling projects. The ability to fashion reliable joints, laminating multiple layers and knowing how to correct damaged metal components or failed joints are other skills that will never be wasted.

LAMINATING

To achieve a deeper level of relief, it is necessary to build up layers of sheet metal, whether by adding a series of small components behind etched apertures, or by laminating a series of thin sheets on top of each other. The process of combining multiple layers also serves to build up a more resilient whole, as is often the case with wagon or carriage sides. There are great cost benefits, as well as added convenience for the modeller, in not offering parts in thick brass sheet, but instead designing several parts to be overlaid from the same fret.

Where large surface areas are involved, it is sometimes easier to glue the parts together with epoxy, being careful not to allow any squeezed-out adhesive to obscure the surface detail. However, gluing these important structural elements makes the soldering of subsequent joints difficult. Therefore, being able to sweat the layers together with solder solves any such problems.

Greater depth can be added on the inside, with recessed windows, or, in this case, mesh screens, fitted behind the apertures. Clamped in position, with flux brushed around the joint, the solder can be deposited around the edges.

Working in sheet metal usually requires several layers to be assembled in order to build up the necessary surface relief. In the simplest form, this may just consist of adding door or panel overlays. Clamped in position, a light run of solder at the top and bottom will suffice with this panel.

Extra raised details, such as handrails, add further realism. A scrap of fret is acting as a height gauge here, ensuring all similar fittings sit consistently above the surface. Solder from the inside to secure the wire.

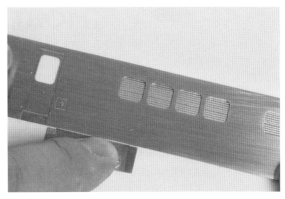

In other instances, larger laminations may be required. For entire vehicle sides, it might be worth considering an epoxy adhesive rather than soldering. However, this precludes any further soldered joints on the bodyshell.

Once overlaid, the reason for laminating two separate sheets is revealed by the pleasant depth created around the grilles.

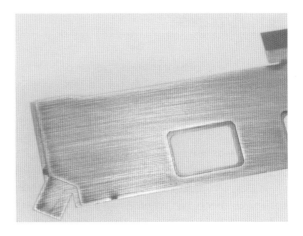

On the inside, too, there is a reason for the task. The smaller inner lamination creates a recess around the window aperture to fit near-flush glazing and the corner butt joints are given a useful step to help locate the ends.

The upper and lower inward faces of each lamination have been pre-tinned and flattened with a file. Brought together and clamped, plenty of flux has then been added and the two parts sweated together, working on an inch or so at a time. The job can be speeded up by heating with a mini-blowtorch, such as the Dremel tool featured in Chapter 11.

As already mentioned, a kit's level of difficulty is down to its design as much as the materials. This MARC Models ferry van incorporates folded tabs to ease alignment and bonding of the corner joints. Temporarily fixing the floor to the ends with bolts allows the body to be fitted out squarely in little time.

A quick tip for cleaning up corner joints is to use a coarse abrasive drum in a mini-drill (wearing goggles is a must). Refine the edge with a fine file and abrasives.

WHITEMETAL PARTS

The first task before assembling a whitemetal kit is to examine all of the parts to ensure that they are straight and true. Being rendered in a soft material, parts are liable to twisting or bending during storage or transit, especially long, thin components such as solebars or wagon sides. Kits packaged in loose bags are the worst culprits and, in extreme cases, parts may arrive broken. Repairs can be effected, but replacements should preferably be sought and will usually be sent free of charge, depending on the policy of the supplier. Straightening parts is not difficult, but the metal must be handled carefully. Whitemetal is soft and fairly flexible, but it is also brittle if roughly treated.

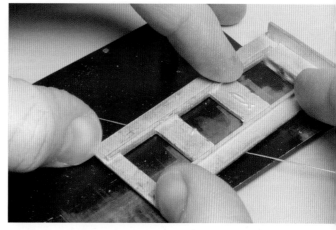

Whitemetal parts are liable to be slightly misshapen when taken out of the box and structural components will have to be corrected. Laid on a flat surface, such as a sheet of glass or metal, it will be possible to discern where the component needs attention. Exerting pressure over a length of brass wire will help iron out any kinks.

Check with a straight edge and set square and repeat the process until the parts are completely true.

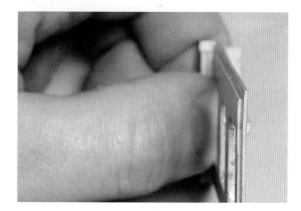

WHITEMETAL SOLDERING

The previous chapter highlighted the need for soldering whitemetal with a much lower temperature than when working with brass or nickel silver. The constituents of the whitemetal alloy have low melting temperatures and, especially with thin or delicate components, there is a real risk of them being reduced to a molten blob if overheated. However, with a temperature-controlled iron and the correct grade of solder and flux, we can work with the most intricate whitemetal parts with confidence.

Lending itself to the production of solid castings, whitemetal can be found in many brass rolling-stock kits, most commonly in the form of detail components, such as battery boxes, brake cylinders, buffers and gangway connectors – basically anything that would be impossible to recreate effectively in sheet metal form. Alternatively, some kits may be exclusively rendered in whitemetal, the fairly simple and cheap production process being attainable for small, cottage-industry producers. Quality really does vary, but when they are done well, whitemetal kits can offer an extraordinary amount of detail.

As also mentioned in Chapter 12, the quality of temperature-controlled soldering irons is variable and, as often as not, the quality is reflected in the price. A quick look on the Internet turned up a handful of tools for less than £30, although their effectiveness and longevity may well be in doubt, especially if used for long periods. From personal experience, it is important to know that the tool is up to the job, especially when building a kit that may have cost a pretty penny or two.

The luxury of controlling the temperature of the soldering iron's tip makes whitemetal work much more straightforward. Larger parts, like floor units and bulky bodysides, can be joined with the iron at a higher setting, before the tool is turned down to treat more delicate components.

Soldering whitemetal requires a temperature-controlled iron and units with digital temperature read-outs are a real boon. Heat is controlled at the touch of a button or the turn of a dial. Expect to pay between £80 and £200 for a good-quality tool. According to the size of the components to be joined, the iron should be set at a temperature between 90°C and 180°C.

Preferably, a unit that can be turned down to around 80°C should be sought, although my current soldering station has a minimum setting of 150°C, which has been fine for the OO and O gauge whitemetal kits that I have built recently. However, rather than take a risk with very small or thin parts, I opt to fix them with cyano glue.

Joining whitemetal

The act of soldering whitemetal does not differ greatly from the techniques employed for other metals, save for the lower temperature and different solder and flux formulas. The fundamentals of thoroughly prepared surfaces and close-fitting parts are equally vital, with whitemetal also being prone to forming a solder-resisting tarnish. A scrub with a fibreglass pen will soon have the metal's surface shining and ready for bonding.

Cleanliness is vital and all whitemetal parts should be washed thoroughly before use. The material tarnishes easily and a scrub with a scratch brush before every joint is to be recommended.

Longer components will need an initial tacking approach, making small bonds every inch or so, checking that the parts stay aligned correctly as you go. The joints can then be refined if desired, using the iron and flux to spread the molten solder along the joint.

I find that tinning delicate parts, prior to bringing them together, makes for more successful bonds. With plenty of flux applied before the tinned parts are heated, the solder tends to flow

Working with whitemetal involves the same processes as already demonstrated, save for the temperature and types of flux and solder employed. After brushing Carr's Yellow label flux into the joint, melt a little Carr's 70 (or similar) solder on to the iron's tip and introduce it to the metal. The solder will soon flow into the joint. Remember that the metal has a low melting point so do not linger with the iron for too long, especially if there are smaller, delicate castings in close proximity.

quickly and efficiently, thus reducing the time that the hot iron needs to be in contact and lessening any risk of overheating.

Something to be aware of is the time that the solder takes to harden in the joint. Depending on the temperature of the iron and the type of solder in use, it may take longer for the solder to cool, so keep watching for it to turn back to a dullish grey colour before moving the workpiece. Disturbing the joint while the solder is still liquefied will seriously weaken the bond, as well as potentially misaligning the parts.

Many low-temperature solders require a higher temperature to remelt after application to the metal's surface, so any adjustments or corrections carry with them the dangers of excess heat. 'Tack' soldering is always recommended in order to form a quick bond before the parts are rechecked for alignment. Working in a patient, gradual fashion reduces the risk of errors and the need for annoying alterations. If corrections do need to be made, reheat the joint gently and, as soon as the solder appears to liquefy, either make the adjustment, or, to be on the safe side, break

continued overleaf

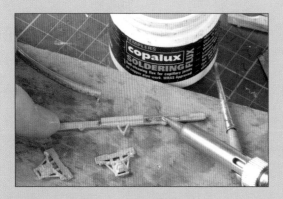

This wagon chassis needs the axle guards overlaying on to the solebars, so both joint faces must be tinned.

the joint and remove the iron immediately. The parts can be cleaned up with a file or fibreglass brush and the joint attempted again.

Also in common with 'normal' soldering, thorough cleaning afterwards is also vital, to remove any traces of flux and grimy deposits. A good habit to get into is of wiping away excess flux immediately with a damp swab, keeping a bowl of water and a box of swabs on the workbench. Then, at the end of every work session, bathe the model in warm water. When assembly is

complete, a good scrub with an old toothbrush and a little detergent, or proprietary neutralizing fluid, should shift any remaining chemical traces.

Joining whitemetal to other metals

Bonding whitemetal to brass or nickel silver sees both surfaces needing to be tinned beforehand, albeit with different types of solder. The whitemetal can be tinned with low-temperature solder, while the brass or nickel silver must be treated with regular 60/40 grade at the usual temperature of about 200–300°C. This is required as a preventative measure, avoiding the risk of the antimony contained within the whitemetal from reacting adversely with the zinc content of the brass and nickel silver.

Once the tinning is complete, bring the parts together and use the low-temperature iron, flux and solder to make the bond. Interestingly, a new low-temperature solder from Australian firm DCC Concepts (branded as Sapphire 100) has been tailored for use with whitemetal, although its melting point of 100°C is higher than most other whitemetal solders (usually 70°C). However, it can also be applied to brass at a higher temperature, allowing both parts to be tinned with the same solder.

A clothes peg and scrap of wood make an improvised clamp and, with plenty of flux paste applied, the joint can be soldered. With the parts held fast and the tinned parts allowing the solder to flow throughout the joint, the resulting bond is incredibly strong.

To join whitemetal to other metals, tinning is essential. In the case of assembling a set of metal bogies, the etched brass frame is assembled first and tested. The outer faces of the sides are then tinned with regular 60/40 solder.

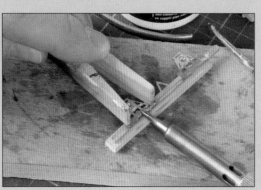

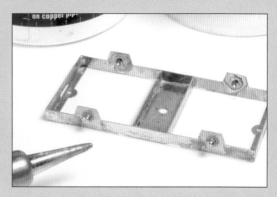

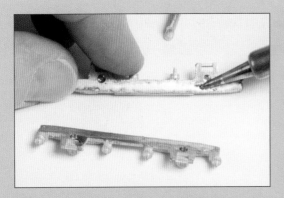

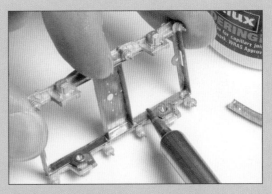

The iron must then be turned down to a lower temperature and the bogie overlays prepared. Check that they fit and then tin the joint face with low-temperature solder.

With the parts brought together and clamped, add flux and apply the iron to the brass frames (still on a low temperature of about 150°C). Watch for the solder to start melting and move the iron across the sides to ensure that the joint is made all the way along.

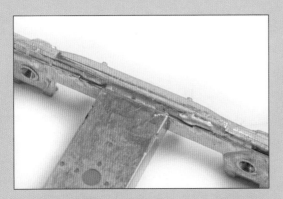

Do not worry if a bit of excess solder oozes out of the joint. Allow it to cool and dress with a file.

Even small brass detail fittings need to be tinned before fixing to a whitemetal base. These wire tie-bars have been tinned in the centre, where they are joined to the suspension unit. I haven't fixed the wire to the axle guards as this would make the bogie too rigid; instead, the wire sits just behind the castings.

There are times when you have to admit defeat – the sections of plastic angle on this ballast hopper reveal my struggle with the whitemetal originals. Once the material has been damaged by excessive heat, it is extremely difficult to affect a repair, making replacement a more viable option.

continued overleaf

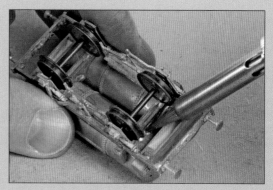

Improvised construction aids like this are perfect for tackling awkwardly shaped structures, taking all the hassle out of alignment and clamping the parts during soldering. For the sake of ten minutes spent on building a jig, the job can be speeded up by hours.

Working inside confined spaces with a hot iron has its perils, especially where whitemetal kits are concerned. Therefore, keeping joints brief and perfunctory is the key, ensuring that the shaft of the iron is kept away from the material. Many gas-powered irons emit the exhaust through the side of the shaft, just above the bit, making them a risky proposition in enclosed spaces.

TRICKY JOINTS

Forming plain butt joints at corners of vehicles is not easy and neither does it offer the most resilient bond. Even building up a generous fillet of solder along the inside of the joint offers little extra strength, as solder is a soft material. Getting the parts aligned is another worry, yet sometimes a kit leaves no other option.

Quite a few kits have passed my way that have been excellent, yet produced as scratch-building aids rather than fully fledged assembly kits. In virtually every case, I have tried to fit some form of reinforcement to these inner corners, usually with nothing more complicated than a few short lengths of brass angle, soldered to one part of the joint first, then used as an aid to lining up the other element before the joint is soldered properly.

The roof-to-body joint is another tricky task. Whitemetal kits are usually fine, as the thicker material has a more positive seat when dropped into place. Brass vehicles may sport a few tabs to help locate and fix the roof, ensuring that it sits atop

the sides and ends satisfactorily. This is not often the case, however, and careful alignment will be necessary before tack-soldering the roof in stages. What is usually the biggest hindrance with fitting

Assemblies of complex shapes can be time-consuming, but must be treated methodically, ensuring that each subassembly is correct before trying to put them all together. Note that the edges of the end and side have been tinned ready to make the butt joints.

Preferably, soldered corner joints should be made on the inside, leaving the outer edge as clean as possible. However, this is not always possible. Here, the multifarious end assemblies made it hard for the iron to reach inside, so the joints had to be treated on the outside. These were duly cleaned up with files and a scratch brush.

Another hint for getting brass roofs correctly aligned is to tack one end in place at a time. Just a small blob of solder at the top will suffice. Check that the sides are sitting square to the body, remelting the solder and adjusting if necessary. Once you are happy with the location, start adding more tack joints around the sides and ends to secure the bond permanently.

roofs, however, is finding space inside the body in which to wield the soldering iron. Heat builds up within the closed space alarmingly fast and, especially with whitemetal kits, great care must be exercised. Working in a small area at a time, leave a few minutes of cooling time before treating the next area.

As long as the parts sit correctly, there is no need to worry about leaving any gaps between parts, as they can be filled in later. Solder is not really a filling agent, so leave this task to epoxy putty, applied after the soldering has been completed and the parts thoroughly cleansed.

REPAIRS

The beauty of soldered joints is that, in theory, they can be broken just as readily as they were made in the first place. This statement is partly true, in that enough heat applied in the right place will remelt the solder, but pulling parts free is not always so simple, especially large components where a long joint has been made. Hence the reason why tack-soldering has been promoted so far in this book, as the smaller bonds allow for simple adjustments to be made as you go, before committing to flooding the joints with more solder.

Reheating has its problems: other surrounding joints may be affected; some solders need a higher temperature to melt a second time; and there is the difficulty of accessing the joint if the model is at an advanced stage of construction. Breaking solder joints in whitemetal kits offers similar problems, with the extra heat factor being even more critical.

It is possible, though. Patiently applying heat will eventually soften the solder enough for the parts to be drawn apart. Be gentle – parts can easily be distorted from too much toing and froing, or from excessive heat. Once apart, dress the joint faces with a file and try again. There is no need to remove all traces of old solder, as the remnants will save you retinning each face. As long as the parts meet cleanly, add fresh flux and try soldering the parts again, tacking in place first, then checking that all is well.

If the brass or nickel silver parts do end up distorted, try to flatten them as much as possible, rubbing with a piece of flat steel bar over a hard surface. Persistent problems can be minimized with the annealing technique, softening the metal to allow the creases to be ironed out. Twisted whitemetal components can also be reshaped using the method described at the beginning of this chapter.

Breaking glue joints can be trickier unless, of course, cyano has been used; cyano debonders are freely available to match the different brands of adhesive. Epoxy bonds, however, are a difficult prospect, with intervention taking a more mechanical form. A stout blade or small chisel, jimmied under the glue, should break the bond with gentle persuasion, again being careful to avoid damaging the parts if possible. The only way to remove the glue from each component is to abrade with a file; the surfaces need to be spotless before attempting to reglue, or possibly solder, them

Melted whitemetal parts are not easy to remedy, especially detailing components such as brake cylinders or buffers. Once they have lost their shape, there is little chance of reinstating it. Craters and other minor distortions, however, can be remedied in a similar manner as addressing dents in car bodywork. Some epoxy putty and plenty of abrading will flatten the surface and any lost surface detail reinstated with new rivets fixed in place (see Chapter 14), or panel lines re-scribed.

CONSTRUCTION TIPS

Putting all of the foregoing theory into practice, presented here now are some useful illustrated tips to cope with common features of metal kits. For example, fitting captive nuts to floors and chassis is a convenient means of making kit-built rolling stock easy to dismantle, although this demands a considered approach for a reliable bond and to prevent the threads of the nut from being flooded with solder. Tips for decorative tasks are also included, such as ensuring that all handrails sit consistently proud of the surface, or that small details can be sweated into place without being smothered by solder.

METAL BOGIES

Metal bogies are either rendered purely in whitemetal, or a composite of brass or nickel silver frames and whitemetal overlays. Pinpoint axles and bearings will be required, as per the plastic bogies assembled in Chapter 7, and the same requirement for accuracy in the assembly of the framework applied here.

Whitemetal bogies can be quick to put together, the central bolster helping to gauge the sides and, with the axles in place, everything can be soldered or glued together with little fuss. Brass frames, meanwhile, need folding and soldering before checking that the axles are perfectly aligned and running freely before fitting the cast overlays. Either glue or sweated solder joints are possible, the latter offering much more strength. Incidentally, resin bogie sides are cropping up more and more, needing to be glued to brass frames in a similar fashion.

Internal reinforcements help to keep the thin sides from bowing inwards through rough handling. Scraps of fret, cut squarely, are the ideal material.

Placed strategically, where they are not visible through windows, they create a rigid and resilient structure.

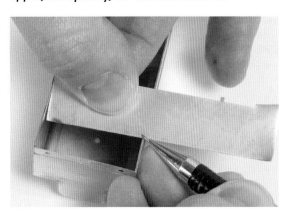

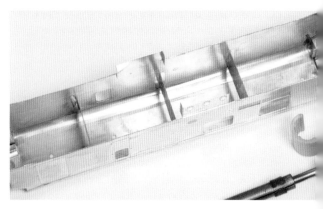

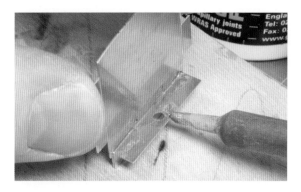

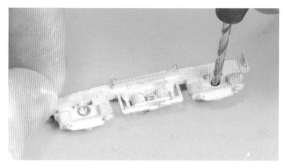

Many metal kits call for the use of captive nuts to allow the floor to be removed for maintenance purposes. The bond has to be secure, so the job needs doing properly. Start by tinning around the hole.

Construction of wholly whitemetal bogies offers a simpler alternative to brass–whitemetal composites and assembly can be swift. The holes for top-hat bearings are likely to need opening-out with a drill and the brass units tinned before being soldered into position (or they can be glued with cyano).

File the face of the nut to give a clean surface and thread it on to the bolt, but only by a couple of turns. Carefully tin the dressed face of the nut, being restrained with the flux and solder so as to prevent it flowing into – and blocking – the threads.

After checking the fit of each component and loose-fitting the wheels, one bogie side can be soldered to the centre stretcher, ensuring that the parts meet at a right angle.

Retain the nut in place on the floor brackets with either a clamp, or, for more precision, with the bolt fitted tightly. Coating the threads of the bolt with candlewax will prevent solder ingress. Add more flux and heat the joint until the solder begins to flow.

Drop in the wheels and place on a flat surface to get the axles trued-up. Holding or clamping the assembly together, make a small tack-solder bond with the other bogie side. Check again that all is well, then make the solder joint properly, keeping the parts tightly clamped until the solder has cooled.

What is also critical is how the metal bogies interact with the rest of the chassis. Matching floor-mounted bolsters are the optimum, as all you need to do is screw or bolt each bogie in place. However, if adding bogies as separate accessories, some degree of improvisation may be necessary. The bogies must ride at the correct height, while also having enough clearance beneath the floor and solebars to rotate freely on level and graded track. One thing not desired is that the body rocks from side to side while the vehicle is in motion; some bogies cater for this by having fold-up brackets, incorporated into the top of the bogie. These act as bearing faces on the carriage's floor, allowing a small amount of travel before the swaying action is corrected.

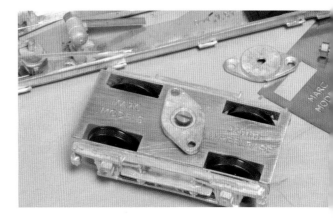

Most bogies come with a suitable bolster-bearing arrangement, allowing the unit to move freely without causing the body to wobble.

Sometimes the modeller is left to resolve the bogie-bearing issue. Adding loops of brass wire into pre-drilled holes, either side of the bolster pin, is a quick remedy, standing high enough to meet the bogie floor. To even out the stabilizing effect, the other bogie on this vehicle has the hoops fitted fore and aft of the bolt (rather than either side as shown here).

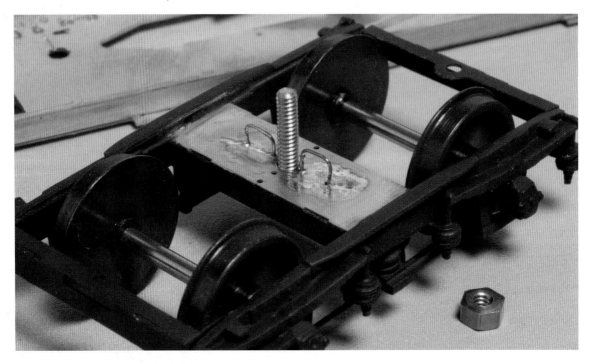

CHAPTER FOURTEEN

ADVANCED TECHNIQUES

Having now covered most of the fundamentals of plastic, resin and metal kit building, a number of advanced techniques can be considered. Compensation sounds very technical, and indeed it can be, although kit builders are not short of outlets offering aftermarket products to make the job easier. Before we get into these matters, however, we can have a look at upgrading more mundane features of a kit. Items like buffers are ripe for improvement, as are other smaller fittings like door hinges, handles, ladders and support brackets. Perhaps rows of moulded rivets have been lost during bodywork repairs or filling glue joints, with replacements necessary.

EXTRA DETAILS

There are few kits, whether in plastic, metal or resin, that cannot be improved in some way. Even the best products will benefit from a few refinements or modifications to get the best out of supplied parts. Replacing less resilient materials may also be prudent, such as whitemetal brake pipes that are notoriously easy to snap off. Instead, fabricating your own from metal wire or guitar strings offers a greater chance of longevity (see Chapter 9).

Aftermarket detailing parts are available to cover a vast range of components and vehicle types. Battery boxes, dynamos, brake gear, builder's plates and even interior seats and tables are offered from the likes of Comet, MJT, No Nonsense Kits and Alan Gibson. It really is a question of adding what you see fit, using prototype references for information as where a kit can be improved. Parts may be crafted to complement a specific kit, or they may be packaged in generic kits, such as Mainly Trains' packs of etched parts common to most privately owned mineral wagons.

Either the kit's original mouldings will need trimming to accommodate the new parts, or the extra bits are making up for the kit's omissions. Handling and fettling metal and plastic parts has already been covered and the basic techniques are relevant here, with components probably needing folding or shaping, drilling or trimming before fitting.

Cyano is the most versatile adhesive as far as detailing is concerned, especially the thicker, slower-setting formulas that allow a modicum of adjustment before setting hard. Epoxy still has its uses, especially for larger tasks, such as fitting heavy metal castings

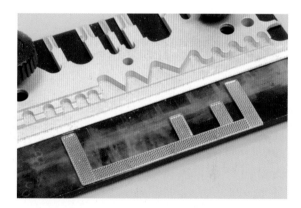

C-Rail's own range of ISO container kits can be enhanced by a set of etched parts from the same manufacturer, this etched walkway being part of an upgrade kit for a 'tank-tainer'.

After folding up the various mounting brackets and strengthening ribs, the metal parts can be added with a tiny amount of cyano.

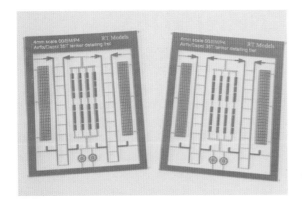

Another detailing pack for a specific kit subject is this ladder and walkway upgrade for the Airfix/Dapol Class B 35t tank wagon. The etched-nickel-silver sets are produced by RT Models.

After preparing the part-assembled wagon, by filling in the moulded recesses and sanding the surface smooth, the location of the new parts can be carefully marked out. A pin is used as a centre punch to guide the drill bit, starting with a bit half the size of the eventual hole and working up in increments for total accuracy.

It takes time to get the various mounting brackets shaped and fitted correctly, checking alignment with a straight edge.

The ladders need forming to the distinctive curved profile before folding-up the brackets. Use the rod-and foam-mat method of gently rolling the parts to shape, concentrating on the upper section only. Using one of the kit's original mouldings as a rough template helps in gauging the desired shape.

After a few trial runs, the ladders can be fitted. Again, take the time to locate and drill the mounting holes. Happily, this detail kit came supplied with comprehensive instructions, but this is far from universal.

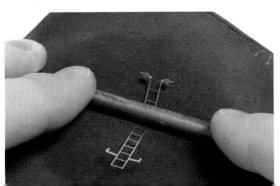

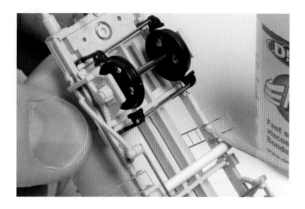

Check that the ladders are sitting vertically with a set square before fixing the lower brackets behind the solebars.

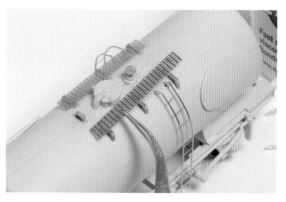

When fitting etched parts like these, use the absolute minimum of cyano on the brackets, or the glue will clog the perforated walkways.

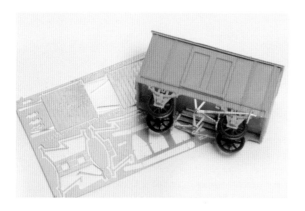

Other detailing packs for off-the-shelf rolling-stock kits may also introduce an element of 'conversion'. In this case, a set of *Model Railway Developments* parts will transform this Ratio kit into a different version of the GWR Mink van.

The same rolling method is again employed, taking care to keep the rod perpendicular to the ends. Keep checking against the model to gauge the correct radius.

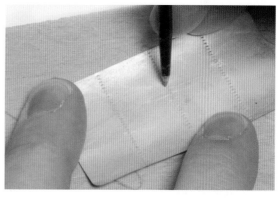

An etched roof overlay replicates steel plating, but the rivets need punching out from the inside. A slightly blunted scribing tool is employed here, using just hand pressure over a scrap of plywood to support the metal.

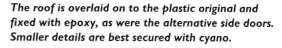

The roof is overlaid on to the plastic original and fixed with epoxy, as were the alternative side doors. Smaller details are best secured with cyano.

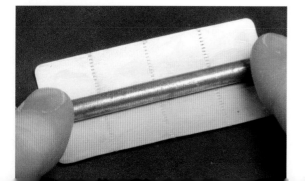

A simple upgrade for plastic wagons fitted with Morton-style brake gear is to cut away the solid safety loops just behind the brake shoes.

After fitting the brake assemblies in position, form new loops from strip brass (such as scrap material from a kit's fret), folded to a flat-bottomed U-shape and fixed with cyano. The visual improvement is significant.

or large sheets of metal on to a plastic base. Plastic details fitted on to a plastic background can be fixed with either cyano or liquid poly-cement, although applying the latter in very small quantities is a little difficult unless dispensed through a pinpoint applicator. Resin detailing parts are becoming increasingly common and these require fixing with either cyano or epoxy. For the most delicate of detail additions, though, clear varnish can be a surprisingly effective adhesive, applied with a small paintbrush and leaving an invisible bond.

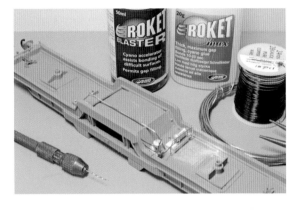

Some kits offer little or no renditions of underframe equipment and separate components are available from various sources. This Genesis wagon kit has received air tanks from Inter City Models, with plumbing added from brass and nickel jewellery wire.

Solid plastic or whitemetal brake handles can be rather crude, but etched replacements are available. This set is from Mainly Trains.

Brake pipes are seldom included, especially airbrake hoses. This Genesis Flatrol has been fitted with modern-style air hoses, as well as a vacuum through-pipe (from Shawplan). Check your prototype, as some modern stock carries either a single (red cocks), or twin reservoir hoses (red and yellow cocks).

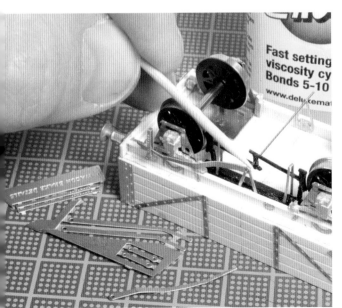

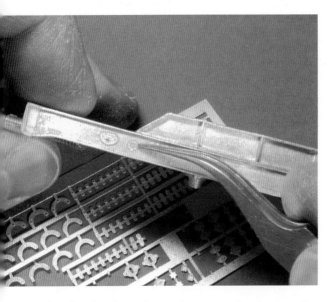

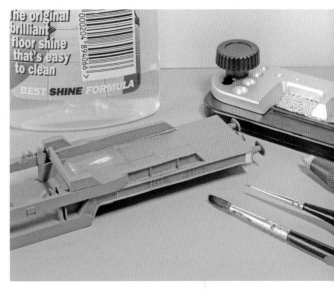

Smaller details are just as important for the overall effect. Even the pattern of builder's plates may differ and a kit may have them incorrectly rendered (or not there at all). This etched pack from Mainly Trains includes all sorts of fittings and plates.

Where modifications or repairs have been carried out, surface relief, such as rivet heads, may have been lost. However, they can be reinstated with a Nutter tool. Rivet and bolt heads are simply punched from thin metal foil.

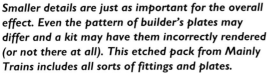

Adding cast details to a brass underframe requires each joint surface to be tinned before soldering, although epoxy or cyano glues can also be employed. However, for items like this dynamo belt (from scrap fret), soldering offers the strongest bond. Do not forget to check that the bogie will rotate unhindered.

Having marked out their position, use a fine paintbrush and clear varnish to pick up and fix the rivets in place.

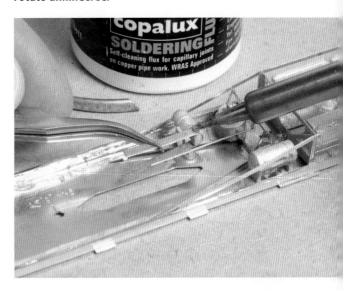

Other detail additions to consider for coaching stock are filling pipes for roof-mounted water tanks, as well as lamp brackets and emergency brake valve apparatus (the wire looping over the gangway), both of which can be fashioned from fine wire. Note also the brake rodding around the vacuum cylinder below the floor.

SPRUNG BUFFERS

Chapter 9 described some useful techniques for improving the buffers on plastic kits, although working sprung buffers are a viable option for even more realism. Moreover, if you will be operating scale couplings, then the model's buffers will really come into play and performance can be improved if they operate like the real thing. Absorbing the various shocks as trains come to a halt, or during the shunting process, gives the vehicles more chance of staying on the rails. Also, as tight curves are negotiated, the shorter gap between vehicles poses less of a problem if the buffers can retract under pressure.

Removal of existing buffers follows the same processes already outlined, although the fitting of sprung replacements may require a different approach, depending on the products employed. The heads and shank are rendered separately, the latter being fixed to the buffer beams in the usual way, although the hollow internal channel must be kept free of adhesive or solder. It helps to test-fit the heads, to

ensure that the tails have a free passage through the shanks, but wait until the model has been painted and finished before fitting properly.

The buffers will be retained with coil springs in the shank channels, by either a threaded bolt or by simply bending over the end of the wire tail. A tiny drop of oil into the shanks will ease their movement

Sprung buffers come as standard on some OO and O gauge kits and are available as aftermarket details in most other scales. Consisting of a metal head and shaft, the separate shanks can be plastic or cast metal.

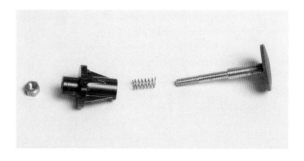

A coil spring is fitted into each shank and the shafts are retained with either miniature nuts, or by bending over the tails. Check that the buffers operate before removing the heads and springs and refitting after painting, so as not to clog the moving parts. Retain nuts with a drop of Loctite 603 fluid, as they are liable to work loose in operation.

and, if threaded retaining nuts are fitted, a drop of Loctite 603 retaining fluid will stop them working loose.

COMPENSATION

Assembling metal bogies, with a form of compensation, demands an extra level of precision in terms of shaping components, soldering and assembly. The same can be said for compensated single axles, with a number of important variables having to be in

place if the vehicle is to perform correctly. It must sit squarely on the rails, without a discernible lean to one side; it must negotiate curves and gradients without hindrance; and it must offer appreciably smoother running characteristics, otherwise there is no benefit over fixed axles.

Compensation is not a priority for the majority of modellers. Indeed, it is often seen as necessary only in the finescale gauges of EM, P4 and Scale Seven. For the humble OO, N and ordinary O gauge enthusiasts (along with the various narrow-gauge offshoots), it can be viewed as a luxury exercise. However, having built a number of compensated vehicles – in OO and O – there has always been a tangible improvement in ride quality. While my uncompensated vehicles stay on the tracks just as well, those with added suspension seem to glide over the rails in comparison. Small lumps or bumps, especially at crossing Vs and baseboard joints, are absorbed more effectively by the springs and, more importantly, the 'clickety-clack' sound of the wheels is a little more convincing.

As laid out at the beginning of this book, it was not my intention to produce a manual for the finescale modeller, so the subject of compensation has been treated a little curtly. Indeed, it would fill a good few chapters if covered in anything like the depth that the subject truly deserves. But hopefully what is included in the illustrations in this chapter may whet readers' appetites and inspire them to pursue the subject further.

Compensated chassis do not have to be complicated and simple upgrades for scratch-built or kit-built models are available. This set, from Comet, provides material for three wagons, with a separate unit for each axle.

The underside of the floor needs to be absolutely flat, so cut away any moulded ribbing, following with a flat file.

Deduce the vehicle's longitudinal centre line and the wheelbase. Mark the points where these factors intersect, drill a 0.35mm hole and fit short stubs of 0.33mm wire into the floor. The support brackets feature etched locating holes for these wire stubs to aid alignment.

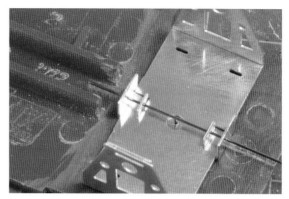

Glue the support to the floor, checking the alignment with the longitudinal centre line. The axle guard unit then sits inside, with a length of 0.33mm wire threaded through the side brackets. Check that the axle guard pivots freely, but do not fix the wire yet.

Whitemetal or plastic axle boxes and springs must be sourced to finish the axle guards (these are from MJT/Dart Castings), with top-hat bearings being soldered into the axle holes. The castings can be glued or low-temperature-soldered in place.

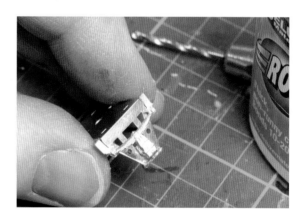

With the axle guards and wheels fitted and tested, the solebars and brake gear can be added. The pivoting wires do not need fixing into the brackets, just cut to length and folded at each end to stop them sliding out.

The kit's solebars will need modifying to fit around the compensation units, with unwanted material cut away and the backs of the solebars filed flat.

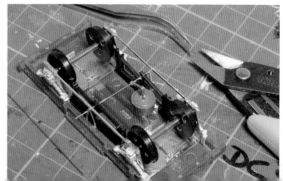

Other kits offer similar compensation units for fixed axles. This MARC Models version slots over a support bracket. Note how the inner folds of the axle guards have been reinforced with solder – this is essential with any such units.

After checking the location and operation of the axle guards, the solebars can be fixed. Here, the brass and whitemetal parts were each tinned before being brought together.

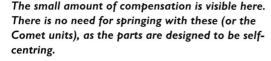

The small amount of compensation is visible here. There is no need for springing with these (or the Comet units), as the parts are designed to be self-centring.

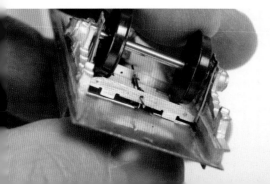

To allow enough free movement for the protruding axle bearings, as the compensation unit pivots vertically, the axle-box overlays will need milling out on the inside. Take care not to go through the material by being overeager with the mini-drill.

In this instance, the pivot wire must be fixed to the prongs of the support bracket, but not the axle-guard unit. Use only a small amount of flux and clean up the parts thoroughly to remove any residue.

The compensated axle guards incorporate locating holes for brake gear. In this case, the brake shoes are threaded on to wire supports fixed to the axle units, with all parts being free to move with the axles and avoiding any binding issues.

For bogie vehicles, there are many ways in which each axle or bogie is compensated. This Dave Bradwell kit is perhaps an extreme example, as it features both primary and secondary suspension. Each axle is sprung, with piano wire fixed to each top-hat bearing. The bogies themselves are then also compensated, with longitudinal wires bearing on a U-section bolster. The resulting ride quality is exceptional.

With all compensation systems, a little lubrication promotes smoother running and less wear and tear. Wait until the model has been painted and finished before using a precision applicator to dispense a drop of light model oil to all working surfaces, including bearings and metal bogie bolsters.

CHAPTER FIFTEEN

KIT BASHING

Perhaps readers are aware of the meaning of this chapter's title, referring as it does to the art of taking a model kit and 'bashing' it about in order to create something a little different. This gives a clue as to the purpose of the following pages, being offered as a guide to what is possible with a little imagination. Hybrids of kits and ready-to-run models are considered, along with some notes on scratch-building as a means of creating new components or even complete models. Assembling a plastic or metal kit has many rewards, but the sight of something that you may have greatly improved or even crafted from scratch generates another emotion entirely – especially if it turns out well.

RTR/KIT HYBRIDS

Carriage-building in metal requires a degree of aptitude, especially to get the bodysides correctly shaped and assembled. However, a viable alternative is to take a ready-to-run (RTR) model and replace the crude plastic underframe with an etched kit. Coupled with a detail upgrade of the body and interior, some attractive models can be produced. Freight wagons can be similarly treated, with impressively rendered bodies liberated from their stodgy underframes in favour of plastic or metal replacements.

Why not take advantage of the various OO wagon underframe kits available separately from the likes of Parkside and Coopercraft to upgrade RTR offerings? Many, including this Hornby mineral wagon, boast nicely rendered bodyshells that are wasted atop fairly crude chassis. The original plastic chassis simply unclips from the body. The underside of the floor needs flattening of all raised detail; a broad, flat file does the trick.

Mark out a centre line and the appropriate wheelbase on to the floor. The solebars need spacing equidistantly from the centre line, with the wheels turning freely between. Typically, in OO, this works out at around 24mm, but will depend on the parts and axles being fitted. A strong adhesive, such as Mek-Pak or Plastic Magic, is essential.

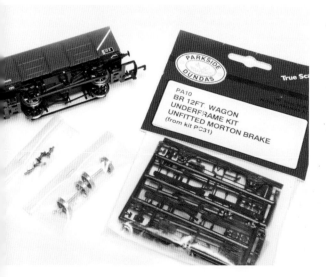

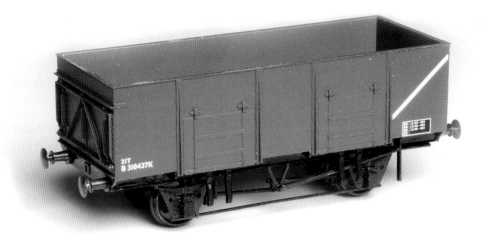

ABOVE: *RTR/kit hybrids offer lots of potential and provide a great way to master the art of plastic chassis assembly, not least as the moulded body provides a perfectly flat reference surface to work from. It is also a great way to bring older or budget rolling stock up to the standards of more contemporary RTR products.*

BELOW: *The transformation of this cheap Hornby wagon is quite astounding. With the cost of the Parkside chassis, new wheels and bearings, plus a set of metal buffers, the upgrade still cost less than £10.*

Building brass carriage kits is not for the fainthearted, especially if curved profiles need to be formed into the sides and roof. An alternative method is to use the RTR/kit hybrid as a skill- and confidence-boosting exercise. Comet Models is an obliging concern, making all aspects of its kits available separately. Here, an aged Bachmann body has been procured, along with a Comet chassis kit, Kirk bogies and assorted smaller details.

The solebars, being long and thin, are not easy to fold up to the required L-shape. A large Hold & Fold makes life easier, with a steel rule being used as a lever to get the fold nice and even all the way along.

If the parts are correctly aligned, flood the joint with longer runs of solder. Fold up the trusses (they are etched into the floor) to sit against the rear of the solebars, then solder these in place, again checking the vertical plane.

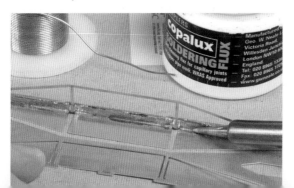

The Comet chassis etch certainly crams all the parts into a small space, making it tricky to cut the brass tangs. With no room for snips, my handy DIY punch (see Chapter 11) comes into its own. Take the time to clean up the parts after cutting from the fret; the tab and slot assembly relies on crisp edges.

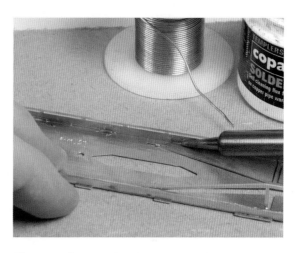

The tabs of the solebar fit into the slots etched into the chassis floor and are tack-soldered in place, starting at one end. Ensure that the solebar is sitting at a right angle, then carry on tacking every 2.5cm (1in) or so until you reach the far end. Keep an eye out for any warping in the chassis, especially when adding the second solebar. Working on a sheet of plywood or glass will help.

Add the lateral stretchers for the truss assembly, followed by the vacuum-brake V-hangers. At this point, the brass chassis will reach full rigidity.

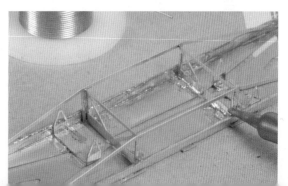

After tinning their respective surfaces, solder the various whitemetal detail components to the chassis. If you prefer not to solder – or do not have a low-temperature iron – use epoxy adhesive.

With the bogies and body temporarily fitted, the vehicle can be given a road test before dismantling and painting.

Converting vehicles to different types, or even modified versions of the same design, adds some welcome variety to your fleet. For modellers of the 1970s and 1980s, steam-age rolling stock reaching the end of its life received some interesting repairs. This N gauge Parkside mineral wagon kit is having its side doors plated over, simply by carving away the raised strapping and hinges with a fine blade.

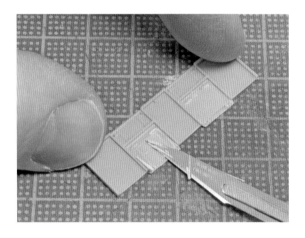

Modified wagons also had the top fairing extended over the site of the upper doors and this was fashioned from plastic strip. Fill the gaps for a seamless finish.

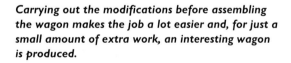

Carrying out the modifications before assembling the wagon makes the job a lot easier and, for just a small amount of extra work, an interesting wagon is produced.

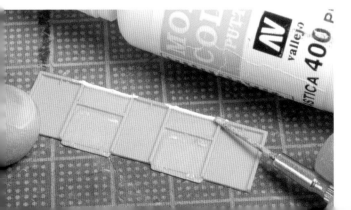

This OO Parkside kit is being modified to represent an LMS loco coal wagon, with repositioned door strapping and riveted corner panels, courtesy of some etched rivet strips from Mainly Trains.

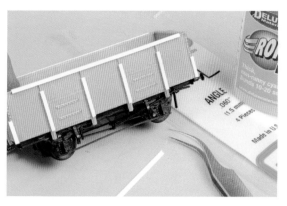

Various sizes of plastic strip and angle section replicate the distinctive plating over the stanchions.

Not the most taxing of conversions, by any means, but this wagon certainly stands out from the crowd.

SCRATCH-BUILDING IN PLASTIC

Although there are many rolling-stock kits and detailing components around, there are times when you may need something not offered in the various ranges (or in your scale at least). Instead of making do with the nearest equivalent, why not have a go at making it yourself? Scratch-building is not always a cheaper alternative and it certainly takes a lot longer, but the rewards are manifest.

Plastic is my preferred scratch-building medium, being significantly cheaper than working in metal. The medium lends itself perfectly to 'dining-table modelling', with only a small area required and no fancy tools or pieces of equipment. Plastic card, section, strip and tube are available in a wide variety of dimensions from the ranges of Evergreen, Plastruct and Slater's. This forms a perfect resource for enhancing kits or scratch-building replacement parts. Even entire vehicles can be crafted from a mix of plastic resources, along with etched-brass axle guards and brake gear.

Working plastic sheet or section is easy, with little special equipment required, other than a variety of measuring, cutting and abrading tools. Accurate marking out is vital, as these dimensions will form the cornerstone of the project and determine how well the various parts will come together. A fine ink

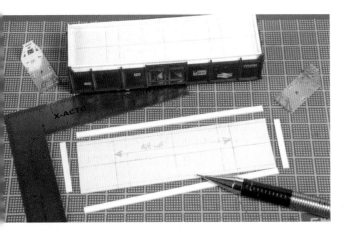

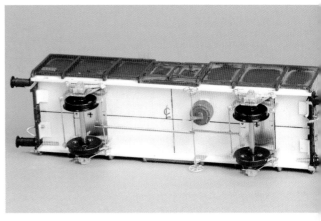

This small fleet of 1980s Lima models had been hanging around for years, but I only recently found a use for them on my fictional wartime Egyptian layout. But the bulky underframes had to go, with a scratch-built unit the only viable alternative. 40thou (1mm) thick plastic card, 3.1mm (⅛in) channel section (Evergreen ref.264), Comet axle guards and plenty of leftover bits and pieces from other kits formed the raw materials.

As well as ensuring the chassis floor is true, the other critical factor is the alignment of the axles. They need to be parallel in the horizontal and lateral planes, as well as perpendicular to the centre line of the vehicle.

The freelance nature of this project allows for some leeway in the underframe's fitments. However, everything should look like it is there for a reason and attention to small details like the addition of vacuum rather than air brakes, and oil axle boxes rather than roller bearings (to suit the period), help to add credibility.

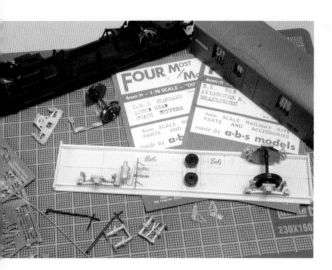

A slightly more complicated scratch-building task was posed by this ex-Lima CCT van, now reissued by Hornby. The original chassis is very crude and something better was needed to complement a detailed and repainted bodyshell. Again, plastic card and an assortment of metal components were assembled from a variety of sources.

A couple of parts from the original chassis gained a new lease of life, being carefully cut away and remounted, with extra plastic packing where necessary. Note the heavy-duty whitemetal axle guards, in contrast to the smaller brass units used on the previous projects; a distinctive feature of the real thing. Whitemetal brake shoes and brass cross-shafts raise the spectre of short circuits unless they are kept a respectable distance from the wheels. Note also the plastic angle reinforcing the rear of the buffer beams – an essential feature if using spring-loaded scale couplings.

pen is better than pencil for marking; just give the ink a few moments to dry to avoid smudging. Thick ink markings, however, cannot help but introduce a certain ambiguity to precise measurements, especially in small scales. Where do you make the cut? Is it along one side of the ink line or the other, or down the centre? In the same way as a craftsman measures and marks out timber, I find it preferable to mark out plastics with a single-edged knife blade, using a light score line as the exact measurement, run along a steel rule. A pinpoint scribing tool or a pin in a hand vice will also do the trick. This recessed line will serve to guide the knife or saw when the cuts are made.

To cut plastic sheet, use several light passes with a knife, exerting only minimal pressure to prevent the blade wandering off course. When the blade reaches halfway through the material, the sheet can be snapped apart, preferably while held over the

edge of the workbench. The edge may need dressing with a flat file to get a truly square edge in relation to the flat faces, but be careful not to make the part too small by overdressing. In contrast, very thin sheets of styrene can be cut more easily with sharp scissors or shears, especially curved or irregular shapes.

Plastic section, tube or rod, needs a sturdy blade to cope with the rigidity of the material and a knife will struggle to leave a square edge on the material. A razor saw, perhaps in a mitre box, will produce more consistent results. All cut edges will need tidying up, including the faces of the material that may have gained a raised burr from the knife or saw. Files, sanding sticks and abrasive sheets are ideal for the job.

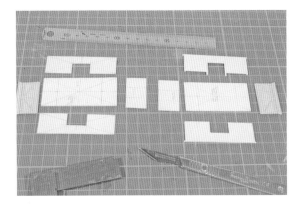

There is no existing source for the 1970s-built 16ton, 10ft wheelbase mineral wagons. Rather than try to stretch an existing kit's bodyshell, it seemed easier to scratch-build the whole thing. Again, sheet plastic was the chosen medium and the parts drawn out and cut with as much accuracy as possible.

The characterful T-section strengthening ribs posed a problem that was solved by laminating 1.5 × 0.5mm and 0.8mm square plastic strip. Long strips were assembled and left to cure before cutting to the required lengths.

Some spares from a Cambrian Models kit were employed for the side and end doors. Smaller details like strengthening brackets, door hinges and sliding locks were all fashioned from different sizes of plastic strip. Softened by hot water or liquid poly, the strip can be shaped and manipulated to create a variety of components.

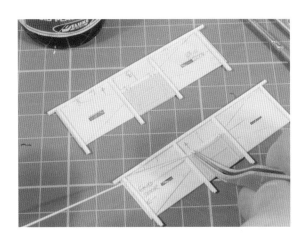

The separate components were left to harden completely before assembly, taking great care to get the body panels aligned square and true. Plastic sheet is liable to warp if used in too-thin section, so 20thou (0.5mm) was employed here, strengthened by the overlaid ribs and fairings, as in real life.

The solebars and buffer beams were again fabricated from 3.1mm (⅛in) Evergreen channel section, spaced to allow fitment of Comet compensated axle guards, as featured in the previous chapter.

The test of a successful scratch-built model – does it look homemade? These were built back in 2007 and are still going strong on my 1980s layout. Incidentally, the real wagons received flame-cut rectangular holes in the sides to prevent overloading when these vehicles had been cascaded into the engineers' fleet and used for carrying dense spoil.

There are times when plastic has its limitations and, when trying to represent bare timber, only expert painting can fool the eye. Therefore, it seemed a logical idea to replace the plastic parts on a trestle wagon with real strip wood. The original Parkside components were retained for use as templates and the half-lap joints of the real things were incorporated.

Assembly was easier than it perhaps looks, with Deluxe Super 'Phatic! glue offering super-quick drying time. It had been planned to use oil-based stains to finish the wood, so great care was taken not to clog the grain with excess glue. A damp swab mopped up any squeeze-out from the joints immediately. Fine embroidery pins were used as clamps, being pulled out once the glue had set.

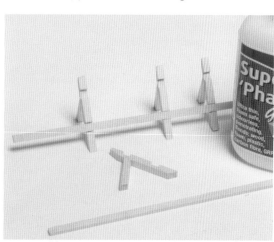

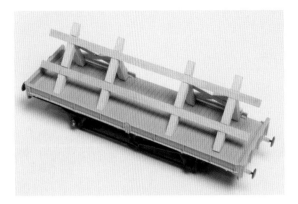

It is important not to try to rush the fabrication of wood parts, as, although the assembly is strong when complete, the glue needed a few minutes to take hold while making each joint. Regular test-fitting ensured that the assembly was correct.

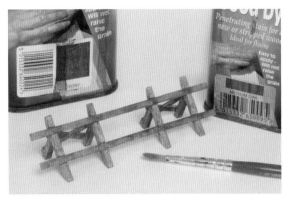

A mix of oil-based wood stains was applied by brush, concentrating darker shades around the joints and wiping away any excess with a swab.

Strengthening plates and brackets are easy to create from 10thou (0.25mm), 2mm wide brass strip, fixed with cyano.

The final touches were small hoops for securing the load shackles, formed from 0.33mm brass wire and fixed with cyano. When dry, the metal parts can be carefully painted and weathered to blend in with the stained woodwork.

Rivets, formed using a Nutter tool, were placed on the brackets with clear varnish and left to set.

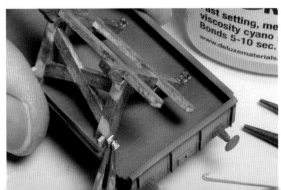

CHAPTER SIXTEEN

PAINTING

Having invested many hours ensuring that a kit is assembled and running perfectly, there is little sense in rushing the final stages. Indeed, the preparation, priming and painting steps can be the most crucial in many respects. The appearance and longevity of a finish is directly related to how thoroughly the model is prepared. Moreover, the quality of the primer and subsequent paint layers all rely on the soundness of the surface beneath. Therefore, taking the time to get each stage right before moving on is the key to success, not being afraid to take a few steps backwards and remedying any imperfections before stepping forwards.

A brief overview of the various factors involved in the painting stage are outlined below, including surface preparation, priming, painting and varnishing, along with a quick look at the properties of different paint formulas. However, readers are referred to my previous book, *Airbrushing for Railway Modellers* (The Crowood Press, 2011), which probes into every aspect of the finishing process in much greater detail.

SURFACE PREPARATION

No matter how expertly a paint finish is applied, if the surface has not been properly prepared, the results will always be poor. Dirt, dust and grease deposits must be thoroughly cleansed and the model perfectly dry before work can proceed. With an assembled kit liable to be covered in all of these unwanted contaminants, we are likely to have quite a bit of work to do.

Joints and areas of filler must be dressed smooth until all surface abrasions have been removed. Files and abrasives leave behind all manner of debris and a good scrub in a bath of warm water and dissolved soda crystals will shift the majority of loose deposits. Solvent-based cleaners, like Model Clean (Just Like the Real Thing) are useful for removing more stubborn dirt and residues left from adhesives, flux or grease. Resin models are especially challenging to finish, with silicone residues from the moulding process being particularly hard to remove. To make

Solvent-based cleaners, such as Isopropyl Alcohol or Model Clean are great for dissolving oil and grease deposits. At least three applications should be made, brushed on and wiped away with cotton swabs. The first loosens the muck, the second removes it and the third makes sure. After cleaning, try not to handle the model again with your bare hands, wearing disposable latex gloves from now on.

Before applying any primer or paint, vital working surfaces such as bearings, power contacts or any fixed glazing should be masked off.

the cleaning task easier, specialist fluids are available, such as Silicon Buster from Finescale Model World (see Appendix).

Leave the model aside somewhere warm and dust-free for a day or two to dry out completely. Models with enclosed spaces, such as vans and tank wagons, may have moisture trapped inside the body or other voids and must be left to evaporate before applying any paint.

PRIMING

A primer forms the perfect intermediate layer between the bare material and the subsequent coats of paint. It has a strong, penetrating bond to the surface and its self-levelling formula dries to a lovely matt finish, giving the more fickle top-coat formulas a better platform in terms of adhesion and allowing their full opacity to be achieved. Some primers even contain micro-filling compounds that disguise any slight surface imperfections.

Grey is the most common shade of primer, the neutral tone allowing any hitherto invisible gaps, scratches or debris to be spotted and redressed with filler and abrasives. A light grey is also an ideal under-colour for most paints, as it will not alter how the final shade appears. Lighter colours, such as white, yellow and pale blue, are best applied over a white primer. Conversely, metallic paints benefit from a gloss black undercoat.

Primers are offered in most hobby paint ranges, in acrylic and enamel format. Spraying paint is always the ideal method, to achieve a consistently flat coating and aerosol primers offer good results. Pre-thinned cellulose or acrylic primers, aimed at airbrush application, are also highly recommended, especially the Alclad II range, which sees plenty of use in the Dent Workshop.

Etching primers, where a chemical within the paint 'eats' into the model's surface to improve the bond, are popular with some kit builders. Available in single- or twin-pack format, application methods vary according to brand and formula, so studying the instructions and safety notes is important. Indeed, they must be handled and applied with great care, as they contain some rather nasty ingredients. Etching formulas are tailored to metal or plastic surfaces, the latter also being effective on the notoriously hard-to-paint polyurethane resin. One thing that etching primers have in common is the price – they are all expensive. With thorough preparation of the surface, I have yet to find any definite benefits of etching primers, although many other modellers swear by them, especially those working in large scales, or whose kits are destined for outdoor railways.

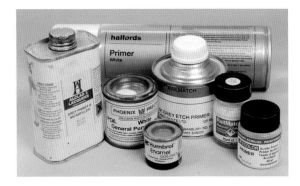

If possible, choose only high-quality primers, as cheaper formulas are difficult to use and frequently offer poor results. Halfords car primers are excellent, as are the aerosols produced by Modelmates and JLTRT. Only use aerosols at a minimum temperature of 15°C, as a cold and damp atmosphere interferes with the propellant.

Shake the can for a good five minutes and spray from a consistent distance of about 20–30cm (8-12in). For best results, build up several light layers, leaving the model for a minute or so in-between. This avoids the risk of the paint running off the surface, or clogging the fine surface detail. Wear a facemask and work in a well-ventilated space.

The performance of a good airbrush is hard to beat, with the flow of paint being controlled more accurately than via a spray can. The massive upgrade in the quality of your painting output will be just reward for the investment. Alclad II primer comes pre-thinned, ready for spraying, and the micro-filler additives go some way to disguising minor surface imperfections.

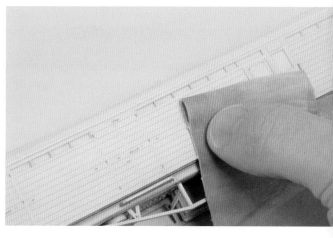

Allow the primer to dry thoroughly and add a little filler where necessary, rubbing down when fully cured. Micromesh abrasives feature a rubber backing and can cope with uneven surfaces without damaging fine detail. Move through the grades, from 3,600 to 12,000grit for best results. Give the model another wash and set aside to dry out. A further light coat of primer will blend in any modified areas.

Build up layers of primer gradually, spraying from the prescribed distance, which is usually 20–30cm (8–12in). It will take a few light coats before the primer takes on a uniform shade. Plastics, resin and filler compounds absorb different amounts of paint, resulting in a patchy appearance. However, it simply requires a number of light coats to achieve an even finish. Getting the primer into all of the model's nooks and crannies is vital and an aerosol often struggles, especially on smaller-scale models. An airbrush has a better chance of dealing with awkward spots and the lower air pressure gives the user much more control over the paint flow.

PAINTING

Applying paint follows the same basic rules as that of priming, with the need for the surface to be clean and dry and the paint layered on to the surface evenly and gradually. The dry primer may need a light buffing to remove any loose particles or dust, or to de-nib any rough areas. Ultra-fine

abrasives like Micromesh are perfect for the job, used wet for best results. Clean the surface down with water or a spirit-based cleanser and allow it to dry completely.

Enamel, cellulose or acrylic paints are the main formulas available to hobbyists and each has particular characteristics. Cellulose paints are expensive and cannot be applied by hand, their rapid drying times being suited to spraying via an aerosol or airbrush. The fumes are hazardous and only a small number of railway-themed colours are available off the shelf.

Oil-based enamels have been around for decades, popularized by the famous Humbrol brand. Railmatch and Phoenix Precision also offer high-quality enamels with a railway theme and the paint is equally suited to hand or spray painting. High-quality finishes are possible, although drying times are long and the paint may contain harmful substances such as lead chromate. White spirit is the usual thinning and cleaning medium for enamels, although high-quality specialist thinners are available for airbrush use.

Acrylics are largely water-based and offer a much less toxic material with shorter drying times and ease of use, whether by hand or airbrush. Brands with good reputations include LifeColor, Tamiya, Vallejo and RailMatch. Acrylic thinning mediums are tailored to specific brands, while brushes and tools can be cleaned in water.

Ordering the application of different colours is important. Working to a general rule of 'lightest first' helps in the decision-making and avoids the need to apply lighter undercoats over darker shades in order to get bright colours to achieve full opacity. Moreover, the more layers of paint added to a surface, the more the fine surface detail will be obscured, so keeping coats to a minimum is the ideal.

Again, building up numerous very thin layers, whether by hand, airbrush or aerosol, will generate a better-quality finish. Rushing to get each coat done and dusted will only result in coarse, uneven finishes. Painting by hand is a time-consuming task, with each layer benefitting from a rub-down before the following coat. Coupled with the use of slow-drying enamel paints, even a basic livery may take several days to achieve. However, airbrushing and aerosol spraying also take time and all paints should be rested at least overnight before abrading, recoating or applying any masking tape.

Paints vary in formulation and performance. Acrylics are user-friendly and dry quickly with few unpleasant fumes. Enamels, however, produce superior results, but require patience. Be sure to employ the correct thinners to suit your chosen paints.

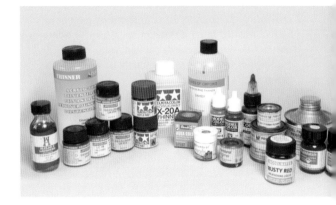

If painting by hand, investing in high-quality paintbrushes is a justifiable luxury, making the job so much easier. Cheap brushes shed their bristles and lose their shape, soon becoming unusable. Sable brushes are preferred and, if looked after, will offer a respectable working lifespan.

Shake or stir the paint thoroughly before use and add a little thinner if necessary – the paint needs to be about the viscosity of whole milk. Apply light coats, using the brush to spread it evenly.

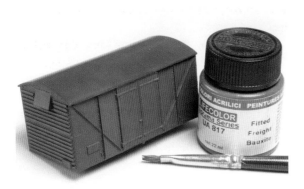

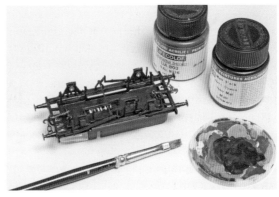

Keep brush strokes running in the same direction and allow each layer to dry thoroughly before rubbing down with Micromesh and applying the next coat. Repeat until the colour reaches full opacity.

Underframes are easier to paint by hand, although having to dab the medium into all those nooks and crannies tends to ruin brushes, so save older tools for this purpose.

Airbrushing is quite a complex subject, with lots of variables to be considered such as air pressure, paint viscosity and distance between nozzle and subject.

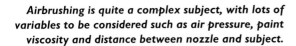

For a successful finish, the paint must be built up gradually, over several coats. With each coat being very thin, there is less chance of smothering fine relief than painting by hand, which invariably leads to thicker layers.

Airbrushing offers far superior results than hand brushing. Work progresses rapidly, as previous coats do not have to be completely dry before another thin layer is applied.

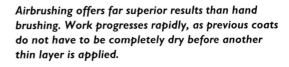

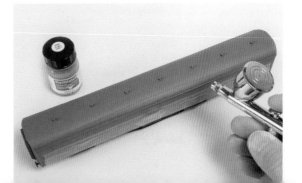

MASKING

Creating 'joints' between different colours requires the use of some form of masking. Indeed, masks also work to protect features such as glazing, bearings and electrical contacts from paint contamination. Masking tape comes in many different forms, sizes and materials, but it is worth sticking expressly to well-known hobby brands, as general-purpose decorator's tapes are not suitable for scale models. Amongst the best all-round tapes are those in the Tamiya range, followed closely by Tristar. Tacky enough to stay in place without damaging underlying paint, they are also fairly flexible and can cope with a degree of surface relief. Vinyl-backed tapes, however, are far more flexible

and can be stretched to cope with all manner of awkward shapes.

Masking fluid is also a vital tool for the kit builder, consisting of a fast-drying latex or acrylic solution that forms a resilient, yet easy-to-remove film. Great for sealing gaps between different layers of masking tape, fluid can also be used to mask tricky areas such as glazing.

A bit of forethought can greatly ease the painting stage, especially if lots of masking stages will be needed. Omitting certain raised detailing parts until after painting, such as handrails, brackets or piping, can all interfere with masking tape, but can be fitted and painted by hand later. Indeed, coach handrails and door handles benefit from being left in their bare brass state, as per the real thing.

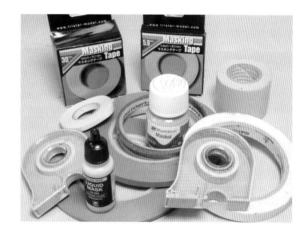

Masking tape comes in various sizes and forms. Vinyl tape gives knife-edge joints between colours and can be manipulated around awkward shapes, while cloth-backed tapes are good all-rounders. Masking fluids help to seal layers of tape and prevent paint ingress, while also being ideal for covering complex shapes or glazing.

Once in place, use the edge of a cocktail stick to press the tape into any recesses and to ensure that the working edge of the mask is firmly in place, lessening the risk of paint creeping underneath. And do not forget to mask the inside of glazed carriages as well as the outside.

To cope with awkward areas, or where cutting individual masks would be too laborious, use masking fluid instead. Similarly, when faced with raised details that interfere with the masking tape, simply cut holes for the parts to protrude and seal with masking fluid.

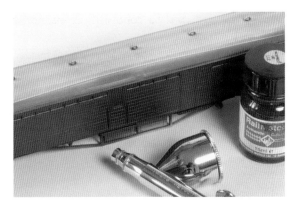

Think about the order in which the various colours will be applied. In this case, the crimson sides have been rendered first. When dry, the areas of 'overspray' on the roof will need to be abraded smooth, as they will feel a little gritty.

The sides can then be masked, with high-quality vinyl tape being used to make the 'joint' around the edges of the ends and roof. General-purpose tape then fills in the gap and masking fluid seals all layers of tape to stop any paint from bleeding through.

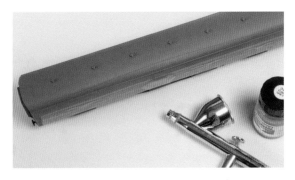

The roof is next to be painted, ensuring that the colour reaches around the raised roof ventilators and other details by changing the airbrush's angle of attack.

After covering the roof with tape, the awkward edges are treated with masking fluid.

Always wait for the paint to dry before removing the masking, or there will be a risk of damage to the finish. Peel away from the edge where the new paint is lying, using a blunted cocktail stick to lift the edges of the tape. Tidy up any rough edges with a little white spirit and a swab.

The ends and chassis are then treated to a few coats of black paint.

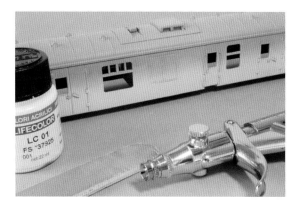

It helps when building up multiple colours to start with the lighter shades. A white undercoat has been added to the lower edges of this Irish Railways van (a Silver Fox resin kit), to give the subsequent layer a suitable base.

The CIE 'golden brown' (or orange, in reality) is a vivid colour that benefits from the white undercoat.

Once the orange has dried, it is masked off for the black of the upper sides. Ruling a faint pencil line along the body helps to keep the masking tape straight over such a long distance. Note the cheaper, general-purpose tape along the lower edge, saving the high-quality red vinyl tape to make the actual paint 'joint'.

Adding the darkest shade last avoids the need for building up thick layers of lighter shades over a darker background. We are aiming for the thinnest layers of paint possible, while still achieving full opacity, but without leaving visible steps when the masking is removed.

Lining, whether by hand or with decals, helps to blend the various colour elements together. The use of a bow pen is demonstrated in the following chapter.

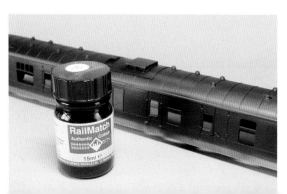

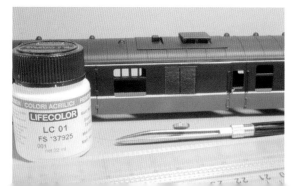

A coat of gloss varnish is essential prior to applying decals. Matt and satin coats are great for a final sealing finish, taking away the unrealistic sheen of the gloss, while also serving to produce a more unified finish.

VARNISH

Once the painting stage is complete, an overall coat of varnish not only blends the various paint finishes together, but also provides a perfect base for applying decals. Varnishes also impart a hardwearing coating to protect against everyday handling. Choose your varnish carefully, as quality really is everything. At this late stage in a kit build, the use of substandard material can have a negative bearing on the final outcome. Poor-quality varnishes tend towards discolouration, usually turning a yellowish shade after a few months, while the compatibility of the formula is also of great import. Certain types of cellulose-based varnishes are not suitable for use over enamel or acrylic paints, for example, so be sure to read the label before use.

Enamel formulas offer highly durable, lustrous coatings, although they can also be the most prone to yellowing. Drying times can be anything from six hours to fourteen days, depending on formula and sheen, with gloss coats taking at least twice as long to cure. Acrylic varnishes lack the resilience and versatility of oil-based formulas, but carry the benefit of low odour and faster drying times. At the top of the range is cellulose clear lacquer, offering the ultimate high-quality coating. Cellulose can only be sprayed, but the quality and toughness of the finish is hard to beat.

Varnish needs a little help to stick to the model and generally prefers a matt surface as a base. A prior rub-down with Micromesh or other super-fine abrasives will help, lubricated with plenty of water.

After a thorough clean and dry, build up the clear coating over several layers, following the techniques already described. Spraying, again, is recommended for an even finish, and a patient build-up of thin coats will produce the best results.

After the gloss coating and decals stage (*see next chapter*), a choice of final finish is up to the individual. Matt and satin coatings offer the most realistic appearance to most miniature models, although some enthusiasts like everything to appear shiny. It should be noted that creating a flawless high-gloss finish requires far more effort and skill than a matt coat, which is much more forgiving.

Whatever the brand or formula of varnish, the finish must be built up gradually over successive light coats. A high-gloss coating is essential as a prelude to applying decals, as described in the following chapter.

CHAPTER SEVENTEEN

DECALS

Unless intending to hand-letter your freshly painted wagon or carriage, adding decals – or transfers, as they are also known – will be the next step in the building process. In the rare instance where a kit has supplied the necessary markings, the correct application method must be followed to get the best out of them. Moreover, the majority of us will have to source our own decals, often from a variety of different brands, to obtain the appropriate running numbers, operating instructions and load-capacity markings. For coaching stock, logo types and classification numerals will also be required, along with any necessary lining transfers.

At the risk of sounding like a football correspondent, there is certainly no shortage of choice in the transfer market. A number of manufacturers offer markings, logos and numerals for virtually all eras and scales, in water-slide, rub-down, Pressfix or Methfix formats. Packs may be tailored to specific subjects, such as late BR coaching stock or 1950s-era cattle wagons, usually offering most, if not all,

the necessary markings to complete at least one vehicle.

Alternatively, more generic packages may work out to be more economical in the long run, offering a larger number of key ingredients like blank wagon data panels, separate numerals and plenty of stripes or BR totems. Quality is generally high across all popular ranges, although there are a few older packs that have been superseded in quality by more recent offerings.

WATER-SLIDE

Water-slide decals will be familiar to anyone who has built an Airfix kit and this format is still the most widely employed transfer medium. A high-gloss finish is vital for the decals to adhere properly and for the clear carrier film to be rendered invisible. Otherwise, if applied to a matt or satin finish, an unpleasant 'silvering' effect is created as tiny air bubbles are trapped between the transfer and the surface.

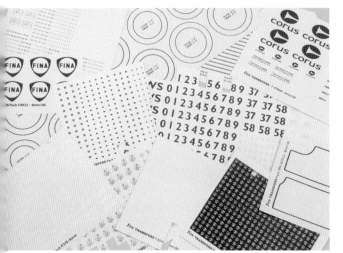

There are masses of decals to choose from, in water-slide, rub-down, Pressfix and Methfix formats.

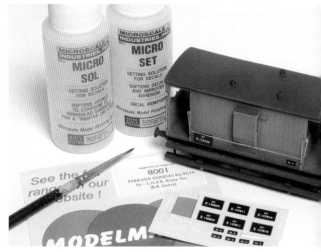

Some brands even tailor transfer packs to specific kit subjects, with the entire Parkside range being complemented by Modelmaster decals.

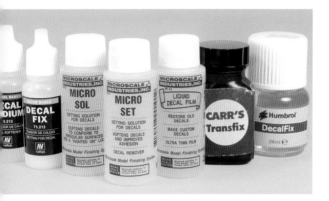

As well as the transfers and a high-gloss surface, you will also need a setting solution to get the best results from water-slide decals.

Water-slide decals are the most popular and user-friendly format. All you need to do is cut out one icon at a time.

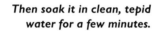

Then soak it in clean, tepid water for a few minutes.

When the decal starts to work loose from the backing – do not let it float off into the water – transfer it to the model and slide into position with a blunted cocktail stick. Try to get it into the right place as soon as possible. The more the delicate film is nudged around, the more the likelihood of damage increases.

An initial coat of Micro Set promotes good adhesion.

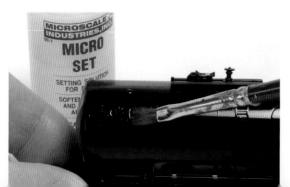

Soak up the excess moisture with a swab, exerting only gentle pressure to squeeze out the water from beneath the film.

Another coat of Micro Set will help seal it in place. Leave to dry out naturally.

On uneven surfaces, the decal will need to be softened. Follow the previous steps and, once the transfer is in position, brush on a little Micro Sol and leave for a few moments.

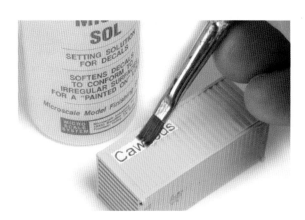

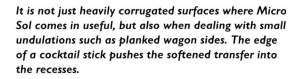

With a swab, cocktail stick and flat brush, the decal can be helped into the recesses while still wet. If it struggles to stretch, add more Micro Sol and try again. When you are happy with the positioning, use a dry brush and swab to wipe away any excess moisture and leave to dry out naturally.

It is not just heavily corrugated surfaces where Micro Sol comes in useful, but also when dealing with small undulations such as planked wagon sides. The edge of a cocktail stick pushes the softened transfer into the recesses.

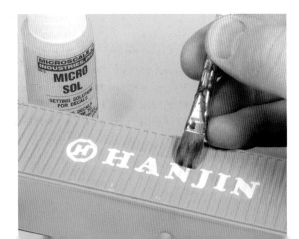

Application is fairly simple – the desired character is cut out from the printed sheet and soaked in water for a few minutes, after which the decal will work loose from the paper and can be slid onto the model's surface. As the water dries, the transfer forms a strong bond and, with a little help from a setting solution, can cope admirably with uneven surfaces. Indeed, when applied in the right way, the best water-slide decals can present an almost painted-on impression.

Setting solutions greatly aid the application process, improving adhesion in the first instance, while also helping the decal to settle on to the surface of the model as it dries out. Products like Micro Set, Humbrol Decal Fix or Carr's Transfix can be viewed almost as an extra layer of adhesive and are intended for brushing on to the surface both before and after application of the decal.

Softening fluids, such as Micro Sol, are designed for use in conjunction with setting solutions and, as the term suggests, they work to make the decal more pliable. Once applied and left for a few minutes, the transfer can be manipulated over awkward surfaces, such as corrugated wagon or container sides, with less risk of tearing.

Fox Transfers, Modelmaster, C-Rail, Precision Decals and Cambridge Custom Transfers are all leaders in the field of British-outline railway decals in water-slide format. Silk-screen printing has more or less given way to modern computer-controlled techniques and quality of reproduction is now universally high. Moreover, these modern techniques allow an infinite number of colours to be rendered in the most complicated designs, making them arguably the most realistic transfers.

FOX

In terms of subject coverage and scales catered for, Fox Transfers offers the most comprehensive range of railway-themed decals, exclusively in water-slide form. Anything from the late 1800s up to the present day is covered, including most of the complex contemporary liveries carried on the privatized railway, reproduced under official licences.

Complete livery packs offer a one-stop resource, while the individual elements are often available separately in bulk packs. These are useful to keep in stock if assembling a large fleet of similar vehicles. Ready-made, or part-made-up, running numbers take a lot of the hassle out of rendering specific wagon or carriage numbers and packs of lining are also available for each of the 'Big Four' liveries, as well as BR's various schemes and a few pre-grouping subjects.

Standards of accuracy and production quality are up in the top echelons of the sector and, as far as railway modelling in the UK, the brand has become a respected household name. Mail order only is offered, although some specialist retailers keep stocks of Fox products and the entire range can be viewed on the company's website.

MODELMASTER

Close behind Fox in terms of subject coverage, the bulk of Modelmaster's water-slide range covers the whole BR period, although a few 'Big Four' and post-1990s subjects are also included. Produced in 4mm scale, these water-slide decals offer a similarly high level of performance to the company's main competitor and the wagon livery Mini Packs are particularly helpful to builders of Parkside Dundas and Cambrian Models kits, covering both companies' entire range of 4mm wagons and parcel vehicles. Everything from coach numbers, lining and overhead warning symbols is available and the quality of the printing is high.

PRECISION DECALS

The clue is in the name, as far as this establishment's mantra is concerned. High levels of accuracy are achieved by meticulous research and the ALRPS wax-resin printing process achieves high-quality results, often without the need for a clear carrier film. The water-slide transfers are more delicate than those of Fox or Modelmaster and are sensitive to many oil- or cellulose-based varnishes. Period coverage is limited to the later BR and post-privatization schemes.

Many transfer packs are tailored to specific liveries or vehicles, with virtually all of the necessary elements provided, along with a spare set of everything in case you make a mistake, which is a nice touch. My favourite feature of the range is the custom-printed wagon data panels, where the necessary information is submitted on the mail order website, saving hours of laboriously adding the necessary TOPS codes, numbers and weight markings individually. Transfers are offered in virtually every scale.

C-RAIL INTERMODAL

Commissioned by C-Rail but produced in the USA by Microscale, this range concentrates on modern intermodal freight subjects, especially the vast range of ISO deep-sea containers that form a ubiquitous backdrop to today's railway. Accuracy, production and performance are extremely good and there are also packs of graffiti for the gritty reality of the modern urban environment. Packs are produced for 4mm and 2mm scale.

NAIRNSHIRE MODELLING SUPPLIES

Also produced by Microscale, this small range of late BR-era logos, numbers and lettering for 4mm scale offers high-quality printing and excellent performance.

CAMBRIDGE CUSTOM TRANSFERS

Another brand with a descriptive tag, CCT offers a custom printing service as well as a comprehensive range of early BR freight and non-passenger carrying stock (NPCS) vehicles in any scale. Typical packs are tailored to one specific (or a number of closely related) vehicle types and each may include enough markings for up to thirty wagons.

The transfers are delicate and must be applied with care. They are also sensitive to some varnish formulas (acrylic coatings being recommended).

The perils of not applying water-slide decals to a glossy surface – the clear carrier film dries to a grey finish, often referred to as 'silvering'. As well as the unsightliness, adhesion will be poor.

Allow the initial layer to dry overnight before applying the bright overlays. The small Red Star logos also received white backing squares and the overall effect is impressive. Use Micro Sol to get the stripes to sit into the door seams and, when dry, run some dilute black paint into the recesses; it is easier than cutting the decals either side of the seam.

Brightly coloured water-slide livery elements applied to a darker backing will benefit from a white 'undercoat'. This can either be painted, or, as is the case here, Fox Transfers supplies suitable backing decals.

Assembling numbers and wagon data panels
with individual characters is a laborious task,
especially when a blank backing 'plate' has to be
applied initially.

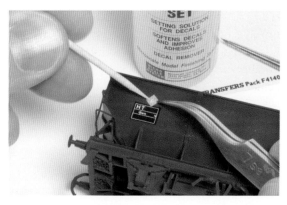

Allow each icon to dry for about ten minutes before
the next one is applied. This seems a long time but,
if treating a handful of vehicles at the same time,
once the last one has been reached, you can then
return to the first model and add the next layer.

I tend to align my decals more by eye than anything
else, especially on grubby freight stock. However,
for more exacting tasks a tailor's chalk pencil and
a straight edge are invaluable. The thin white line
can be wiped away with a damp swab, the soft
chalk leaving no indentation in the paintwork.
Alternatively, a strip of low-tack masking tape
can act as an effective guide, although it may lift
previously applied decals unless they have been
sealed with varnish.

Printed on sheets consisting of a single clear carrier film, trimming each character before application is recommended. The need for a high-gloss surface is even more crucial to disguise the film's presence.

RUB-DOWN

Rub-down transfers are a little simpler, the characters being printed on to the rear face of a sheet of clear plastic. Once aligned, a pencil is rubbed over the chosen icons, thus depositing them on to the model, whence they are sealed by another rubbing, this time beneath a piece of tracing paper. Due to the processes involved, creating multicoloured rub-down decals is not easy and the results are seldom convincing. Therefore, their use is commonly limited to plain numbers and letters, which can look impressive and offer the convenience of application to any surface (a gloss backing is not essential). However, they struggle to adhere to uneven surfaces.

REPLICA RAILWAYS

Replica offers my favoured packs of rub-down numerals, being quick and simple to apply and offering highly realistic results. The range is small, with late BR and some privatized liveries being catered for. A number of water-slide transfers are also available, mostly of logo types for locomotives and rolling stock.

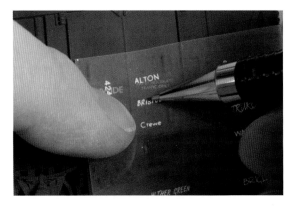

Rub-down decals are simple to apply, although correct alignment is vital – they cannot be manipulated. Use the supplied tracing paper to prevent accidentally applying other characters and employ a sharp pencil to rub over the chosen decal.

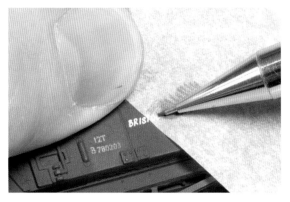

After applying each character, rub the pencil over the tracing paper to seal the decal in place.

RAILMATCH

Paint supplier RailMatch developed a complementary range of rub-down decals a few decades ago and some of them are showing their age. The BR numbering and lettering sheets are fine, their cheapness and ease of use being points in their favour.

PRESSFIX/METHFIX

Pressfix and Methfix are two similar methods of decal application offered by the Historical Model Railway Society (HMRS). Both types consist of characters printed in reverse on to sheets of gummed paper. Cutting out the desired image takes a bit of care, as the knife must not cut right through the backing paper. Once the icon has been peeled away, it retains a semi-translucent coating that makes exact positioning a little difficult. Once pressed into position, the coating is then soaked away with either water (Pressfix) or methylated spirit (Methfix).

Pressfix is a faster option, as the water dissolves the adhesive quickly, plus the process can be further advanced with a few drops of Micro Set or other decal-setting solutions. However, a sticky gum will remain if the process is rushed and the characters themselves tend to stand ever so proud of the surface, being a little thicker than other transfer

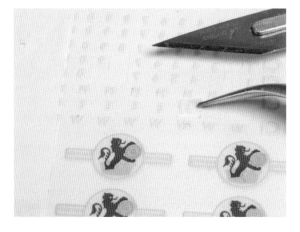

With Pressfix and Methfix decals, cut and peel away the icon from the sheet, being careful not to slice right through the sheet.

Take the time to position the decal as accurately as possible before applying pressure with a fingernail.

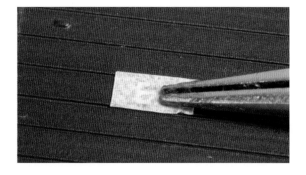

Brush on a little water or Micro Set (Pressfix) and wait for the backing paper to slide away. For Methfix decals, apply methylated spirits to loosen the paper.

Micro Set is more effective than water in removing any traces of gum from Pressfix decals.

types. The Methfix version is for the more exacting modeller, taking much longer for the paper to float away, but producing a much better end result. Incidentally, Parkside supplies Pressfix-style decal sheets with its range of 7mm scale plastic wagon kits.

MAKE YOUR OWN

Because of the vast array of railway vehicles and liveries employed over the past 200 years, even the largest decal ranges will have some gaps, especially for the more obscure subjects. Happily, the home-made option has become much more viable in recent years, with white-backed or clear water-slide transfer papers being available for use with home inkjet or laser printers.

With some reference images, a decent printer and a modicum of IT skills, it is possible to create your own realistic graphics, although it takes a bit of practice to get them looking good and scaled correctly. Printing off plenty of test runs on plain paper and thoroughly checking before using the expensive decal paper is recommended. A coating of clear varnish needs to be applied over the printed decals before use, so as to seal the ink. To be waterproof, an enamel varnish is necessary, preferably sprayed from an aerosol or airbrush.

If the DIY option does not appeal, there are a number of companies who can produce bespoke transfers on your behalf, such as Precision Decals and Cambridge Custom Transfers (*see* Appendix).

IF IT GOES WRONG

Readjustment is possible with water-slide decals for a few minutes after the first application. However, once the transfer starts to dry out, it will become brittle and extremely sensitive, tearing easily and losing its adhesive qualities if disturbed.

A very small degree of adjustment is possible with Pressfix and Methfix decals, while they are still wet, while water-slide icons can be manipulated for a few minutes as long as they are kept wet. Only one chance exists with rub-downs, however.

Micro Sol solution is a handy medium, as it can also remove unwanted decals without any need for mechanical intervention. Just brush it on and let it soak under the characters. A few applications may be required before the transfer can be wiped away with a damp swab. The fluid will work on water-slide, rub-down and Pressfix decals provided, of course, that they have not been sealed with varnish.

HAND-LETTERING

Not all rail vehicles are immaculately numbered or lettered and there are times when the neatness of decals can look out of place. Moribund freight wagons,

A quicker alternative is to hand-letter your stock with a draughtsman's pen and white or black ink. You need a steady hand and good eyesight, but it offers a less than pristine appearance that is ideal for scruffy freight stock.

A look through prototype images will reveal much in the way of amateurish attempts at applying markings to BR stock and this shock-absorbing van is receiving just such a scheme, using a Rotring ink pen to form the distinctive warning stripes.

After ruling the outlines, the ink pen is then used to fill them in, using a prototype image for reference.

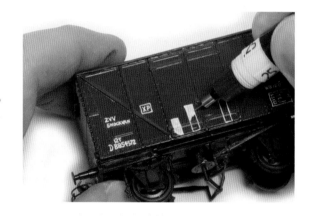

Use a wood block or spare hand to steady the pen as you work. Working on a gloss surface allows any mistakes to be wiped away with white spirit.

It would never win any awards for signwriting, but this fairly messy job of lettering is a close copy of the real wagon late in its life.

especially those near the ends of their working lives, or those employed in industrial environments, were often given running repairs necessitating the original markings to be replaced with more crudely applied versions, sometimes applied via stencils or a large brush. Others may have temporary markings chalked on, or the more ominous 'COND' lettering, for condemned stock. A steady hand and a fine paintbrush can replicate this sort of feature well, but a draughtsman's pen and some white ink will do the job better.

LINING

Passenger stock has long carried lining in some form or other, with pre-1940s schemes ornately highlighting the various timber panels along the carriage sides. The more austere BR livery still required lines separating the crimson and cream, while the later plain maroon called for a straw and black horizontal lining arrangement. Even the drab blue and grey saw a fine white line following the join between the two colours.

Lining miniature models can be a make-or-break stage in the finishing process. Done well, it will look lovely, bringing together all the various livery elements into a cohesive whole. A less than perfect application, however, will draw attention and potentially spoil the overall effect.

Ruling the individual lines with a bow pen and paint offers supreme results, but the technique can take time to master and the quality and set-up of the tool are paramount. My own tool is a few decades old, being initially purchased while studying technical illustration. Years of use has seen the jaws 'worked in', with the tips worn to fine points, rather like the edges of an artisan's plastering trowel. Indeed, taking a brand-new implement, regardless of the price, is unlikely to produce perfect results without first being dressed on an oilstone.

Lining is a very useful skill to have up your sleeve and I would recommend having a go, even if using it for little more than orange cantrail stripes on modern stock, or adding the odd white diagonal line on a mineral wagon. The paint must be stirred

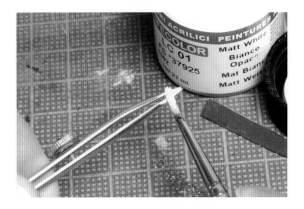

Lining with a bow pen is not as tricky as it looks, as long as the tool is of sufficient standard. Stir the paint thoroughly and load the pen with a brush, wiping away the excess.

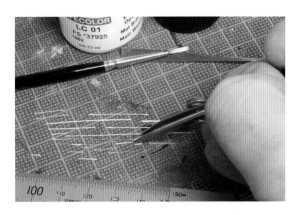

Adjust the thumbwheel and test on a scrap of plastic or card to gauge the correct thickness.

Ensure the model is secure and improvise a hand rest from wood or a pile of books. With a steel rule aligned correctly, simply run the bow pen along the edge. Always work on a gloss surface and wipe away any mistakes with white spirit.

thoroughly and free of any sediment – a fresh tin is recommended – and the tool cleaned out thoroughly after every stroke. Enamels are probably the best formula, as the slower drying offers easier working. I do use acrylics, especially LifeColor shades, which are free-flowing but they do dry quickly, usually before reaching the end of a long line. For smaller jobs, however, acrylics are fine. Lining by hand deserves more space than we have at our disposal in this volume, although the basics are illustrated here.

A more accessible approach to lining is to make use of water-slide decals. Easily trimmed into the necessary lengths and with a vast array of preformed corners and curves available, a cut-and-paste job can be achieved quickly and easily. Accuracy is important, though, and a tailor's chalk pencil and straight edge should precede the transfers, marking out their intended location, and getting the horizontal and vertical lines dead straight is vital.

Of course, the beauty of using water-slide decals is that they can be manipulated for a few minutes if kept damp, allowing for plenty of fine-tuning. Schemes that rely on layering different colours of lining need a tentative approach, as rushing will simply loosen the decal beneath. Instead, apply the base layer as needed and allow it to dry out, using a decal setting solution to help things along. Once dry, apply another thin coat of gloss varnish and leave this to cure also. The next stage in the lining can then proceed without any risk of disturbing the underlying layers.

Applying long, thin decals takes a bit of patience. As soon as the decal begins to work loose from the backing paper (do not let it float away in the water), place it in position on the model and push it off the backing paper a little at a time, using a damp paintbrush to move it into its exact position. Working a few centimetres at a time keeps the job under control and requires the decal to be manipulated as little as possible.

Lining is also offered in Pressfix and Methfix format, but these are more difficult to apply, not least as the exact positioning of each element is obscured by the translucent backing paper and there is very little margin for error.

SEALING COATS

Whatever type of decal or lining has been employed, the model should be left overnight to dry out completely before a sealing coat of matt or satin varnish is applied. Protecting the decals from damage, the varnish will also present a pleasing uniform finish over the whole model. Choose the varnish formula carefully, checking the application instructions supplied with your decals, as some are sensitive to oil- or cellulose-based coatings.

A sealing layer of varnish prevents the decals or lining from being damaged and presents a unified overall finish.

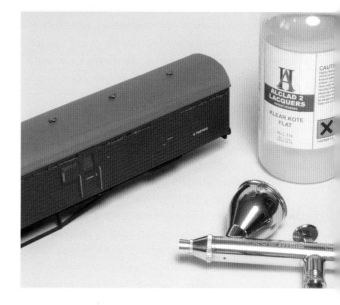

CHAPTER EIGHTEEN

FINISHING TOUCHES

This final chapter offers a guide to a number of useful techniques for adding those final touches to a model, for example wagonloads and their attendant shackles, destination labels, interior details and glazing. A brief look at weathering techniques is also included, although, as mentioned in Chapter 16, readers are pointed in the direction of my book *Airbrushing for Railway Modellers* (The Crowood Press, 2011) for a more thorough treatment of this subject. It can be argued that it is these last stages in a model's assembly that can produce a truly lifelike appearance, giving the impression that the vehicle is actually doing what it was created for.

GLAZING

Vehicles with windows rely on whatever clear material is employed looking the part, both in its inherent appearance, but also in how it is fixed into each aperture. Preferably, it should be sitting as close to flush with the surrounding surface as the windows do on the real thing. Suitable moulded or etched recesses are usually incorporated on the inside, allowing the windows to be fitted in a realistic position. If not, the modeller is left with some tricky work to do.

Plastic kits featuring glazed windows invariably offer clear polystyrene components, yet they are seldom crystal clear and the brittleness of the material leaves them at risk of serious damage before they have even been removed from the sprue. Even specialist sprue-cutting shears can cause the clear plastic to splinter; a mini-razor saw is a much safer bet, cutting through the material gently and gradually. Buffing the clear parts with fine abrasives, lubricated with water, can greatly improve the transparency of the glazing. For supreme results, try one of Tamiya's tubes of polishing compound, available in a variety of grades and perfect for use on most types of plastic glazing.

Sheet styrene, as supplied in metal kits or freely available separately, can be treated in a similar way, as it is equally susceptible to scratches. If cutting out individual panels, a knife will cause splintering around the edges, so it is a good idea to use either a razor saw or to cut the parts oversize, then trim them back with files and abrasive paper or sanding sticks.

Vacuum-formed glazing is offered with many resin kits, being rendered to fit into the deep apertures of the bodysides, so that from the outside the windows appear flush. This soft material is much more flexible than styrene and less liable to damage. However, do be careful handling it and avoid getting any sticky fingerprints on the windows, as they will be hard to remove.

Regardless of what the glazing is made of, avoid solvent adhesives such as poly-cement or cyano, as both may cause the clear material to turn cloudy. Instead, a dedicated glazing adhesive, such as Deluxe Glue 'n' Glaze, will offer a strong bond, while any excess will dry absolutely clear. Such adhesives can

Vacuum-formed glazing offers fairly convincing results. The material is thin and can be cut with scissors, with each unit having to be fitted individually. Use a good-quality glazing adhesive such as Glue 'n' Glaze, applied with a Micro Tip applicator or cocktail stick.

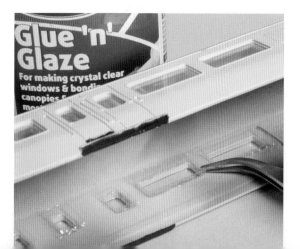

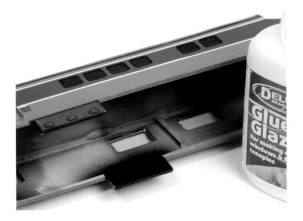

It is simple to craft your own glazing from clear styrene sheet, although the material can be easily scratched. Polish the surface with ultra-fine abrasives, or a polishing compound, for best results. Dipping the glazing in clear acrylic varnish or Johnson's Klear floor polish improves its appearance.

Another alternative for smaller apertures is a liquid glazing compound, such as Glue 'n' Glaze. Run a bead around the inner edges of the aperture, then use a cocktail stick to draw the film across. It takes practice to get it right, but the effects are impressive, albeit sensitive to rough handling.

also be used to form the glazing in smaller apertures, running a bead around the edges and then drawing the film across with a cocktail stick. Provided the model is not handled roughly, these 'windows' can look very convincing.

INTERIORS

Carriage interiors are ripe for enhancement, as they are often highly visible through large windows. Creating a convincing wood-panelling effect is probably wasted in the smaller scales, but the use of an airbrush and stippling actions by hand combine to produce effective finishes for the interior walls and upholstery.

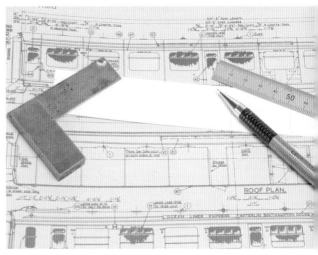

Carriage interiors are usually highly visible from the outside, so put in the effort to get them looking right.

Plan books are a great help and the raw materials for coach interiors are available from Comet, if not supplied with your kit.

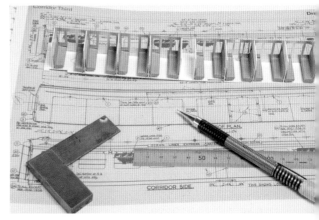

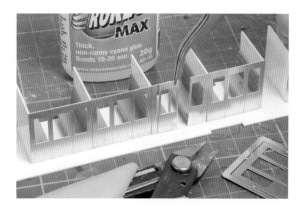

Preformed corridor units or bulkheads save hours of scratch-building work and they can be customized readily. The odd half-open door adds some extra realism.

Researching the correct interior colour schemes and interior fixture layout is also worthwhile. Mirrors (kitchen foil) and framed pictures (cut from miniature posters) break up the monotony of the mock-timber panelling.

Passengers, with their newspapers, drinks and assorted detritus, add a human element to our rolling stock. All can be quickly created from scrap material.

Other details, such as mirrors, framed prints and passengers, along with items of luggage, drinks and newspapers, all combine to complete the scene of a busy express or spartanly populated local branch-line service.

WEATHERING

The term 'weathering' refers to the mimicking of how a real object is affected by being operated outdoors, in harsh conditions, for a given amount of time. It is not only dirt and grime accumulation, but also fading of paintwork from exposure to sunlight and extremes of temperature, or areas of damaged paintwork and corrosion.

Weathering is not for everyone, but it has been growing in acceptance over the past decade or so, helped in no small part by the availability of factory-distressed RTR models. There will always be some of us who prefer our trains to be pristine, but for those who want a little more 'grit' in their miniature recreations, the process of weathering can appear daunting – not least after spending many hours building and painting an item of rolling stock. But, fear not, it does not have to be difficult and the main key to success is to find the medium in which you are happiest working and to invest the time in practising on scrap items before letting loose on a prized model.

The place to start is by looking carefully at prototypes in order to glean an idea of how the real

Weathering is a big subject, but there are some quick, basic techniques to take the shine away from newly finished kits. If you do not own an airbrush, try spraying an aerosol on to a sheet of paper, with the model placed close by to intercept the 'overspray'. Some subtle effects can be created.

An airbrush is essential for anyone with serious weathering aspirations. Combining light layers of varying 'dirty' shades creates highly realistic results.

vehicles weathered. Freight commodities obviously played a part in how the wagons conveying them appeared. Dust from coal, iron ore and aggregates have their own signature stains, while oil or bitumen tanks were left with characteristic deposits. Coaching stock, however, was cleaned on a much more regular basis. although this was usually confined to the sides. As a result, underframes, roofs

and ends could be thick with years of accumulated grime, making for an interesting contrast.

Weathering is deserving of an entire volume, such is the vast array of materials and possible techniques. In the meantime, a number of different approaches are outlined here by way of an introduction.

PRE- AND POST-SHADING

Applying part of the weathering before the livery coat has been painted may not occur to many modellers, but it is an effective method adopted from the military and aviation hobbies. Particularly suited to vehicles with plenty of surface relief, such as planked sides or with pronounced recessed panel joints, the pre-shading technique depends on a decent airbrush for success.

Dark shades are applied into the areas where dirt would collect, or where shadows naturally appear. The livery top coats are then applied with the paint thinned a little more than usual and sprayed in light layers to tailor the amount of the dark pre-shading showing through. The visual effect can be quite stunning even at this early stage, but subsequent weathering will heighten the appearance even further.

Pre-shading is a technique that can only be achieved with an airbrush. It consists of spraying a mix of dark shades into all the nooks and crannies before the livery is applied.

Once the top coats are added, sprayed in very light layers, the dark pre-shading still shows through, exaggerating shadows and bringing out the best of the surface relief.

Post-shading is a way of creating similar effects, but with the darker paint added after the livery coats. This demands far greater accuracy with the airbrush and a more sensitive choice of weathering shade.

Post-shading, unsurprisingly, refers to the creation of darker areas of paint after the livery has been applied. Greater accuracy with the airbrush is necessary for post-shading (rather than pre-shading) and there is an increased risk of applying too much paint into confined areas, leading to runs or the obliteration of fine surface detail. In practice, a judicious combination of both techniques can be highly effective.

POWDERS, PIGMENTS AND WASHES

Weathering powders require little in the way of expensive equipment, with just a handful of decent paintbrushes being required. Powders adhere best to a matt surface and can give pleasing dusty effects, as well as being built up into a textured sludge if mixed with turpentine or paints (read the instructions of the powders to check compatibility). A less-is-more attitude works best, as it is easy to get carried away and apply too much powder at once. Again, a bit of practice will do wonders for your technique.

Weathering powders and pigments are a great way to add texture to a weathered finish; similar results to airbrushing can be achieved with practice. Use only good-quality powders and brushes for best results.

Using a variety of subtly different shades adds greatly to the effect and the powder can be worked into awkward corners with a fine brush.

Freight wagons, such as this Prestwin, can look very effective with heavy deposits of powder around the discharge apparatus and underframe. Powders cling best to a matt surface.

Do not be tempted to blow away excess powder with your breath, as this will stain the surface with moisture. Instead, use a large, soft brush to clear away the unwanted pigment.

Soft colouring pencils are also great for weathering. Areas of bare metal can be replicated with silver or light grey, ideal for heavy traffic areas such as walkways or handrails.

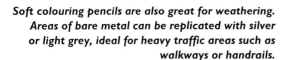

It is important to seal powders and pigments in place with a fixative solution. Different brands of powder specify different mediums (or no sealer at all), but MIG's liquid fixative can simply be sprayed through an airbrush at a very low pressure, so as not to disturb the effects.

Keep weathering powders away from moving parts, including bearing faces. Small strips of masking tape will keep them clear during the painting and weathering stages.

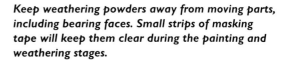

Acrylic and oil-based weathering washes are designed for application by hand, either to create grimy or rusty streaks, or to highlight panel seams or areas of raised detail. They can be brushed over a large area and then manipulated with water or thinners – according to formula – to create a variety of staining or shading effects.

Other materials can be equally effective for creating specific visual effects, including coloured pencils, coal dust, ash and talcum powder.

FILL YOUR WAGON

Although freight vehicles often run empty, a model is soon brought to life with accurate renditions of the various commodities that are still a feature of railway life. As part of the common-carrier legislation, Britain's railways were obliged to carry any freight that was offered, leading to some weird and wonderful payloads. Anything from coal, iron ore, livestock, military vehicles and even tree trunks

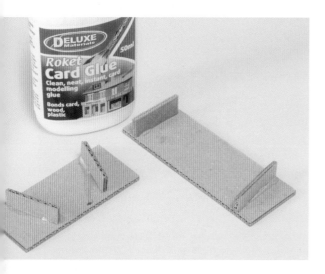

Fitting realistic loads adds a further dimension to a model. Geoscenics offers wagon-fill kits that include stout card from which to cut false floors to fit inside open wagons.

With the card floors in place, the commodities can be added. Real coal and stone are offered in various grades to suit your scale and type of material.

Push the loose material into all corners and create a realistic mound if the prototype demands it. Apply a dilute mix of PVA adhesive, water and a drop of washing-up liquid, via a syringe or eyedropper.

Leave the loads to dry for a day or two, then shake off any loose material for reuse. The Geoscenics loads are hard to match for aggregate or mineral traffic.

Another distinctive wagonload that is easy to replicate is steel. Plastic angle, strip and section, glued into piles, can be painted with metallic paints and suitably weathered.

Enhance the load further with accurate renditions of a wagon's shackles. This modern-style vehicle features tensioned nylon straps that are recreated with thin strips of electrical insulation tape, fixed with cyano.

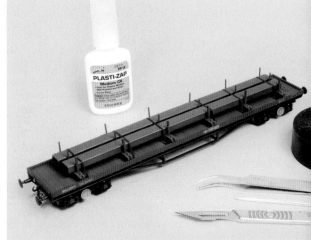

could be glimpsed aboard the humble railway wagon, right up to the late 1970s. Even today, there is still plenty of interesting freight handled, with containers, steel, motorcars, breeze blocks and aggregates and so on being visible in hoppers or open wagons.

A number of off-the-shelf wagonloads are available, including cast-resin products in Hornby's Skaledale and Bachmann's Scenecraft ranges. While of acceptable standard, these can be improved upon either by covering with tarpaulins or making your own. Using natural materials has a tremendous effect on the appearance, especially where mineral traffic is concerned, and the use of scenic scatter material on false floors can offer great results. Geoscenics, in particular, produces some highly authentic wagon fill packs, complete with the card to fill the wagon's payload bay.

Bespoke, ready-made wagonloads are produced in HO and other scales by Czech firm Duha, and

Miniature brass chain is ideal for older-style wagons. Look at the prototype to determine how and where the loads were shackled.

A mix of real and artificial materials is employed for these two timber loads. The smaller logs are a plaster casting from Ten Commandments, painted with various wood dyes. The larger 'tree trunks' are branches from a hawthorn bush.

ABOVE: *Again, look at how the real thing was secured, with sawn timber often sheeted with a tarpaulin that was itself tied down in a specific manner. Roger Smith's offers a range of paper tarpaulins and, after scrunching them about, they can look highly realistic, especially with securing ropes formed from thin wire or cotton thread.*

BELOW: *A distinctive wagon with a distinctive load – this Genesis girder-carrying set has been loaded with a Ratio plastic bridge girder, complete with chain shackles and screw links, copied exactly from a prototype image.*

ABOVE: *Another case of careful prototype study – note the wheel chocks, cut from scraps of stained balsa wood, and the chains wrapped around the buffers.*

these are very attractive, although aimed at the Continental market. Steel, timber, minerals and even scrap metal are rendered in believable loads, all of which can be lifted in or out of open wagons. Other possible sources include Ten Commandments and Harburn Hobbies.

Creating your own wagon fills is not difficult, making use of all manner of materials to get the job done. Plastic section, from the likes of Plastruct or Evergreen, can be painted and weathered to mimic steel, real tree branches harvested to represent log traffic or scale vehicle kits assembled for military or civilian loads.

OTHER FINAL TOUCHES

In the days when general merchandise was a key part of the railway's economy, and when a large number of freight trains ran in daylight hours through busy stations, many companies saw fit to paste advertising posters on BR's vans containing consignments of

their goods. Contemporary household names like Spratt's pet foods and Fyffes bananas are just two examples. Adding some suitable replicas of these bills creates an extra dose of realism.

Moreover, these bills can help to highlight particular traffic flows or reinforce a reference to a geographical location in a layouts. Some examples include chocolate traffic from a Fry's or Rowntree's factory, bagged cement, agricultural fertilizers, or perishable goods, each packed in the appropriate type of vehicle (fruit vans for perishables, ventilated vans for foodstuffs, pallet vans for cement).

Ready-made wagon posters are available in O and OO from Hollah Models, distributed by Parkside Dundas, but, like the possibility of DIY decals, making your own is a viable alternative if your desired brand name is not obtainable. Perhaps your layout is a fictional rendering with a key industry at the heart of it, therefore suitably branded wagons would be a pleasant addition.

In the days before computer-controlled freight operation, the destinations of individual wagons or parcel vans were often simply chalked on to the side of the vehicle, with previous legends crossed through. Various decal makers offer water-slide or rub-down renditions of these markings, although they can just as easily be applied by hand, especially on larger-scale models; printed versions may appear just a bit too neat.

And finally, how about adorning the end vehicle in your freight or carriage rakes with a suitable tail lamp. Springside Models and others offer a choice of oil-lamp patterns, as employed by the various steam-age railways (BR and Big Four), as well as the modern battery-powered versions. Indeed, there are also working, illuminated versions that can be powered from a cell battery or from a DCC chip, power being collected via the vehicle's wheels.

Wagon posters add an extra something to van traffic, with a variety of period brands depicted in the Hollar range for OO and O.

Distressing the posters slightly and pushing them into any recesses with a cocktail stick creates a more believable recreation.

Chalked destination or instruction markings were a common sight on the railways until privatization; a range of relevant decals is available in rub-down or water-slide form. However, using a fine ink pen, they can look more effective if applied by hand.

The traditional tail lamp is still an everyday sight on the modern railway and miniature replicas are available to suit a range of eras and regions.

AFTERWORD

The foregoing pages include all of the fundamentals of wagon and carriage kit building, in all of the popular materials and scales. There is still far more for us to learn and the next volume in this series, dealing with locomotives and multiple units, will introduce a number of further techniques.

As already mentioned throughout this book, there is no substitute for practice. Indeed, the art of kit building is something to be developed over time, offering hours of pleasure, challenge and reward. Do not forget that making mistakes is all part of the continuous learning process and, hopefully, this book has offered sufficient encouragement, advice and enough tips and tricks to remedy (or avoid) any problems that you may face along the way. The most important aspect of any hobby is fun. Kit building can be one of the most enjoyable and educative pastimes around, so remember to enjoy the experience.

There are many variations in kit-building techniques, dictated by the nature of the kit in hand. However, all are based on the fundamentals outlined within this book and, with a bit of practice, there should be nothing that cannot be tackled. After building a few items of rolling stock, you may be tempted to branch out into locomotives and multiple units, which will be covered in Volume Two.

USEFUL CONTACTS

MODELLING SUPPLIES

The Airbrush Company Ltd
79 Marlborough Road
Lancing Business Park, Lancing
BN15 8UF
Tel: 01903 767800
www.airbrushes.com
Airbrushes and equipment, tools, paints and
finishing sundries

Crafty Computer Paper
Woodhall
Barrasford, Hexham
NE48 4DB
Tel: 01434 689153
www.craftycomputerpaper.co.uk
DIY decal materials

Finescale Model World
Tel: 07780 097503
Email: finescalemodelrailway@gmail.com
Specialist cleaning fluids for plastics, resin and metal

Fox Transfers
4 Hill Lane Close
Markfield Industrial Estate, Markfield
LE67 9PN
Tel: 01530 242801
www.fox-transfers.co.uk
Transfers and RailMatch paints

Gaugemaster
Gaugemaster House
Ford Road, Arundel
BN18 0BN
Tel: 01903 884488
www.gaugemaster.com
Deluxe Materials adhesives, fillers and applicators
and model kits

Howes Models Ltd
Unit 2C/D Station Field Ind. Est.
Rowles Way
Kidlington
OX5 1LA
Tel: 01865 848000
www.howesmodels.co.uk
Kits, components, RailMatch paints and transfers

Model Hobbies
Unit 2, Bank Works
Warren Street, Stoke on Trent
ST3 1QB
Tel: 0845 643 1304
www.modelhobbies.co.uk
Paints, glues, tools, accessories and kits

Modelmaster
31 Crown Street
Ayr
KA8 8AG
Tel: 01292 289770
www.modelmasterdecals.com
Rolling stock transfers

Phoenix Precision Paints
PO Box 8238
Chelmsford
CM1 7WY
Tel: 01245 494050
www.phoenix-paints.co.uk
Paints and finishing sundries

Rapid Electronics
Severalls Lane
Colchester
CO4 5JS
Tel: 01206 751166
www.rapidonline.com
Antex soldering irons and equipment

Relish Models
9 Ferriby Close
Herringbrough
Selby
YO8 6YX
Tel: 0844 3510777
www.relishmodels.co.uk
Kits, tools, adhesives, paints and sundries

KITS AND COMPONENTS

Alan Gibson
PO Box 597
Oldham
OL1 9FQ
Tel. 0161 678 1607
www.alangibsonworkshop.com

Cambrian Models
10 Long Road
Tydd Gote
Wisbech
PE13 5RB
Tel. 01945 420511
www.cambrianmodels.co.uk

Chris J. Ward Model Railway Parts
The Shires
Gloucester Road
Corse
GL19 3RA
Tel. 01452 849051
www.chrisjward.co.uk

Comet Models
Charnwood
Firs Road
Ross-on-Wye
HR9 5BH
Tel. 05602 602188
www.cometmodels.co.uk

Cooper Craft
Broom Lane
Oake
Taunton
TA4 1BE
Tel. 01823 461961
www.cooper-craft.co.uk

C-Rail Intermodal
Morven
Roome Bay Avenue
Crail
Fife
KY10 3TR
Tel. 01333 450976
www.c-rail-intermodal.co.uk

Dave Bradwell
South Muirnich Cottage
Gorthleck
Inverness
IV2 6YP
Tel. 01456 486377
www.scalefour.org/bradwell

DC Kits
111 Norwood Crescent
Stanningley
Leeds
LS28 6NG
Tel. 0113 256 3415
www.dckits-devideos.co.uk

Genesis Kits
Waveney Cottage
Willingham Road
Market Rasen
LN8 3DN
Tel. 01673 843236
www.genesiskits.co.uk

Geoscenics
30 Berkshire Drive
Woolston, Warrington
WA1 4EX
Tel. 07811 673341
www.geoscenics.co.uk

Hurst Models
PO Box 158
Newton-le-Willows
WA12 0WW
www.hurstmodels.com

Inter-City Models
1 Halvosso Vean
Longdowns
TR10 9DN
Tel: 01209 860851
www.intercitymodels.com

Just Like the Real Thing
26 Whittle Place
South Newmoor Industrial Estate
Irvine
Ayrshire
KA11 4HR
Tel: 01294 222988
www.justliketherealthing.co.uk

MARC Models
15 Hadley Highstone
Barnet
EN5 4PU
Tel: 0208 440 5918
www.marcmodels.co.uk

Model Railway Developments
www.emardee.org.uk

Parkside Dundas
Millie Street
Kirkcaldy, Fife
KY1 2NL
Tel: 01592 640896
www.parksidedundas.co.uk

PH Designs
www.phd-design-etchings.co.uk

RT Models
75 Yew Tree Close
Spring Gardens
Shrewsbury
SY1 2UR
www.rtmodels.co.uk

Shapeways
www.shapeways.com

Shawplan
2 Upper Dunstead Road
Langley Mill
NG16 4GR
Tel: 01773 718648
www.shawplan.com

Slater's Plastikard Ltd
Old Road
Darley Dale
Matlock
DE4 2ER
Tel: 01629 732235
www.slatersplastikard.com

Steam Era Models
c/o Post Office Rhyll
Victoria 3923
Australia
Tel: +61 3 5956 9389
www.steameramodels.com

Springside Models
2 Springside Cottages
Dornafield Road
Ipplepen
Newton Abbot
TQ12 5SJ
Tel: 01803 813749
www.springsidemodels.com

Ten Commandments
20 Struan Drive
Inverkeithing
Fife
KY11 1AR
Tel: 01383 410032
www.cast-in-stone.co.uk

Wizard Models
PO Box 70
Barton upon Humber
DN18 5XY
Tel: 01652 635885
www.wizardmodels.co.uk

USEFUL WEBSITES

George Dent Model Maker: A Model Maker's Diary
http://georgedentmodelmaker.blogspot.com

Model Rail Magazine
www.model-rail.co.uk

SCALE SOCIETIES

2mm Scale Association
www.2mm.org.uk

3mm Society
www.3mmsociety.org.uk

Double O Gauge Society
www.doubleogauge.com

EM Gauge Society
www.emgs.org

Gauge O Guild
www.gauge0guild.com

MOROP (for NEM standards)
www.morop.org

N Gauge Society
www.ngaugesociety.com

NMRA
www.nmra.org

OO9 Society
www.OO9society.com

Scalefour (P4)
www.scalefour.org

Scale Seven Group
www.scalesevenorg.uk

PROTOTYPE SOCIETIES

Diesel and Electric Modellers United
www.demu.org.uk

Great Western Study Group
www.gwsg.org.uk

Historical Model Railway Society
www.hmrs.org.uk

LMS Society
www.lmssociety.org.uk

LNER Society
www.lner.info

Midland Railway Society
www.midlandrailwaysociety.org.uk

Railway Correspondence and Travel Society
www.rcts.org.uk

Southern Railways Group
www.srg.org.uk

BIBLIOGRAPHY AND SUGGESTED READING

BOOKS

Bartlett, P., Larkin, D. & Mann, T., *An Illustrated History of British Railways Revenue Wagons, Volume One* (OPC, 1985)

Bixley, G., Blackburn, A., Chorley, R. & King, M., *An Illustrated History of Southern Wagons, Volume Four* (OPC, 2002)

Burkin, N., *Modern Wagons in 4mm Scale* (Warners, 2008)

Dent, G., *Detailing and Modifying Ready-to-Run Locomotives in OO Gauge, Volume One: British Diesel & Electric Locomotives, 1955–2008* (The Crowood Press, 2009)

Dent, G., *Detailing and Modifying Ready-to-Run Locomotives in OO Gauge, Volume Two: British Steam Locomotives, 1948–1968* (The Crowood Press, 2009)

Dent, G., *Airbrushing for Railway Modellers* (The Crowood Press, 2011)

Essery, R.J., *LMS Wagons, Volume One* (OPC, 1981)

Essery, R.J., Rowland, D.P. & Steel, W.O., *British Goods Wagons, from 1887 to the present day* (A. M. Kelley, 1970)

Gamble, G., *British Railways Vans, Volume Two* (Cheona, 2000)

Harris, M., *LNER Carriages* (Noodle Books, 2011)

Hendry, R., *British Railways Goods Wagons in Colour* (Ian Allan, 1999)

Hendry, R., *British Railways Coaching Stock in Colour since 1960* (Ian Allan, 2006)

Jackson, A. & Day, D., *The Modelmaker's Handbook* (Pelham Books, 1987)

Jenkinson, D., *British Railway Carriages of the Twentieth Century, Volume Two* (Patrick Stephens, 1990)

Jenkinson, D. & Essery, R.J., *LMS Standard Coaching Stock, Part Three* (OPC, 2000)

Kent, G., *The 4mm Wagon, Part One* (Wild Swan, 1991)

Larkin, D., *Working Wagons, Volumes One to Four* (Santona, 1998–2002)

Macaulay, J. (Ed.), *Modern Railway Working, Volume Five* (Gresham, 1913)

Marsden, C., *Rolling Stock Recognition: BR and Private Owner Wagons* (Ian Allan, 1984)

Parkin, K., *British Railways Mark I Coaches* (Pendragon, 1991)

Rice, I., *Locomotive Kit Chassis Construction in 4mm* (Wild Swan, 1993)

Rowland, D., *British Railways Wagons, The First Half Million* (Leopard, 1996)

Russell, J.H., *Freight Wagons and Load in Service on the GWR and BR(WR)* (OPC, 1981)

Smith, T., *British Railways Air Braked Stock, Volume Two* (Cheona, 2003)

Stevens-Stratten, S.W., *Bulleid Coaches in 4mm Scale* (Ian Allan, 1983)

Tatlow, P., *A Pictorial Record of LNER Wagons* (OPC, 1976)

Tatlow, P., *Historic Railway Carriage Drawings, Volume Three* (Pendragon, 2000)

Tourret, R., *Petroleum Rail Tank Wagons of Britain* (Tourret, 2009)

Twining, E., *Indoor Model Railways* (Newnes, 1937)

Weiss, A., *Plastics for Modellers* (Nexus, 1998)

Welch, M., *The Art of Weathering* (Wild Swan, 1993)

Williams, S., *The 4mm Coach, Part one* (Wild Swan, 1994)

ARTICLES

Beattie, I., 'BR MkI CCT', *Railway Modeller* (July 2002), pp344–5

Dent, G., 'Red Rust and Coal Dust', *Model Rail* (June 2005), pp36–40

Dent, G., 'Mineral Matters', *Model Rail* (June 2007), pp60–64

Dent, G., 'Paint Supertest', *Model Rail* (February 2010), pp74–81

Dent, G., 'Varnish Supertest', *Model Rail* (March 2010), pp74–80

Dent, G., 'Glue Supertest', *Model Rail* (August 2010), pp68–78

Dent, G., 'Ultimate Guide to Soldering', *Model Rail* (April 2012), pp52–7

Goodwin, D. & Oldfield, R., 'BR 16ton Mineral Wagons, part 2', *Railway Modeller* (March 2000), pp116–8

Goodwin, D. & Oldfield, R., 'BR 16ton Mineral Wagons, part 3', *Railway Modeller* (May 2000), pp240–3

Larkin, D., 'British Railways 21ton Mineral Wagons – The Re-building Programme', *Model Railway Constructor* (November 1983), pp637–41

Larkin, D., 'British Railways 21ton Mineral Wagons', *Model Railway Constructor* (December 1983), pp708–11

Larson, E., 'Clear as Crystal', *Airfix Model World* (June 2012), pp72–8

Paterson, I., 'Let's Look at Couplers', *Model Trains* (July 1981), pp346–7

Senior, J., 'Looking Back at LNER Parcels Stock', *Model Rail* (June 2000), pp36–7

Spiegelhalter, P., 'Knuckling Down to Coupling Conversion', *Model Rail* (August 2006), pp34–8

INDEX

RELATED TITLES
FROM CROWOOD

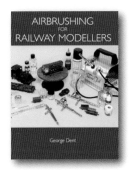

Airbrushing for Railway Modellers

GEORGE DENT

ISBN 978 1 84797 265 1
224pp, 500 illustrations

A Practical Introduction to Digital Command Control for Railway Modellers

NIGEL BURKIN

ISBN 978 1 84797 020 6
192pp, 400 illustrations

Planning, Designing and Making Railway Layouts in Small Spaces

RICHARD BARDSLEY

ISBN 978 1 84797 424 2
144pp, 130 illustrations

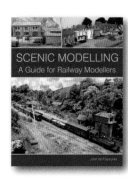

Scenic Modelling

JOHN DE FRAYSSINET

ISBN 978 1 84797 457 0
160pp, 230 illustrations

In case of difficulty ordering, contact the Sales Office:

The Crowood Press Ltd
Ramsbury
Wiltshire
SN8 2HR
UK

Tel: 44 (0) 1672 520320
enquiries@crowood.com
www.crowood.com